This Luckiest of Women

Margaret Emily Cantlay

Published by Bewley Publishing
Copyright © Judy Watson, 2021
All rights reserved.

No part of this book may be reproduced in any form by photocopying or any electronic or mechanical means, including information storage or retrieval systems, without permission from the copyright owner and the publisher of this book.

ISBN 978-1-3999-0750-7

First Printed 2021

Kestrel Press
25 Whittle Place, Irvine KA11 4HR
www.kestrelpress.com

Layout
Kestrel Press

Edited
Judy Watson & Laura Hamilton

Order your copy by email: bewley@bewleypublishing.com
or online at bewleypublishing.com
Prices and availability subject to change without notice.

"This Luckiest of Women" is my grandmother's story of her life in India during the first half of the 20th century. Written from her diaries, and typed up shortly before she died, it attracted some interest from a publisher but sadly, never went to print. The manuscript then lay forgotten until many years later, I rediscovered and now share, this extraordinary woman's fascinating account of a bygone age.

Margaret Emily Cantlay known as Madge, or Oma to her grandchildren, was born in 1892 to British parents living in Ceylon. When six years old, she was sent to Scotland to be educated by two elderly relatives. Here she endured a somewhat bleak experience until, aged sixteen, she returned to her parents now living in Kerala. In 1911 she married the manager of a neighbouring tea estate to whom she bore two children. Amid vivid descriptions of wildlife, she describes working tirelessly to improve the workers' health and welfare particularly woman and children. The tea estates of Kerala remained her home until 1948 when Madge and her husband Jim moved to Scotland where her love of hill climbing, gardening and wildlife continued until she died in 1976.

Judy Watson

This memoir is dedicated to the Dravidians of South India who after centuries of oppression and poverty, have shown that given the opportunity, they can become valued citizens. They are now able to laugh though heaven knows, there's still little to laugh about…

Thanks are due to Oxford University Press for permission to quote from Jim Corbett's book 'The Man-Eaters of Kumaon', and to Dr K Caddick, without whose encouragement I would not have had the temerity to send this memoir to be published.

Margaret Emily Cantlay
1962

Contents

Childhood Memories	1
Passage to India	4
Onwards by Bullock Cart	7
A Return to Life on the Tea Plantations	10
Forays with my Father and Encounters with Dangerous Beasts	11
Tigers	15
Friends, Neighbours and Unusual Company	17
A Haunted House and Engagement to Jim	19
Superstitions, Traditions and Defending Caste Honour	21
To Pastures New	24
Special Celebrations in our New Church	29
Dealings with a Devil and Drunkards	32
Married Life, Ooralies and a Naval Captain's Ghost	35
Babies, Health Scares and the Onslaught War	38
Return to Post-War India	43
Cloudland	47
Adventures with Peramal	49
Battling Malaria and Encounters with Bears	55
Consecration of our New Church	61
More Malaria, a Family Reunion and the Curse of Munaindy	63
The Arrival of Colonel C, Cholera and the Hydrodam	66
A Trip to Calcutta and the Ganges	70
Snakes in the Hydrodam, Rainstorms and Floods	75
The Lull after the Storm and an Attack at Sea	79
Jungle Treks	83
Local Hill Tribes	87
Cochin, Friends and Chance Encounters	91
A Plague, Thieves and a Move to High Wavys	97

Leeches and More Amenable Locals	101
Bobs, a Seaside Excursion and Building a New Factory	107
An Earthquake, A Leopard and A Cardamom Plantation	111
Madura	116
Trouble	122
The Trail of Sher Khan, the Trial of Savrimuthu and the Jewels of Madura	128
Animal Rescues and the Rise of Sagunam	133
Kolar Rowther, Ooty, Mysore and the Surili Falls	136
Land Surveyance, Ratnam and Doctors	141
Medical Matters	147
The Opening of the New Factory	155
Sewing Classes and Corruption	157
Yurghese	159
Remembering Elephants	163
Wives, Mothers and Daughters	167
A New Houseguest and Entertaining at High Wavys	173
Christmas Plays, Other Dramas and the Arts and Crafts School	177
Java	181
The Splendours of Kashmir and the Taj Mahal	187
Wartime Rationing	192
Angus, Snakes and a Troublesome Tiger	196
Rajan, Rabid Dogs and Donkeys	199
Riots and the Dawn of Independence	203
A New India and a New Road	206
Final Adventures and Ongoing Injustices	209
Farewell to Forty Years in India	214
Acknowledgements	217

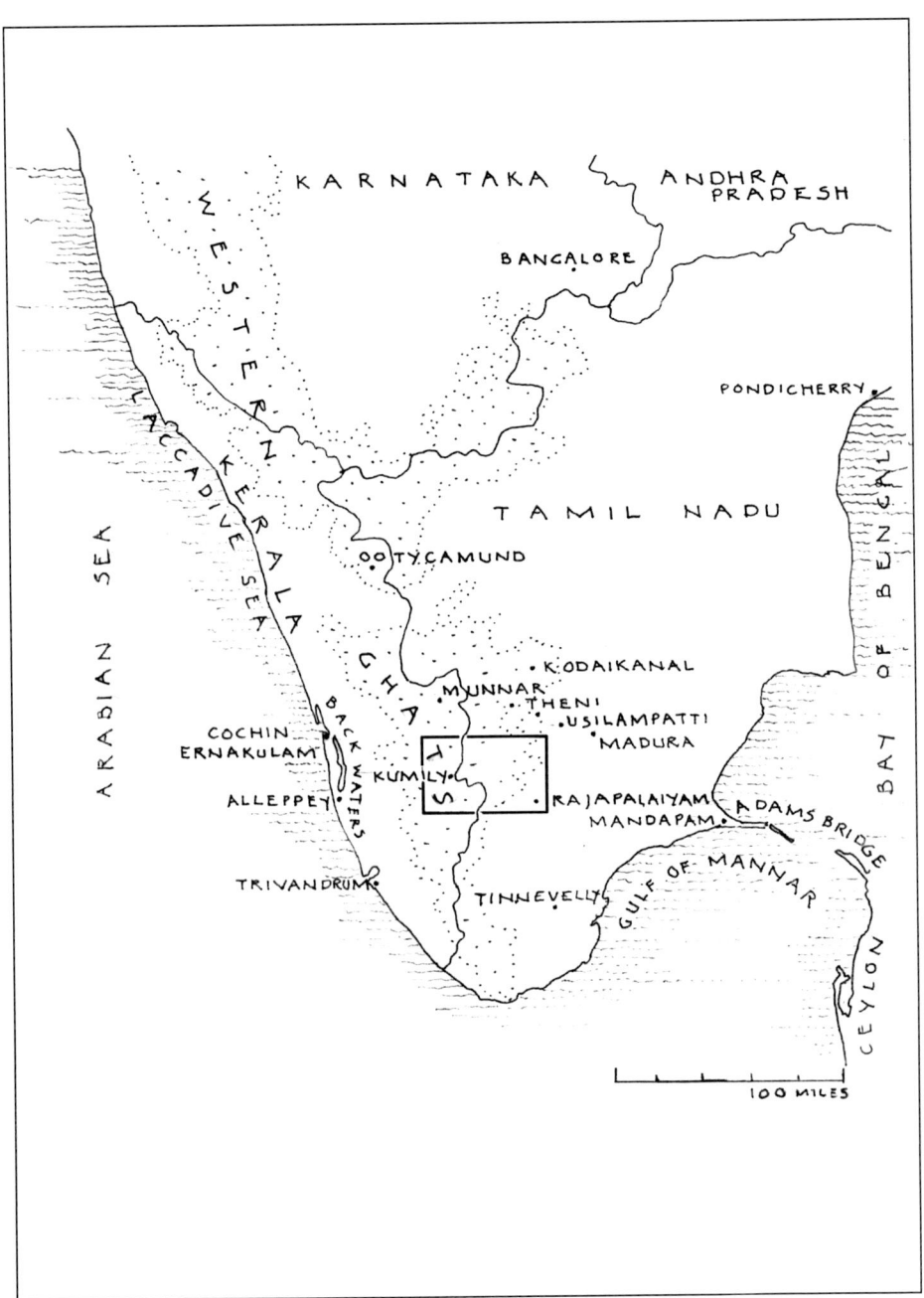

Introduction

'This Luckiest of Women' is my grandmother's story of her life in India during the first half of the 20th century. Written in longhand and typed up shortly before she died, it attracted some interest from a publisher but sadly, never went to print. The manuscript then lay forgotten until many years later, I rediscovered and now share, this extraordinary woman's fascinating account of a bygone age.

My grandmother Margaret Emily Cantlay, known as Madge, or Oma to her grandchildren, was born in 1892 to British parents living in Ceylon. When six years old, she was sent to Scotland to be educated by two elderly relatives, alongside other children from colonial families. She endured this somewhat bleak experience until, aged sixteen, she returned to India and subsequently in 1911 married the manager of a neighbouring tea estate, James Cantlay, to whom she bore two children.

Her story, peppered with heartbreak, love, humour and adventure, follows one woman's life on and around the tea estates, mapping challenges posed by the climate, disease and wild animals, as well as her deep affection for the Indian estate workers and those she treated in her dispensaries. Imbued with an independent and pioneering spirit, she had the courage, determination and imagination to reject convention in order to work tirelessly to improve the lives of the labour, and in particular, the women on the estate.

Amidst vivid descriptions of her love of the outdoors, the flora, fauna and her encounters with wildlife, she provides a poignant insight into cultural differences, including the impact of the caste system on relations between workers, and the impact of superstition on the acceptance of change, such as the introduction of electricity in the factory and the construction of dams.

Living through both world wars, she describes the resilience and adaptability of the estate workers in times of great hardship, the heart-breaking decision to send her two children, when only five and six, to Britain, and the eruption of the riots leading up to India's independence in 1947.

My grandmother's forty years in India ended just one year later, when she and my grandfather Jim came to live in Dollar, Scotland, in a cottage at the foot of our family home. Her love of hill climbing, gardening and wildlife continued until she died in 1976.

Judy Watson

Childhood Memories
1892-1908

My story begins in Ceylon where I was born in 1892. My father George Bewley was the manager of a tea estate and it was here that I spent the first six years of my life. Recollections of this time are formed of unconnected pictures. I remember clearly our bungalow and garden, and the horse my father rode. I can still visualise the face of Vellachi, our old sweeper-woman, yet none of our other servants.

The image of the estate factory itself is clear and I remember sitting on a table in my father's little office, playing with toys as he worked, and my delight in feeding flies to a tame gecko. I have clear recollections of the road to our nearest neighbours along which we used to drive a trap drawn by Father's horse, the Mighty Atom and remember too, the day when protecting her calf, a fierce little native cow gave chase and came far too close for comfort!

One of our neighbours had a parrot which intrigued me. From outside the room in which it was kept, I could hear it whistling to the dog, cackling like a hen, calling the 'boy' and making all sorts of fascinating sounds, but as soon as I entered, its cage was hurriedly covered with a dark green cloth. It was only many years later that I discovered the reason. The bird had been bought from a sailor and had a wonderful and very clearly enunciated vocabulary of swear words which were considered unfit for my infant mind!

Another clear picture is of a rest-house or Dak bungalow and sitting with my parents on the verandah whilst a temple elephant was brought up to see us. He salaamed and 'spoke' to us when ordered, and managed to unearth first a five-cent coin and then a needle buried in the dust, with the 'fingers' at the end of his trunk.

I can still see myself as a small girl with my dark hair held back with a snood, wearing long black stockings, strap shoes and a starched, frilly white cotton dress. I'm sure I was a good child. I don't remember ever being very naughty and my mother told me that I was never any trouble. This sounds horribly dull, and indeed, I suspect I was rather an unenterprising, stolid little person.

Zig-zagging through all these memories are recollections of lying-in bed in the nursery listening to Mother singing in her very fine mezzo soprano voice during our frequent musical parties. Before they began, she would always visit me in bed, looking very beautiful in her evening gowns. I especially remember a scarlet dress, very décolleté with little black bows down the front, which made of stiff silk used to rustle delightfully as she walked.

There was however, one song which I dreaded hearing: Grieg's 'The Worker.' It used to break my heart, and whenever she sang it, I would put my head under the bedclothes, weeping bitterly. It was a sad song, but I think it was something in the musical accompaniment that moved me, rather than the lyrics. Curiously enough, when I returned to India as a young woman, that same song used to affect one of our dogs in the same way and he would sit and howl as if being beaten.

I adored my father and he and I were always very close friends. A fountain of information, he had plenty to tell a small girl bursting with curiosity. He always had a sensible reply to a "why" or a "how" and never tried to foist me off with funny stories nor tell me anything that wasn't true, to the sort of persistent questioning which irritated other grown-ups. In 1898, when I was six years old, I was taken by my mother and father, along with my brother and baby sister to Britain. As there were no schools in Ceylon, I was then left with relatives in Scotland to begin my education. I sorely missed my father and also the freedom afforded by the outdoor life of the tea plantation. My new life, like that of other children whose parents were in the East, was inevitably circumcised and bound by rules and regulations. I especially hated the long, dark winter evenings. Back then we had no electric lights and the alarming curves and odd shapes cast by the small gas jet at the turn of the stairs made trips to the bathroom particularly fearful.

At the beginning of the 20th century, children's lives were very different to those of children today. We girls spent our evenings sewing whilst one of my aunts read us stories. We were expected to be quiet little people and as I recall, very sedate and prim! In Scotland, Sunday was Sunday with a capital 'S'. Always a day of joy in Ceylon, since Father was not at work, Sunday was now a day of quiet repression. Our aunts did their best to make things more bearable by providing special toys and books to keep us amused, but even in summer, games in the garden were prohibited for fear of disturbing our neighbours' Sabbath rest and walks in the country were discouraged. Holidays were spent at the seaside, but despite being severely disciplined, we children had fun one way or another and as a rule, managed to enjoy ourselves.

In those days, taking leave from the East was not easy, and our parents were due home but once every five years. I was left during one leave, then five years later my brother joined me. The household soon grew to nine and within a few years to ten when my sister Kathleen joined us. As we grew older the evening sessions of reading aloud altered; the smaller ones had the usual sewing, while we did our homework. Then, once the youngest had been put to bed, we older ones were spread flat-out on 'back boards' on the floor, to straighten our backs for half an hour, whilst our aunts, who were very good readers, kept us in a wonderful state of suspense with 'Treasure Island', 'Westward Ho!', 'Uncle Tom's Cabin' and books by Ballantyne and Henty. We also had animal stories by Earnest Thompson Seton over which I wept buckets and I vividly remember the feeling of tears trickling into my ears as I lay on the floor mourning some tragedy.

I attended a small private school run by two elderly aunts. Back then, education for girls was not considered very important. I had learned two of the three 'R's (the third R always eluded me) and had a smattering of Geography and History, which as I recall, came from just two textbooks: 'Tales of a Grandfather' and 'Little Arthur's England'.

All the girls in my aunt's household were dressed identically. In winter we wore red merino blouses with high ruched necks, blue serge skirts, heavy dark coats and black velour hats, and in summer, somber cotton frocks and stiff sailor hats. But oh, how I longed and even prayed for a floppy hat that 'trembled' like those I had seen other small girls wearing. So, in the summer of 1903 when my parents were home, I persuaded my mother to get me one and shall never forget my joy in that hat for as long as I live! The other older girl Zoe, who was also given one, had a great advantage over me: the delight of curly hair! Mine was long, heavy and uncompromisingly straight, and whilst she looked charming whatever the condition of her hair, I was always in trouble for looking untidy. I remember wetting my brush, straining my hair off my face and plaiting it tight, but try as I might odd bits would escape making it appear as unruly as before.

Passage to India
1908

I returned to the East at the age of sixteen to help and be a companion to my mother, who was unwell and feeling lonely, living as she was on an isolated tea estate. By then, my parents who were now almost strangers, had left Ceylon for South India and it was a wrench to leave Scotland and the life to which I had grown accustomed to venture alone to a strange land. However, once the initial parting was over and since they had arranged for friends to look after me, I enjoyed the voyage, at least, when I wasn't seasick! In those days, most of the tea planters in South India and Ceylon travelled to and from Britain by Bibby Line, and it was a Bibby boat that took me out in 1908.

Despite anxiously trying to appear worldly-wise, I must have looked quite a prim and proper young miss in my pigtail when Father met me off the ship in Columbo, but delighted that none of our old camaraderie had been lost, I felt more than ready for whatever adventures lay in store! Colombo itself was fascinating and although I had forgotten the smells and sights of the East during my ten years in Scotland, they met me like old friends on the jetty, in the hotel and all around the town.

We left by ferry steamer for Tuticorin that night and oh dear, how sick I was. My father was never happier than when aboard any ship and though thankful to have him by my side, I found the overnight voyage purgatory and our arrival at Tuticorin, pure hell. The weather was rough and due to insufficient depth along the coastline, the ship had to anchor, lurching and straining, three miles offshore. We then had the agony of standing on deck in the dim morning light, waiting for a small craft to collect passengers and their luggage.

When it eventually arrived, I watched in horror as waves threw the wildly heaving tug to the top of the gangway, then crashed back down into a trough that seemed to plunge to the very bottom of the ship. Past caring what would become of me, I looked on as the other women passengers were slung over the side in a sort of basket affair and expertly deposited on the deck of the violently leaping tug. My overwhelming desire was for a moment of stillness, to regain control of my insides. Beyond being sick, I just wanted to lay down and die, but in a trance-like state duly allowed myself to be bundled onto that chair-like contraption. As I began to swing over, the waves that had crashed so far down as to leave the sides of the ship streaming with water, reared up at express speed to snatch at my heels. I was utterly terrified and having survived being deposited on that horrible craft, stinking of oil, had yet to suffer three miles of rolling sideways, climbing waves and shooting down troughs. It was without doubt, the last straw! After what seemed like hours to cover a relatively short distance, we finally reached shore and anyone who's ever been really seasick will appreciate my joy in standing still without any lurching, heaving or weaving up and down underfoot!

Being young and healthy, it did not take me long to recover. With much yelling and shouting, coolies rushed to lower the gangplanks, and offering their services as porters, soon had us boarded on the train standing ready nearby. Although hot and humid, it was pleasant to lean back in the carriage and enjoy being back on solid ground. The scene outside was one of noisy chaos and although I had never been here before, the atmosphere felt curiously familiar. The Indians selling their wares were Tamils, the same race as the labour on the Ceylon estate where I had spent my early childhood, and brought back memories of how Tamils do nothing without a great deal of noise. When moving anything heavy, the men would chant a sort of sing-song refrain rather like a sea shanty, and when not working, were always ready with vociferous advice to which nobody appeared to pay the slightest attention.

Amidst the shouts of porters and cries of vendors, skinny mangy dogs yapped as they wandered through the melee, hotly contested by hundreds of screaming gulls whenever they picked up titbits dropped by passengers. Everywhere I looked, vendors sang out their wares in wailing nasal tones, whilst constantly having to brush off the flies that swarmed around trays of Indian sweets and pieces of melon and mango. Glasses of coffee and tea could be bought for a 'pie', a tiny coin worth about a farthing, and it was fascinating to see them being poured from a great height from long-spouted pots, perfectly aimed to produce a bubbly head.

Brisk trade continued up and down the long train until it was time for its departure. We then set off through flat, arid countryside with few landmarks and very little cultivation bar plantations of toddy palms. A popular drink in South India, toddy is produced by tapping sweet sap into earthenware vessels tied to the trunks. When fresh, it tastes delicious, but once fermented becomes intensely intoxicating and smells quite revolting. The heat increased as the day wore on and the glare became almost unbearable. If we were hot in our comparatively cool compartment, I couldn't bear to think how the poor folk in the crowded third-class carriages were feeling. However, watching them tumble onto the platforms at the infrequent stations, laughing and chattering as they pumped water into their cupped palms to splash over their faces, feet and legs, I almost wished l could do the same.

Cultivation increased as we continued north-east and fields of rice and varieties of millet, and plantations of coconuts and bananas made the view more interesting. We finally reached our station at about 4.00pm whereupon porters, who crowded around our carriage, got our baggage out in a trice. Followed by quite a regiment of these men, we then walked off the platform to a nearby rest-house.

Onwards by Bullock Cart

My father ordered a meal and a bath, and once freshly clothed and feeling a little cooler we rested on the verandah until 6.30pm when three bullock carts trundled into the compound. Each was drawn by two bullocks and had been arranged to take us on the next leg of our journey. Two had mattresses onto which my father and I crawled whilst our luggage was piled onto the third. Then, with much shouting and tail twisting, our carts clattered out of the courtyard and onto the wide road shadowed by huge trees.

Let me describe a bullock cart. Ours were rather superior types with fancy decorations round the hood and springs. Above the springs, albeit too poor to shield us from every bump and hole in the road, were flat boards beneath an arched hood of bent cane and cane matting, or sometimes in superior models, linoleum. A single pole protruded from this platform with a crossbar which lay over the necks of the bullocks – a variety called Zebu with pronounced humps – and by pushing against the crossbar with these humps they were able to pull the cart with its huge wooden wheels. The driver or 'jehu' sat on the pole, either near the cart or further forward, balancing his weight so that the crossbar neither pressed too heavily on the necks of his beasts nor tipped too high as to slip above their humps.

The evening was clear with a cool soft breeze and it was fascinating to be lying alone on the floor of the lurching cart watching the arch of the hood swaying above me. Looking ahead I could see the head and shoulders of my jehu, and as it grew dark an arc of starlit sky through the back. We stopped every eight miles or so, and with a lot of noisy shouting that sounded like violent abuse, our bullocks were changed for fresh beasts then off we trundled once more. We crossed two rivers, the first of which presented a major problem. Flowing between two low banks it was particularly wide with a bed of sand some twenty feet deep. On our approach the cart's wheels began to sink, warranting shouts from our jehu to scare even the most lethargic of beasts. Fortunately, a few men from the village appeared and by manhandling the wheels we eventually arrived at the opposite bank. Around midnight we had a longer wait; I called to Father and was told that having reached halfway the men who had driven us thus far would go no further.

We arrived at the second river later that night where we were met by a gang of men who, despite sounding like a band of brigands bent on our destruction, had come to assist us across. The banks were steep and rocky, and we bumped and rattled our way down the deep stone path to the river's edge. Our bulls did not like the look of the surging torrent nor to be candid, did I, but with screams and shouts, tail-twisting and other encouragement they were persuaded into the water which welled up to their bellies and swirled and bubbled around the floor of my cart. Several men splashed on each side keeping it upright until with much effort we managed to slither and lurch our way to the other side. Apart from a little splashing we were dry, which was something of an achievement considering the amount of water in the river.

That journey, now taken by car, is far more comfortable and comparatively short, but gone are the excitement and romance of those early days which I must confess I relished!

The rest of the night passed peacefully bar the regular changes of bullocks. There were no more rivers to cross and though the road continued to deteriorate the ground was softer and less stony, and hence less uncomfortable. Around dawn, I caught my first glimpse of the mountain range which we would later traverse. Rising 7,000 feet above the plains and silhouetted against the clear, pale sky, it looked unbelievably beautiful in the early morning light. Black shadows lingered in the fissures and over the deeply scarred grey rocky faces, and here and there, patches of water glittered like mirrors in the sunshine amidst vast swathes of soft green scrub and grass.

We stopped at a village rest-house for breakfast and a wash then, since the road ahead was unfit for even these tough and sturdy vehicles, we left the bullock carts behind. My father was given a horse sent down from the estate, whilst I was carried in a dhooly: a cross between a sedan chair and litter slung on poles carried by four stalwart men with four more following behind as replacements. Our luggage was carried by other porters and the whole cavalcade began to wind its way along the road, making straight for what appeared to be an impassable rocky face. As we approached the mountains the sun grew ever stronger and hotter, and after a few miles we began our steep ascent, zig-zagging our way up a narrow track barely wide enough to accommodate my bearers walking side by side. Sitting in my dhooly I had the luxury of being able to enjoy and appreciate my surroundings, but it must have been tough for the men carrying me on their shoulders. Jogging up the steep and stony path they began to sing a local shanty with one man chanting a recitative and the rest joining in with exclamations of "Ram! Ram!". It was an exhilarating experience. My father rode ahead on his sturdy sure-footed pony, sometimes disappearing round a hairpin bend as I followed in his wake, first through thorny scrub with mimosa-like flowers, then through rough grassland. Well up the mountainside, we began to hear the musical sound of running water and emerging from a cool, dim forest, at last reached the pass that led to a green rolling plateau, beyond which lay the estate managed by my father.

While sitting eating our picnic lunch, I gazed in delight into the soft shadows under the trees, admiring the foliage and the undergrowth. Suddenly, in flew a pure white bird, trailing behind him two slender, waving white feathers. I watched spellbound as his plumage changed from soft white to dazzling silver as he fluttered from the shade into the full sunlight; a miraculous sight which took my breath away. I would later encounter many of those birds, but have never forgotten my first sight of the male Paradise Fly Catcher in his third year of life. There is a delightful legend about this bird. It is said that at one time he was a true bird of Paradise, but grew so vain and haughty that God became angry and took away his flowing tail feathers and turned his face black. The bird repented and in due course God forgave him, reinstating two of his flowing tail feathers to float behind him as he flew, and decreeing that in his third year of life his deep chestnut plumage apart from that on his head would turn pure white. He was however, given two sky-blue eyelids to shine like jewels on his dark face; and so it is to this day.

Once fed and rested we resumed our march, this time on smoother tracks which wound through the valley, covered mainly with waving elephant grass, often six to eight feet high in the hollows. Now and then my father stopped to point out huge droppings on the side of the path. "Elephants!" he told me, "There are plenty of them in this valley." Excited, I kept my eyes open hoping to see them but was disappointed. The road rose again, zig-zagging up through a tea-field until just after teatime I caught sight of the bungalow and my mother at the edge of the garden, looking stouter and a bit older than I expected. After my long and adventurous journey I had a wonderful sense of home. My father and I received a joyful welcome from Mother, our two magnificent cats Rajah and Jeremiah, and Mac the dog ecstatic to see Father, his god, after three days' absence.

A Return to Life on the Tea Plantations

I had now embarked on a new life, which though lonely at times was freer and far more exciting than anything I had ever experienced under the restricted regime of a small Scottish town. I abandoned all study, something I still regret, and set myself to helping Mother in the house, and whenever possible accompanying Father when he rode to the tea fields.

We had two servants in the house and another in the kitchen none of whom spoke any English, so I, perforce, picked up Tamil at least enough to manage in the house and garden. The head 'boy', Savrimuthu, was a small, elderly and faithful man. He had been with my parents for many years, and considered himself responsible for both my wellbeing and behaviour. He understood more English than he cared to admit but spoke none to Mother or Father, and only the odd word, almost unrecognisable in its pronunciation, to me when I issued stores for the day's meals. He never laughed at my stumbling efforts at Tamil, but an occasional "Tch, Tch, Tch" made me realise that I had made some especially stupid mistake.

On days when Mother was feeling well I went out with my father visiting the weeders: men and boys scraping the surface of the soil with mattocks. In the fields worked by the female pluckers many of the trees bore strange fruit: babies slung in grimy fragments of old saris, suspended from the lower branches. Now and again an arm or leg would be seen waving about, or the whole contraption would begin to jerk, often accompanied by lusty wails of protest as some small body began to object to their confinement. If the volume increased the mother would abandon her work to suckle her infant before returning it to its shady hammock or leaving it lying on a blanket to kick in the sunshine.

Working quickly and with great precision, the pluckers made their way through the low, flat- topped bushes, discarding coarse leaves whilst deftly throwing handfuls of the younger, more tender, sweet-smelling leaves into baskets slung over their backs. I had all but forgotten the intense aroma of freshly plucked tea leaves and their scent when rolled and fermented in the factory. However, at first sniff I was returned in an instant to my childhood and the tea factory in Ceylon I had left ten years previously. After all these years it remains the most perfect scent I know and even writing about it fills me with nostalgia.

Forays with my Father and Encounters with Dangerous Beasts

On occasion, we would eat a picnic lunch in a shady strip of jungle in an area bordering cardamom and coffee plantations. The little coffee estate also grew other crops, including coca from which cocaine is made. It was the only place I ever saw it and when I came across it for the first time my father told me to nip off one of the pale green leaves and place it between my teeth. Almost at once the tip of my tongue and lower lip began to feel numb and I never tried it again!

The cleared boundaries of the estate were places where one had to walk warily since they were used by the game as highways; there were usually hidden traps and snares set by the coolies, and now and then our dogs would be caught, leaving them bruised and sore. One common trap, shaped like a small narrow cage and open at both ends, was roofed by a delicately balanced stone or log of wood which, as soon as a creature triggered the mechanism, fell down killing it instantly. I hate all traps, but like the one above, most of those used by the jungle folk are less cruel than those used by trappers to collect skins. These vicious steel clamps, designed to break an animals' legs, inflict so much pain that the captor will often chew off a limb in order to get free, and thus maimed are unable to flee their predators.

One day, we found ourselves sitting on a rock close to a fallen tree, the top of which had lodged in the branches of a neighbouring tree. Father was smoking his pipe, but the moment we heard galloping in the distance he put it aside and put his finger to his lips for silence. The sound came closer and a sambhur stag came into view; a magnificent animal with spreading antlers and as big as a polo pony. He cleared the fallen tree in one effortless bound and quickly disappeared into the jungle, followed a few moments later by a small pack of wild dogs who were the same breed as those in Rudyard Kipling's 'Red Dog'. They were fortunately too intent on their chase to notice us.

After they had gone Father explained that these dogs were the terror of the jungle, fierce and implacable hunters, who would pursue everything except elephants. They had even been known to attack a tiger; surrounding him, dogging his every footstep and keeping all game from him until, weakened from their harassing tactics and hunger, he is unable to defend himself against their concerted attack. They fear nothing and will attack and destroy anything that comes between them and their prey, including men with guns. Though beautiful, they are considered vermin in the State of Travancore as well as in many other parts of India, and in those days a royalty of some five rupees was paid per tail.

On another excursion, looking down into the valley from a path high on the hillside, we saw the largest herd of elephants I have ever seen. We counted fifty-nine, but there may have been many more. In those early days, elephants were among the chief pests pioneer tea planters had to contend with. As a rule, they were not dangerous if left undisturbed, but the amount of damage that a playful party of elephants can do has to be seen to be believed. The tea nurseries with their thousands of seedlings protected only by light covers from the heat of the sun were particularly vulnerable. Watchmen, positioned in trees to guard the nurseries at night, used anything that made a noise to try and scare off the elephants and when that failed resorted to old muzzle loading guns, but the elephants soon became accustomed to the racket and simply ignored it. I shall never forget my first sight of the devastation caused, nor the delighted squeals of the culprits, as they shuffled off into a nearby patch of jungle!

My mornings with Father were always interesting, if not always adventurous. The estate he managed was mainly tea, but also grew some coffee; a particularly pretty crop in any season. The bushes are pruned so that two crowns of branches, one at the top and one half way down, droop all around the main stem, and when in blossom are covered with masses of sweet-scented white flowers not unlike jasmine. The berries then turn a brilliant red and when ripening, families of monkeys, mainly black-haired Wanderoos, would 'camp' in neighbouring trees ready to raid the bushes at night. Each berry contains two coffee beans, encased in a strong parchment-like envelope which is impervious to the digestive juices of the monkeys, resulting in the fields being strewn with droppings full of untouched coffee beans. These Wanderoo monkeys, with their black hairy bodies, long tails, and grey faces, whilst obviously unpopular with the planters, were the greatest fun to watch and I loved to hear their deep "hoo, hoo, hoo" ringing through the jungle.

The jungle is a noisy place, alive with an infinite variety of calls from different animals: the repetitive hammering of the barbets, boring holes in the trees, the eerie bark of the muntjacs, and the clear 'bell' of the native sambhur deer. Loveliest of all is the pure and penetrating ring of the Malabar, the largest of the squirrels. One of the handsomest animals in the forest, it has a black upper coat and bushy tail, deep chestnut flanks, and a creamy-yellow underside spreading under the neck to the chin and face. Unlike the monkeys who crash about and chatter constantly they move about silently, and it is only when the eye catches some movement that one becomes conscious of their presence. Sometimes, if lucky, we watched as they made tremendous leaps from branch to branch, but travelling their own highways high up in the trees they were generally hard to spot.

Once, on one of my solitary rambles, I left my horse and wandered off into some tall elephant grass. The weather was hot, dry and airless and as I sat on a boulder watching the birds and insects, I spotted a crested lizard with a blood red throat, bobbing his head up and down, perhaps to attract a mate or to scare off some enemy. Then, out of the corner of my eye I suddenly became aware of something moving about fifty yards away, and turning around slowly I saw a magnificent black leopard leap atop a rock and after a good stretch and a wide yawn proceed to have a wash and brush up! My momentary fear was surpassed by the sheer beauty of the animal and a sense of my astonishing luck in being privy to such a wonderful sight. Sitting as still as I could I watched this fierce wild creature behave exactly like our domestic cat, Rajah, also sleek and black. The afternoon sunlight illuminated both the black rosettes on his slightly rusty coat and the ripple of his powerful muscles as he licked himself fore and aft, before spreading his legs, his tummy.

Time lost all meaning, but after a while mosquitoes began buzzing around me and I realised that the sun was getting quite low. I could not move until he left and if he chose to have a snooze on that nice warm rock I would just have to stay where I was. Leopards are short tempered and far more dangerous in a situation such as this than a tiger would have been. Mercifully he had other plans and with a final stretch and yawn, which revealed his great teeth, he leapt lightly into the long grass and disappeared. I could see the grass moving as he passed and the chatter of monkeys at the edge of the jungle told me where he was headed.

As soon as I felt safe I jumped down and hurried off to where, about a quarter of a mile away, my horse waited patiently. I was full of what I had seen but only told Father. Mother would have been scared to death and might have put an end to my happy wanderings.

Many of my outings with Father were quite without incident but our adventures were frequent enough to keep me ever alert. One day, whilst walking single-file along a narrow jungle path, we encountered a wild boar; an event which gave me a wholesome respect for these dangerous beasts. Running ahead and into the jungle Mac must have found himself too close to a sow and her brood. We heard angry grunts then watched as the dog sped towards us, hotly pursued by a huge boar, with gleaming murderous looking tushes and small angry- red eyes. I was rooted to the spot but immediately responded when Father shouted: "Run as hard as you can and climb up that rock!" We tore along the path, up between the tea bushes, and scrambled up the steep sides of a large round rock as if the devil himself was after us, as indeed he was. It didn't take long for the boar to catch up and raising himself on his hind legs, forefeet on the rock, he stood glaring at us furiously. He might have kept us there for some time, but after just a few minutes and having possibly heard calls from his family, dropped to all fours and hurried back to the jungle, but not without threatening backward glances to warn us to keep our distance. I have never been nearer to a wild pig, and neither would I wish to. Looking down, I didn't like anything about him: his rough skin, the way his coarse hair stood up, the big yellowish-white tushes that gave his mouth a wicked twist, and his evil little eyes. No, I didn't like him, and yet he was only defending his family, poor fellow. In all my years in the jungle I lost my fear of all other creatures bar the wild pig.

Tigers

There were two more memorable adventures with wild animals during my first year in India. One morning, Father and I were riding over a high path to a neighbour's bungalow when we heard shouts and the lowing of cattle and looking down saw a clearly agitated herdsman frantically waving his arms. The next moment, we spotted a yellow and black striped body, then a great snarling head appeared from out of the grass near a small black bull. The bull reared its head and the cattle stampeded. The herdsman continued his shouts, to which Father added his, and scared by the noise, the tiger abandoned its kill and slipped away. The bull lay on its side, with its neck broken and head flung back almost to his spine, bearing just two deep tooth marks as evidence of how it had died.

It had been Father's intention to build a raised platform or 'machan' close to the kill, and when it returned, attempt to bag the tiger. However, by the time we returned from our visit the labour had butchered and eaten the entire animal. No other kills were reported and the excitement died down. Given the volume of cattle grazing the hills around South India's tea estates the number killed by tigers is surprisingly small, and in this instance we suspected that the culprit was a tigress driven by desperation to feed her cubs.

The second adventure, if it could be called such, also concerned a tiger. On that occasion I was riding back alone from visiting a neighbour when my horse Tommy, that staid and stolid old gentleman, snorted and stopped still at a point where the path crossed a small strip of jungle or 'shola'. To my astonishment, I saw what looked to be an enormous tiger standing in our way but after gazing at us for a moment, curling his lip in a slight snarl, he leapt lightly into the undergrowth and disappeared. I suppose I was frightened, but only recall the wonder of seeing such a magnificent beast and the grace with which it bounded away.

In that part of the country, tigers and leopards - or panthers as they were known - were not greatly feared. They had all the game they required, and hence no need or desire to seek food elsewhere. The Indian labour felt comfortable walking alone and our postal or 'tapaal' runners travelled long distances from the plains with no protection other than a short spear furnished with jangling bells to scare away bears.

Tigers, through careless and ill-informed hearsay, have acquired a reputation which is quite undeserved. Tigers, leopards, and in fact all carnivores, with the exception of humans and their domestic animals, kill only for food and only enough to satisfy their hunger. The only exception is a tigress teaching her cubs to hunt and this has led to stories of tigers killing for killing's sake. I later came across a book titled 'Man-Eater', published in 1944, in which Jim Corbett sets the record straight in this abbreviated account:

"When I see the expression 'as cruel as a tiger' or 'as bloodthirsty as a tiger', I think of a small boy wandering through jungles of the terai and bhabarin carrying an old muzzle-loading gun, its stock and barrels kept from falling apart by lashings of brass wire. I think of him sleeping anywhere he happened to be that night, with only a small fire for company and when wakened at intervals by the call of tigers, throwing another stick on the fire, then falling asleep without one thought of unease; knowing from his own short experience and that of others that a tiger, unless provoked, would do him no harm. I think of him during daylight hours avoiding any tiger he saw, and when that was not possible standing perfectly still until it had passed. I think of him on an occasion when stalking wildfowl, a tiger turned to the boy with an expression on its face which said as clearly as any words: "Hello kid; what the hell are you doing here?" then walking away without a backward glance.

I have not seen a case where a tiger has been deliberately cruel, where it has been bloodthirsty to the extent that it has killed without provocation or has killed more than it has needed to satisfy its hunger or the hunger of its cubs."

Corbett's account is echoed by another I heard about in India. Many years ago, two young men decided to watch over a bull that had been killed by a tiger. They sat themselves on a small rise of ground some distance from the kill and as there was moonlight had no need of lanterns. They were hard-working assistants on a tea estate and feeling very weary by nightfall soon fell asleep. The tiger came to his kill, had a good meal then walked between the sleepers, leaving bloody pawprints as he went on his way.

A tiger only becomes a man-eater if for some reason it has been forced to kill someone and gets addicted to the taste. When animals are deprived of their hunting grounds by tree-felling and land clearance they will raid cultivated crops for food and, in turn, those which prey on them. Thus, man's actions bewilder the forest-dwellers and force them to behave unnaturally.

Friends, Neighbours and Unusual Company

Our nearest neighbours were great friends of my parents, so we saw a good deal of them. Their attractive young assistant and estate manager James C was also a regular visitor! Up until then I had not felt any need to look more grown-up but now my pigtails bothered me and I harangued my mother to allow me to wear my hair up. It was such a performance that I almost regretted my pestering, but the joy it brought made it all worthwhile! It was a tremendous occasion, a rite of passage of sorts, no longer experienced by girls of today. One felt like a butterfly bursting out of its cocoon. Grown up at last!

We were due to go 'home' in July and one day in the midst of packing, a herd of elephants turned up in the small valley overlooked by my bedroom window. During the night I was awoken by squealing, stamping and a queer rushing sound, and in the morning discovered the cause. Some of the elephants had eaten practically everything in our vegetable garden, and the youngsters had amused themselves by sliding down the nearby hillside on their large behinds, creating a miniature landslide and uprooting almost half an acre of tea in the process. How I wish I could have seen them; it must have been a wonderful sight!

Many of our friends in the district were Scottish and great company. One day, a neighbour sent one of his guests to call on us, probably to get him out of the way for a bit. The type of stolid Scot of storybooks, he had no sense of humour and a ponderous personality that was very hard to entertain. Father had him most of the morning and when they came in for lunch looked thoroughly worn out. In an attempt to entertain his guest and perhaps raise a smile Father laughingly told him the full names of our animals. "This cat", he said, "is known as Rajah, but his real name is the Maharajah of Cooch Behar, and this one goes under the name of Jerry, but is really Jeremiah, Son of Daphne the Grahamite since he was given to us by Mr Graham as a kitten." No smile from our guest. "Now the dog," continued Father desperately, "is really the McNabb of Ballywhakan, County Fife." Having failed yet again to raise a smile, Father gave up the struggle and turned his attention to his food. After a long silence our guest turned to my father, tapped him on the arm and said in a sepulchral voice "There are no McNabbs in Fife." This was too much for Father, his face grew red and unable to contain himself any longer, burst into peals of laughter, laughing till the tears ran down his face. I don't think our guest saw the joke and if he did, gave no indication of it!

My father's furlough began and waved off by James C we boarded a ship of the North German Lloyd from Colombo to London. I had an upper berth in a cabin, shared by a very large German fraulein; an odd girl, who knew no English. We tolerated each other and exchanged smiles until about six days out we ran into very rough weather. Her character then changed immediately, wild-eyed and excitable she persisted in coming into the cabin whenever I lay prostrate on my bunk, and leaning against it, repeating slowly and deliberately: "Top side better". Terrified that she would actually assault me, I was far more frightened of her than any wild animal. She was obviously deranged and, moreover, three times my size. Finally, when I could bear it no longer, I rang for the stewardess and asked that the doctor be sent for. At first, he didn't believe my story since she wasn't there, but mercifully she appeared just in time, more wild-eyed than ever, gesturing for the doctor to help remove me from my bunk. She was duly transferred to the ship's hospital and I was left alone in peace. When the weather calmed she returned, but even though she troubled me no more, I never felt quite at ease.

A Haunted House and Engagement to Jim
1910

On our return from six months in Britain, mainly in Scotland, my father was transferred to another estate, not far from the one to which I had come originally and approached by the same road. The climate here was far better, but the bungalow was not nearly as nice. It was also reputed to be haunted, so Father and I decided to try and see the ghost. We did all the right things, went to all the right places, at the right times, but in the year and a half that we were there we heard and saw nothing. One night, however, I was convinced I heard it. Queer scrunching noises continued for some time outside my bedroom window, followed by an odd swishing sound, as if something were brushing past the rose bushes on either side of a narrow path. I didn't like it one bit, and must admit I put my head under the bedclothes and kept it there. The next morning, I learned that a tiger had killed a big calf during the night, partially eaten it on the path near my bedroom window, then taken the remains through the garden to the edge of a nearby small lake. So much for my ghost!

It was whilst staying at this bungalow by the lake that I became engaged to our old neighbour, James C. He had moved to another district by then and only visited occasionally when his work permitted, riding for many miles over the plains or through jungle highly populated by elephants. I remember him arriving one weekend, absolutely worn out, with his pony caked in mud. Elephants had been having mud baths all across the path in a small valley through which he had to pass, the pony had sunk up to her girth in liquid mud, and he had had great difficulty in extricating both her and himself. Mercifully, the elephants themselves had moved on.

Our new bungalow was much closer to the little village which boasted a European Club and a store selling everything from shoelaces to ham, and to which a runner was sent once a week for groceries, meat etc. It also stocked paraffin for lanterns and lamps, the only form of lighting in the houses and the factory.

Twice a year, when the weather was dry, the Club held a three-day "meet"; a festive event that attracted planters from the many surrounding tea estates. It was all great fun, and I very much enjoyed the gymkhana, the inter-district tennis challenges, the races at which my fiancé distinguished himself, and the dances in the evenings with music played on a rather tired piano by anybody who could manage a dance tune of some sort. What I loved most, even more than the festivities, was coming home over the hills, under the starry sky. There was often frost on the ground so we would get very cold, and because the roads were too rough to trot or canter at night, we would abandon our mounts to the horse-keepers at the top of the hill, then run hand in hand down the last mile or so to the bungalow. Now and again, we would hear the 'bell' of a sambhur or the bark of a muntjac, but probably because of the noise we made, laughing and talking, never met any game. It was usually light by the time we arrived, and after hot baths and breakfast, we didn't bother going to bed but just got on with the day.

Looking back, our horse-keepers had a hard life. Wherever we rode they followed on foot, ready to feed and water our horses on arrival at our destination. It was, however, a popular job, so evidently the men preferred the long walks, grooming and caring for the horses, to labouring in the tea fields. It also afforded them a certain level of prestige. There was only one slight problem. Indians are very superstitious about markings. A horse, dog, cow, or indeed any animal blessed with auspicious marks would always find devoted attendants, but those with unlucky marks were usually neglected and it was quite a job to get a man to look after them. This used to apply to children too; a child with lucky marks could look forward to a rosy life as far as circumstances permitted but the opposite was also true. We knew the eldest son of one of the rajahs in South India, a grand person who would have made a fine ruler, but when his father died and because he had unlucky marks, the 'gadhi' or fortress along with the title of rajah, were inherited by his younger brother.

Superstitions, Traditions and Defending Caste Honour

Around this time, there was great excitement in the district over the building of the first electrically powered factory. There had been murmuring among the Indians that it could not work, or if it did would be at the cost of human sacrifice. It was amazing how little the labour was considered in those days, and because the estate managers knew so little about them, I doubt whether anybody realised the extent and depth of their ingrained beliefs. Be that as it may, the factory was finally completed, and a grand opening ceremony planned.

As ill luck would have it, the afternoon of the opening was overcast, with thunder grumbling in the distance and a heaviness in the air. People had gathered to see the switches turned on and as they waited for the arrival of the general manager, the head fitter, an Indian responsible for a great deal of the work, rode up on his pony just as the storm broke in a tremendous flash of lightning and crash of thunder. The fitter entered the building, the general manager arrived, and the ceremony began. Outside, the storm continued to rage, and before the final speech, a man came running in to say that the fitter's pony, tied under a nearby tree, had been struck by lightning and killed. This was the last straw. Frightened murmurs swept through the factory and one after another, the Indians fled into the storm to escape the Europeans' terrifying magic.

The ceremony proceeded without a hitch, the lights and machinery were duly switched on, but the next morning we learned that three children were missing from the nearby lines. It was impossible to persuade the labour that they had not been sacrificed to provide the magic necessary for the running of the factory machinery, and feelings ran high. Looking back over the years, I feel sure that much of the resulting unrest could have been avoided had someone had the sense to explain matters to the Indians and take the trouble to calm their fears. As it was nothing was done, and for some weeks it was unsafe for women to go out alone. Armed men attacked the labour involved in building the factory, and thus in some way responsible for killing the children; there were even one or two murders. After a lengthy search of the district the children were eventually found alive and well hidden in a village in the plains. It transpired that they had been kidnapped for their own safety by stalwart believers that the engines were driven by magic and the machines would not work without human sacrifice. The safe return of the children brought an anxious period to an end. The factory ran well, the people who worked in it came to no harm, and their fear abated. It had been a highly unpleasant period, but as time went on, more electrically driven factories were built without any ensuing fuss.

The people who had taken over the estate on which my fiancé had previously worked became dear friends. Both were accomplished horsemen, and we spent many wonderful weekends participating in their small private gymkhanas held on a flat piece of land close to the tea factory. A few jumps were set up, we joined in some tent pegging and most enjoyable of all, played a game known as 'pig-sticking'. A sack was filled with straw, tarred all over, and once attached to a length of rope, was handed to the rider of the slowest horse in the party. He or she then set off ahead, dragging behind the black sack, whilst the rest of the riders followed, brandishing long poles tipped with whitewash. Their job was to try and spear the 'pig' as often as possible. Few self-respecting horses were prepared to venture near the bouncing black object, and partly due to the horses' fear and partly because their riders were usually helpless with laughter, the 'pig' was seldom touched. By luck, my horse was unperturbed by the bobbing sack and until disqualified from riding him, I always won!

Mrs. Frode side-saddle and was one of the most natural and beautiful riders I ever encountered. Watching her exercise her young, lively thoroughbred mare on the flat, and seeing Rainbow bucking, jumping about and shying like a kitten from imaginary terrors, was a joyful and unforgettable sight. When staying with them I also helped Mrs. F with her hounds. The couple were keen on hunting and their pack of hounds often became involved with porcupines, with distressing results. Though not prepared to hunt, I was always happy to help dress the hounds' wounds, pull thorns and quills from their paws, and nurse them when they became sick.

Then, during one of my visits, tragedy struck. When Jim worked on the estate he had had a servant named Sebastian. He was one of the best, and had he not had a family living locally, Jim would have taken him with him. Sebastian was a Syrian Christian; a member of a very old Christian community in South India which considers itself a special caste, and a high one at that. He was, therefore, greatly perturbed by his sister's marriage to a very low-caste cattle keeper on the estate, and one day, arrived at Mr F's office carrying a shotgun. He admitted to borrowing it, handed it over and announced: "Sir, I have just shot my sister and her husband. Please call the police." He went on to say that his sister was with child, and he could not tolerate the birth of a low-caste baby into his high-caste family.

This naturally caused huge consternation to the F family. How could Sebastian, that perfect servant with his gentle manners, even temper, and natural gaiety, do such a thing? It just wasn't credible but sadly true: our benign Sebastian was a murderer! The police took Sebastian away and we tried to get on with our lives. It wasn't easy since the thought of Sebastian weighed upon us all. I heard afterwards that he had written to Jim, both before his arrest and several times afterwards, as he awaited his trial and eventual execution. The whole affair was tragic and keenly illustrated the tremendous hold of the caste system over the Indian people, including those who were Christians.

To Pastures New

It was soon after this that my father was transferred to yet another estate. Located on the main 'cart road', we would be living still nearer to the Club, the one and only shop, and other Europeans. Although supposedly 'more civilized', I didn't like it nearly so well, and in some ways, neither did Father as we were both far too enamoured of wild places. Mother, on the other hand, was far happier. She was able to get into the little village easily, return to singing at local concerts, and taking part in district gaiety. She described the move as a chance to "get some of the jungle loneliness out of my bones". Brought up in London, she had never liked the lonely hills of the tea estates, and it must have taken a deal of grit and determination on her part to tolerate living in such places for so many years.

As soon as we had settled into the new bungalow and gone through the usual cutting-up of curtains to fit new windows, altering covers for furniture etc., Mother and I decided to visit my fiancé for a few days. Nowadays, the journey would be considered quite an undertaking, but back then such things were accepted as a matter of course. We left the bungalow early one morning, Mother in a dhooly, and I on horseback, arriving in the village in time to catch the small train that ran to the top of the hill once a day. This part of the journey took about two hours and was quite adventurous in its way. Winding its way along the hillside, the track crossed frail-looking bridges and sometimes on the inward bends, practically doubled back on itself to the extent that, sitting in the front carriage, we could almost have shaken hands with the guard in the rear! Once at the top, our baggage was taken by an overhead ropeway to the foot of the next hill, followed by Mother in a dhooly, and I on foot. It was a fairly long walk of about six miles on a narrow path that zig-zagged so steeply down the face of the hill, that there were sometimes only twenty feet between one zig and the next. By the time we finally made it to the bottom, our luggage had been packed onto two bullock carts waiting to take us on the next leg. As on many previous trips, we trundled slowly along, stopping every eight miles for a change of animals, and enjoying views of the starry night sky through the curve of the roof.

Sometime around dawn, we arrived at a small forest bungalow to which Jim had sent down some food for our breakfast, a dhooly for Mother, and a pony for me. After eating, we left as quickly as we could in order to cross the plains before the sun became too hot. As the sun rose, it filtered through the roof of branches of the Banyan trees, dappling our path with delightful strips of light and shade. and turning the range of forested hills ahead a glorious gold and green. Excited by the prospect of seeing a new part of the country, and especially the place which would become my new home, I found the whole journey a joy.

Some seven miles later, we began to climb into the hills again but this time the road was wide, less rutted and of a reasonable gradient. On the way, we met several bullock carts carrying chests of tea from the estates in the district above. The bullocks leant backwards, straining hard to keep the crossbar behind their heads and avoid being overrun by the heavily- laden carts. A few carts had 'shoe' brakes, but the majority had none. It was amazing how the light-boned bullocks managed to hold back the loads as they did, but by travelling relatively short distances, at a slow pace, they were able to cope with the strain. Once on the plains, the carts travelled by night, and in the days to come, we got used to seeing long lines ambling along with their drivers asleep inside.

After climbing for a mile or two, we became aware of the ever-increasing roar of a waterfall and the jungle became thicker and greener, with a thorny mimosa-like shrub sprawling beneath the trees and over the hillside. Below us, on our right, a stream boiled and rushed down its steep rocky bed and the higher we climbed, the more deafening the sound, until all of a sudden, we came upon a great cataract of water. Tumbling over huge rocks in a welter of spray, it roared its way under a bridge and down the hill to the plains where it was used for irrigation. The road took us over the bridge and stopping to gaze at the foaming water, we were soon soaked by the spray bouncing off the branches of the trees. The whole forest sparkled and glistened in the sunlight, and rays falling on the water made it glitter like jewels. It was such a magnificent and awe-inspiring sight that we were loath to leave. We later learned that this water came from the other side of the hill through a tunnel from a dam, which built years previously had flooded over thirteen square miles of forest and grassland.

Continuing our ascent, we spotted evidence of elephants. 'Eeta', a kind of bamboo, had been torn down, filling roadside drains with earth from the banks where the elephant had dug their tusks. Mother didn't like it at all, but we saw nothing more alarming that day. We soon came to a frontier post on the boundary of the state of Travancore and having given the guards our names and assurances that we had nothing to declare in the way of firearms, tobacco or spirits, we were free to wind our way through a beautiful valley.

After enjoying a mud-bath the previous night, elephants had trouped over the road, making huge holes and depositing mud all over its surface. As we continued down the valley, we came across further signs of elephants at regular intervals. At one point, they had made a huge chasm in the road that even the stout bullock carts could not negotiate, necessitating the need for loads to be carried across and then reloaded on the other side. Such were the roads in the tea districts of Travancore where elephants were protected; the consequence of an astrologer's forecast that the reigning house would prosper as long as elephants roamed free.

At mid-day, we stopped to eat and give the ponies and bearers a rest, then resumed our journey in the heat of early afternoon. The first time we asked how far it was to Munji, where Jim was to meet us, we were told six miles, but when we asked a second time, after travelling for at least ten miles, we were again told six miles! Feeling increasingly weary, we got the same answer the third time we asked, and it seemed as if our destination was retreating further and further into the distance. At last, when we had all but given hope of ever getting there, we came to a village with a fine bridge over a river, and beyond the river the blessed sight of a tea factory.

Our spirits rose immediately and as I rode up to the factory to ask the way, I spied my fiancé on his chestnut mare trotting towards us. How glad we were to see him! It was somewhat of a blow to then discover that we had not yet arrived at his estate and had another twelve miles' journey to Pamba. Having just completed twenty-four, we and our bearers were completely worn out, so, after one last hill, were thankful to be welcomed into a beautiful bungalow where we would spend the night. Hot baths, drinks and dinner followed, and we went to bed early, dog tired.

The next day, Jim and I rode ahead on our ponies by a shortcut, leaving Mother to make the journey in her dhooly by road. Our trail led through grassy downs and tea fields, then along the edge of steep rocky cliffs falling many hundreds of feet to the jungle plains below; an area then marked on maps as "Impenetrable Forest: Unsurveyed". We sat on our ponies and gazed out over this vast tract of forest stretching westwards and even though the sea was some seventy miles away, Jim told me that on a clear evening, it appeared like a silver streak surprisingly high on the horizon. Between the sea and the forest lay the great Empanada Lake and the Travancore backwaters; salt waterways, widely used for transport. Rising to no more than 4,000 feet above sea-level, the hills were covered in grassland with hollows filled with scrubby little date palms which are irresistible to the native, surly sloth bear. When ripe, the thin skin of this fruit, covering a hard seed, tastes exactly like the dried pressed dates one buys in neat little boxes, but is completely without nourishment.

We came at length to another village from which we rode past a tea factory, and then further uphill, finally arriving at the bungalow that was to be my first marital home. The location was lovely, offering nice views over rolling grassy hills, and dominated by huge magenta bougainvillea. The garden, though small, was fine. I loved it all but oh, the bungalow, or rather its sparse and ugly furnishings! The large sitting room had a tiled floor, on which reposed one very small rug by the fireplace, two heavy, carved rosewood chairs, more suited to a church than to a house, one broken cane 'easy' chair, a funny little three-shelf bookcase in one corner, and nothing more. The 'boys' came to greet me, and at the same time give me a look over to assess their likely fate under my jurisdiction! In due course, Mother arrived, and we had lunch in a large, high-ceilinged and rather gloomy dining room. During our week's stay we met several of the neighbours, and Jim and I went off on many long walks and rides through the tea fields and down to the factory to see the pluckers bringing in the leaf. The time then came to return to Father and to my joy, Jim got some leave and accompanied us all the way, even gallantly joining us in the bullock carts, when ordinarily, he would have ridden alone across the plains or through the jungle on the hilltops.

Old Savrimuthu, Mother's cook, probably wondered why Jim and I rode and walked together so much, but when Mother told him that we were officially engaged to be married, he looked horrified, shook his head and said that was no good. Surprised by his reaction she inquired why he should say such a thing, to which he replied in a sepulchral voice: "That master's kitchen no good; only two saucepans". Laughing, she appeased him by explaining that 'Missie' would have more given to her! A funny little chap, he never quite got over feeling responsible for me and because he considered me terribly giddy and irresponsible, I'm afraid I used to tease him by pretending to be giddier than I was!

That was the last estate on which I lived with my parents. I rode about on Tommy Horse visiting neighbours, but although I had quite a gay time it was far too civilised for my taste and I sorely missed the wild. I had been given a bulldog puppy named Bullet, and he and Tommy Horse became surprisingly good friends. That crusty old gentleman put up with more pestering from Bullet than he would from any other creature, and never so much as kicked him, even when I rode up the long road from the bottom of the estate with that little wretch holding onto Tommy's tail growling fiercely and worrying it violently.

On his final visit before we married, Jim presented me with an adorable flea-bitten, half-Arab mare. She had been given to him by his brother, who had been unable to manage her, and Jim, a magnificent horseman, had taken her in hand and trained her to both behave herself and take a side-saddle. In my trousseau was a new riding habit, and I was very proud when I was allowed to wear it and ride my new pony up to the village to show off.

Marie, as I called her, was just the right sort of pony on which to show off. She was a fairy-like creature, all spring and spirit. Her tail swept almost to the ground, and her mane which had never been cut, flowed like silver silk over her graceful neck. Full of life, she was an interesting ride and I had a wonderful time going about on her.

She did, however, have her off-days and on one particular evening she dented my pride. I had been visiting a friend on the other side of the river that flowed through the village and past the club, and on my return saw a number of people sitting outside on the verandah having drinks. The road I was on ran behind the club, into the village across a bridge, and down the cart road, but there was also a riding track in front of the club which forded the river, cutting off a couple of miles. I would not have thought of crossing the ford had I not wanted to show off Marie, but the chance seemed too good to be missed.

As I rode past my audience and down the track to the river, Marie danced along like the lovely little lady she was, and I was sure many envious and admiring eyes were upon me. We entered the river and all went well until halfway across, up went her heels and down went her head, and into the water I went, beautiful new riding habit and all. Having ditched her rider, Marie crossed the river, trotted up the bank and began to graze, as though nothing had happened. Close to weeping with rage and insulted vanity and shivering with cold, I then had to scramble up the bank in full view of the club. Marie made a few short dashes before allowing me to catch and mount her, and then probably feeling that she had humbled me enough, trotted home like an angel, giving me no further trouble.

Special Celebrations in our New Church
1911

In the lonely tea districts of South India, church services were few and far between. Occasionally, a clergyman would come up and hold a service in the clubrooms and later on, in a beautiful little stone church that was built near the village. Particularly memorable was a visit in 1911 by the Bishop of Travancore to preside over our harvest festival. A harvest festival service is always a gay and colourful event, but in this part of the world where the Indian congregation has no money for collections and little or no land on which to grow the 'fruits of the earth' it is quite unique. On that occasion, the service was held first in English and then in Tamil. Each member of the congregation brought along offerings. There were a few pumpkins, marrows and cabbages, but most were some sort of livestock; chickens, ducks, turkeys, goats and even calves, all of which were tied up outside until one by one they were brought into the church to be blessed by the portly and benign bishop at the altar. It was an extraordinary sight! Of no use to the bishop, they were then taken outside to be auctioned and those with money, many of them non-Christians, often paid excessive sums on account of these creatures being blessed. It was all so reverent and grave, with an earnestness and true spirit often absent in the more sophisticated English services.

The Indian men always came in spotless white clothes whilst the Tamil women, as graceful and straight-backed as ballet dancers after years of carrying loads on their heads, dressed in saris of every conceivable colour, with flowers in their hair. In contrast, the Travancore women donned white jackets and white saris with a fan of stiffly starched cotton at the back in place of a bustle. Unadorned with flowers, their hair was worn swept off their faces in either a beautifully coiled bun or a long black plait hanging down their back. I admired the Indian women I met in the village and on the estate, but apart from old Savrimuthu's wife Parkiam and the other bungalow servants I had spoken to none of them. At the time, I was young, thoughtless and in love, living a full and satisfying life, and so my understanding and affection for the locals was yet to develop.

September is a lovely month in the Western Ghats. The long rainy season is almost over, and although the skies are blue, the hills are still filled with the musical sound of running water and are as green as only hills drenched in three months of continuous rain can be. The air feels like champagne, energizing one and all. Each of the seasons has its own charm, but I particularly favoured the months before the beginning of the monsoon with their fine, stuffy mornings and thunderstorms almost every afternoon. During this period, the excruciating noise of the cicadas is enough to drown out conversation and since I was curious to find out more about these insects, a friend caught one for me to examine. The front portion, pale bluish green, vaguely resembles that of a fly, whilst the rear is hollow and cased in overlapping scales of chitin. The loud buzzing is the result of the sound of the vibrating scales being amplified by the cavity.

It was nearing the end of 1911, and preparations for our wedding were progressing. Jim was coming up for the big Christmas gymkhana and staying on till January 16th, our wedding day. It was all very exciting, but I was a defeated woman all the same. I had wanted to be married in my riding habit then ride away from the church to the house that we had been lent for the first two days of our honeymoon. However, since the church was new, and we were to be the first couple married in it, the people in the district forced my parents to have a traditional white wedding.

The morning of my wedding day arrived straight out of Heaven. Mother and I rose early to ride to a friend's bungalow near the church. I was expected to stay behind, pale and tearful, whilst Mother went off to check the preparations, but much to her amusement and the disdain of our hostess, who had expected a demurrer, less matter-of-fact attitude towards my approaching marriage, I felt quite enraged to be trapped indoors! The church was exquisitely decorated with flowers from all the surrounding gardens, and my bouquet comprised white potato creeper and pink antigonon, which, with long hanging streamers of small dainty flowers, were perfect for a wedding. My attendants were some of our friends' children, all suitably attired, but only one small boy managed to brave the long service with the others fleeing to their parents as the ceremony progressed! The whole district turned out to witness the first wedding in their new church, and afterwards walked the few hundred yards to the Club for champagne and cake, albeit battered after its rough journey from Madras!

I think my love of adventure must attract adventure and even our wedding day was not exempt. The sun was still shining when we left, showered in rice, to board the specially decorated carriage that would take us ten miles up the small mountain railway to the bungalow kindly lent by the president of Travancore and Cochin for the first two nights of our honeymoon. However, as soon as we rounded the first bend the sky clouded over and it began to rain quite heavily. Our little engine puffed gamely along, and all was well until on a particularly sharp bend, a large rock detached itself from the mountainside and rolling onto the track, knocked our little carriage off the rails and over on its side. Mercifully unhurt, we scrambled out, Jim firmly clutching one tier of our cake, leaving his bride to manage on her own; an act he has never been allowed to forget! Despite escaping injury, my frock and hat were irretrievably ruined, for soaked by the rain, the gay, paper decorations had bled, staining the white linen with all the colours of the rainbow! Fortunately, our engine driver and fireman were able to reset the carriage on the rails and we were soon on our way.

Dealings with a Devil and Drunkards

Although we had planned to spend the rest of our honeymoon in Madras, just one day after our wedding, we received a telegram requesting Jim's immediate return to deal with an emergency. A month or two previously and against everyone's advice, Jim had accepted the task of reclaiming a tea estate, accessed some ten miles from his bungalow by game tracks over the hills. It had been abandoned for about fourteen years, after malaria had wiped out a large part of the workforce and survivors had bolted, claiming that the place was plagued by a devil.

The emergency that cut short our honeymoon was serious. Given the old estate's bad reputation, the labour was jumpy and easily scared. Although now recognised that malaria was mosquito-borne, we still thought that 'bad air' had an impact, so Jim had temporary huts built high up on the hillside, some distance from the dank valley swamp and the old overgrown fields. Water was piped in from upper hills and as each month passed with no sign of either mosquitoes or malaria, the workers grew more confident and less likely to panic.

All was going well until clearing the undergrowth from the ruins of dwellings in the swamp, workers unearthed the skeletons of fourteen people. The gruesome discovery had unsettled the labour workers to the extent that they were ready to down tools and decamp; their panic was compounded when that very night, a hyena cried for hours outside their huts. Unable to cope, our assistant had sent us a telegram requesting our immediate help.

The day after our return, Jim left at dawn for the scene of the emergency. He eventually managed to persuade the labour to stay, but then as the clearing work progressed, they became increasingly bothered by the elephants and on more than one occasion their huts were destroyed. Jim would frequently encounter the beasts as he travelled alone to and fro, and I must confess that I never felt at peace until he returned in one piece, often late in the evening.

Now and again, I went with him and camped on the hillside in a small tent close to the grass hut occupied by the assistant. The ride over was great fun, but once there, I could not join the men in the 'lantana' or scrub and there was nowhere really for me to walk or ride, apart from the hills above the settlement which had wonderful views over the valley, and the big river running through the jungle and out to the east beyond the spur.

My days at camp, though somewhat wearisome, were not without a couple of scares. I was awoken one night by the sound of snuffling and scratching and as it drew uncomfortably close, pictured an inquisitive elephant bearing down on our tent or perhaps, taking a dislike to it and squashing it flat. The noise soon died away and looking around the next morning, we were thankful to discover that it had been caused not by an elephant but by a sloth bear grubbing for roots nearby.

The next, more alarming incident occurred on one of my first trips. Accompanied by a survey party and the general manager, Jim had gone off, hoping to find the boundary stones of the old estate, hidden within an almost impenetrable growth of dense, thorny shrub about fifteen feet high. Left alone, I amused myself by scrambling about the hillside and not nearly as tough back then, retreated to the hut to sew when it became too hot. The men came in just as it was getting dark, covered with scratches and thoroughly weary, crying out for hot baths and strong drinks before retiring early.

Just as they were leaving early the next morning, there was a bit of a scuffle behind our huts. No one paid any attention but within half an hour of their departure, our new cook staggered towards me completely drunk and demanding money. Having none on me, I tried to distract him but undeterred, he then threatened to burn down the hut. He looked capable of anything and I was terrified. All my attempts to pacify him seemed only to make him worse and although the grass hut would burn like a torch and could offer no protection, I was afraid to leave its illusion of safety.

We later heard that this man was highly dangerous and had stabbed a woman in a drunken rage. I had no idea what to do and shuddered to think what might have happened had I not noticed the general manager's boy Francis, on a path below. He was a slightly built fellow, no more than five feet tall, but strong and courageous and to my intense relief, took in the situation in a flash. Charging up the bank like a fury, he launched into an attack, banging a stout stick hard on the drunkard's head. Standing over him, he then ordered him off the place, and to my surprise and relief, he staggered off never to be seen again.

At once, we sent for and re-engaged Jim's old cook. He too had drunken episodes, but we worked out an arrangement for managing them. I told him, "Veeraswamy I know you drink and you know you drink. If you promise to come and tell me when you need to get drunk, I will give you leave to go away for a few days." He shamefacedly agreed and, on the whole, it worked. Whenever he announced that he wanted to "drink nice medicine," I would let him go. He would then return in a day or two with a fearful hangover, but sober and repentant.

Married Life, Ooralies and a Naval Captain's Ghost

Neighbours came to call, and we had quite a gay time in a quiet way. However, since our bungalow was unfortunately placed midway between one rest-house at Mundakayam and the next at Kumili, travellers would almost invariably want to spend the night with us en-route. It was not uncommon for us to have between one and four unexpected guests, usually because it was unsafe to continue through the elephant-infested jungle after dark. This meant beds, food and drinks for the masters, food and somewhere to sleep for the grooms, and fodder for the horses. Some of our guests were, of course, friends, but many were often complete strangers and now and again rather thirsty strangers to boot! After some weeks of this, I began to keep a record and from mid-February to mid-November we had only six nights alone in our own house. We were not paid handsomely, and although most commodities were cheap, we found that at times our funds ran very low.

It was around this time that a cart road was built through an area inhabited by Ooralies, to link the newly opened estate to the main road. A small settlement of Ooralies lived along the track taken by the new road. Initially, these naturally shy people would run off whenever they saw us, but one day I was able to help a small child with a bad burn, and then later, give quinine and aspirin to those with malaria. The headman of the settlement spoke Tamil, and the others knew a very little, so we were able to understand each other fairly well. We also found that a smile, a little friendly help, and an occasional sweetie were often just as good as language! The Ooralies lived in appalling conditions. During the day they cooked and spent their time in and around small lean-to huts, but at night took both themselves and their belongings up frail ladders into treehouses, where they remained until dawn. The men wore next to nothing and the women, only skirts made from dirty rags of cotton. Beads, usually blue and white, adorned their chests, which were otherwise bare. On the outskirts of every Oorali settlement is a treehouse to which a woman is taken when she goes into labour and where she stays all alone, without any contact with other villagers, until three days after her child is born. I never discovered how many women and babies died either at childbirth or as a result of having no assistance during a difficult labour.

The children, naked and skinny with protuberant tummies caused by malnutrition and hookworm, looked unable to survive to maturity and in fact, when we left India in 1948, there were but a few hundred Ooralies still living in scattered settlements around the Periyar Lake. These Ooralies had become our good friends and whenever we passed, would often ask for castor oil. The children would drink and then lick the spoon clean as though it were golden syrup or something equally delicious, and any remains of doses given to mothers for their tiny babies would be massaged into the infants' tummies or heads. Quinine was less popular but ironically, because of its bitterness they were more convinced of its effectiveness!

At our bungalow at Pamba, women and children were beginning to call in for cough mixture and castor oil. I also attended to cuts and burns, and through experience learned what dressings and mixtures to use, with some success. At the time, estates were visited by an apothecary once a week, and stock mixtures left with the Conductors for distribution amongst the labour. It was a very hit and miss method, and my own was almost as haphazard, but at the very least, I was able to attend to their needs on a daily basis. I never got over my dread of treating burns which were all too common, given that cooking on open fires in cramped primitive huts, made it easy for clothes to be set alight or for large pots of boiling rice to tip over the cook's, and sometimes the children's, bare feet. Usually burns were brought to be treated at once, but if severe, the application of a dressing could be quite painful and victims might wait several days before plucking up the courage to see me, making the process particularly difficult.

The south-west monsoon which arrived early in June, triggered the start of the healthy season. The labour was less prone to sickness, and everyone felt the better for the blustery winds and soft damp air. Work on the abandoned estate continued steadily and despite joining Jim less frequently, I sometimes rode part-way, stayed with friends and returned home with him in the dark, over rolling hills punctuated by small patches of jungle in the hollows. Although over seventy miles from the sea, the valley would often be shrouded in a thick, salty mist carried in by the steady southwest wind. One night, riding home in the bright moonlight with a thick mist below us, I recall watching our shadows, like ghost-riders, accompanying us all the way; a lovely if eerie experience. The months flew by and Christmas came along. The temperature dropped and evenings were spent by the fire, either relaxing in armchairs or standing around the piano with each of us adding his or her contribution to the evening's entertainment. On Christmas Eve, we had a party and singsong, lasting well into the 'wee sma' ' hours. We began with 'good' music, but as the night wore on soon descended to songs and choruses from the Student's Song Book.

Our bungalow had a history and was thought to be haunted. Built by a retired Naval Captain, its sitting room was shaped like the turret in a battleship and even the sash windows were curved. At one end of the room, was a straight 'walk' with a small alcove in the wall at each end that looked as though they had once held statues. We were told, however, that the old man had a habit of marching up and down with a telescope under his arm, spying on passers-by, and in each alcove stood a bottle of beer and a glass, from which he imbibed freely. Should any European dare pass by without coming in for a drink, he would fire a salvo over his head and roar across the valley, demanding that they come in and refresh themselves. The old man had apparently been a champion drinker and must have spent large sums on supplies which in those days, had to be carried on men's heads sixty miles from the nearest shop down by the west coast. Finally, after an attack of DTs, he was ordered to take a voyage around Ceylon and died at sea.

Indians who had known the old man, claimed that his ghost haunted the back room in which he used to keep his beer. We imagined that we could hear him riding down the short, steep hill to the bridge at the foot of our bungalow road, and his horse's hooves crossing the bridge before breaking into a trot then a canter up to the rear of our premises. The sound was so real that we were often fooled. We would sometimes comment "there's the old ghost again," only to find that somebody had ridden up to the stables, but at others, would go out expecting to meet a friend and find no one there. All in all, he proved quite an entertaining old gentleman!

During that period, we had a party of Royal Engineers involved in the Royal Survey of India living on the estate. Their job included an exploration of a great stretch of forest that ran from below the cliffs to the west coast and in the process, they came across a primitive tribe. We had heard about, and discounted, the Indians' fear of these people whom they regarded as devils. Known as Pandarams, they are mentioned in books on India's primitive tribes and described as being rather hirsute with negroid features. Being timid and shy, they were seldom seen, but one of the parties of surveyors managed to catch a poor soul and locked him up in a disused stable, with the intention of photographing him the next morning. The captive however, had other plans and in the night dug himself out from under the walls!

Babies, Health Scares and the Onslaught of War
1913

Early in April, Jim had to go off to Thenga, and as I was pregnant with our first child, due at the beginning of May, I stayed at home sewing and pottering about the house. On the evening after he left, I was working in the stable and stepped on a loose board. It swung upwards, hitting my forehead and I fell heavily to the ground. Though not initially worried, as time went on, I began to feel very ill. I was alone and frightened and when the pain grew steadily worse, I sent one of the horse-keepers for the doctor, who eventually turned up long after dark. By that point, I was past caring what became of me. After just one look, the doctor quickly administered chloroform, just in time to deliver my baby, who owing to my fall, arrived a month early!

I did not realise that as a rule, women are not expected to attend to their babies immediately after giving birth, and so after the doctor had bathed him I got up, ready to do whatever was needed. At dawn I sent a telegram to my mother, and a runner over to Jim, who hurried back that evening eager to see his brand-new son. He too, was ignorant of what should be done on these occasions; it was not until Mother arrived twenty-four hours later, that I was unceremoniously bundled back into bed and kept there for a week. Jim, meanwhile, found an Indian woman from the nearby village to do the washing, look after me and help Mother. As my baby had arrived safely, the nurse ordered for my confinement was cancelled, and the Anglo-Indian nanny, already engaged, was asked to come as soon as possible. Despite her somewhat fierce appearance, we soon grew to love her, and our son adored her. Kind and extremely capable, she was the light of our lives! As a trained nurse, she also helped treat the women and children who came up to the bungalow, and I learnt a lot from her.

When our son Bill was five months old, we were shocked to discover that the sweeper- woman who came up each day to wash nappies and clean out the bathrooms, had been secretly nursing a smallpox patient in her room for several days. With no time to arrange the collection of lymph, we panicked. Telegrams and messages flew hither and thither until a plan was fixed to take him to Bangalore, in the state of Mysore, to be vaccinated. Should the worst happen, he would at least be nearer to civilization and a hospital.

I shall never forget that journey. Bill and I set off in a dhooly, accompanied by Jim on horseback and when we got to the ghaut on the western side of the hills, a deckchair was rigged up on a lorry in which I sat holding Bill. We jolted and rattled along an exquisitely beautiful road past villages nestled in lush plantations of rubber, palms and mango, to the small town of Kottayam at the head of the backwaters. Along the way, we occasionally passed women and children carrying large flat baskets on their heads containing either eggs or chickens, and others driving goats or cattle to market. I also saw for the first time, a flock of several hundred ducks being driven along the road like a flock of sheep. Their owners move from place to place, stopping to sleep wherever their ducks can feed, then after collecting the eggs laid overnight, march on, selling the eggs at villages en route. We got to the backwaters by nightfall, had a meal at a rest-house then settled down for the night in a 'wallum'; a large barge-like boat poled by men along the brackish waterways. I have travelled these backwaters by other means since, but even my anxiety about Bill could not squash my delight in lying on a mattress in the boat and being able to watch the stars and look over the water from the open ends of the matting canopy.

After a wash and breakfast at the station the next morning, it was beginning to get hot and since there were no electric fans in the carriages, the heat became unbearable as our train trundled its way slowly across the plains. Just before dark, we transferred to another train, which proved even more uncomfortable. Our carriage was lit by a paraffin lamp with a very grimy glass reflector, half-full of dirty water and floating with insects, which splashed back and forth with the rocking of the train. We clanked and clattered along in the fading light and then, just as we left the next station, the lamp in our carriage went out, leaving us in complete darkness. Bill, who up until then, had been an angel, took the opportunity to wake up and protest. It was small wonder but trying to deal with the poor little chap in that very hot and pitch-black compartment, was a perfect nightmare. Distances between stations are considerable in India, and it was some time before we stopped once more. I got out and reported the broken light, only to be told that this was a small place and nothing could be done until we got to a larger station two hours further down the line. So, in desperation, I filched a lantern from a railway official on the platform and ignoring his protests, refused to part with it! The chimney glass was black and almost opaque, but though feeble, it was better than nothing.

We finally arrived in Bangalore in the morning, and after freshening up at the hotel, went straight to the hospital where we were all vaccinated. Ours gave us no trouble, but for several days, poor Bill looked as though he had smallpox; his leg was swollen and sore, he had a temperature, and was covered from head to foot with horrible looking pustules which then infected his eyeballs. He was a very sick baby for quite some time. The doctor called every day and Bill recovered, but it had been a very close shave indeed. In those days, Bangalore was a military base and life for the resident regiments was very gay indeed. As mere tea planters we did not 'belong', but since we had friends among the Sappers and in the R.H.A., we had quite a good time once our worries about Bill were over. Then, with no reason to stay, telegrams were sent to make the necessary arrangements for our journey back to the estate, where we were more than happy to resume our old routine.

When Bill was nine months old, I decided to take him to visit my parents. My sister Kathleen was living with them, and I looked forward to showing Bill off to my family, old friends and of course, funny old Savrimuthu. I was weaning Bill at the time, so Mother encouraged me to leave him with her and take the opportunity to catch up with friends I'd made on my arrival in India. It was great fun meeting them all and I spent several days riding all over the dear old place, thoroughly enjoying myself until the time came to bid everyone farewell and face the long trip home.

This time round, it was the leg in the cart that was the least comfortable. Lying in the heat and the dust, Bill became horribly thirsty and the milk I had brought had turned sour. Finding it impossible to find anything safe for him to drink in that primitive countryside, I opened one of those old-fashioned soda water bottles with a pushdown marble stopper and after letting the fizzing die down a bit, offered him some. I couldn't help but laugh when at first taste, he wrinkled up his nose, and am sure it was only his great thirst that drove him to drink it. Poor wee man: he had had a tough time, one way and another, and though none the worse for wear, was due for another spate of ill luck shortly after our return.

He was very late teething, and then his teeth started to appear all at once. The poor babe endured many terrible nights of dark swollen gums and high temperatures and seeing him suffer broke our hearts. I wrote and begged the doctor to lance his gums, but he did not believe in lancing and flatly refused. I was sure that Bill would have convulsions if left untreated and in despair, took the law into my own hands. Shaking with agitation, I collected a small sharp lancet from the estate's dispensary, bound it with white wool to about 1/8 of an inch from the tip and after sterilizing it, took my little boy to our bedroom and locked the door. Despite feeling nervous, I was determined to deliver the poor child from pain and holding my breath, drew the point of the lancet across the front of his gums, top and bottom, where the swelling was preventing the teeth near the surface from breaking through. Blood spurted out, black and turgid, and after gently wiping his gums with boric acid and glycerine, I held him close. He had been crying almost continuously for over twenty-four hours, but within half an hour of his gums being lanced, slept peacefully for almost twelve hours. It must have been a tremendous relief for him and by morning, two of the teeth that had caused the trouble were through. It was probably one of the worst few moments of my life, but I was thankful that I had had the courage to use that lancet.

I had not been home more than a fortnight or so, when one morning, a bullock cart drove up to our back door and out staggered a man looking like a corpse. We discovered that he came from a very malarious place near the west coast and had mistaken our bungalow for the doctor's. I don't know how he survived the journey and as he was obviously unfit to go any further, we put him to bed in our spare room, then sent a runner for the doctor. It turned out that the poor man had had a long spell of malaria and unable to bear being alone in his bungalow, had got himself into a bullock cart, told the driver to take him to the doctor, then passed out. The doctor gave him medicine and ordered him to rest in bed, and there the man stayed for the best part of three weeks. As his health improved, he would come out into our sitting room and sit quietly as though he had no heart for anything. Then one day he asked if he might play our piano, and what a change came over him! His playing was quite exceptional and the many hours he spent playing all the old masters gave us endless pleasure and more than repaid us for anything we had been able to do for him. Each day he became stronger and more able to face life again. It transpired that he had lost his job on a rubber estate, and because he had neither money nor anywhere else to go, he stayed with us through

April until almost the end of May. Then, as my mother and sister were due to pay us a visit and my second baby was expected at any time, we had to ask him to leave, at least for a while.

We were better prepared for my second baby than my first, and there were no excursions or alarms. Bill was now walking, and because Nannie was no longer young and slow, it was decided that she would concentrate on the baby whilst a new nurse was employed to trot after our toddler. Looking back, there was no reason why I couldn't have cared for Bill myself, but in those days, help was cheap, pathetically cheap, and nobody thought anything of employing extra labour for the house or garden whenever it seemed convenient. Lizzie, the new girl, received 10/- a month and even Nannie with all her experience, only £20, plus food and clothing, of course.

    The situation in Europe was becoming very worrying and as Jim had been in the R.H.A and was a trained gunner, there was little doubt that should war break out, he would volunteer for service. My heart sank whenever I thought of what might lie in store for us. Our new daughter Monica was my chief concern. She was a delicate baby, prone to bronchitis and not fit to cope with long trying journeys or barrack life, probably in Britain. We had hoped against hope that it wouldn't happen, but Britain was now at war with Germany and Jim was already in touch with the Company regarding his release. We were all still together when Christmas 1914 came along, though arrangements for our departure for Britain were almost complete. After much deliberation we decided to leave Monica behind with my parents, and with plans to retire the following year, they would bring her to Britain in July. We were due to arrive in wintery February with no idea about the condition of our accommodation, but as it happened, Jim was offered a commission straight away, meaning we would not be living in the barracks after all.

Return to Post-War India
1918

As this is an account of our life in India, and not of our lives as a whole, I will pass over the war years which I spent in Britain, and Jim partly in France and partly in what was then Mesopotamia. On our return to India, Jim was told that he was to take over a small estate in a very malarious valley; a move which presented us with a very difficult decision concerning the children.

Now settled in London, Mother and Father would look after the children if we left them behind, but they were still very small and, in those days, men on the tea estates were only given Home leave every four and a half years, and their salaries were not so princely as to allow wives to visit their children in the interim. However, only too aware of the dangers of exposing the children to malaria, there was no doubt in Jim's mind. Monica, just beginning to grow out of her bronchitis, was very healthy and Bill was a fine, fit and tough little person, so we decided to leave them. It was a hard wrench to bear. They were such sweet children and being apart for such a long time, we would miss so much of the joy of watching them grow up, but Bill was six and Monica five, and under normal circumstances they would soon have been sent to Britain to start school. We never regretted our decision, and over the years as we watched other children in the Periyar valley suffer from malaria, were more than glad not have exposed our two to that insidious disease.

My arrival in India this time was entirely different from my first. I again travelled through Ceylon by train, but instead of that wretched all-night journey and precarious trip by launch from ship to shore, the crossing over to India took only two hours. A new, small flat-bottomed boat now ferried passengers from the Ceylon side across the strait, following the line of the coral reef called Adam's Bridge, to a train waiting on the quay at Danashkudi in India. Then, instead of repeating my previous long journey by bullock cart from the station, Jim and I spent a comfortable night in the rest-house before travelling by car to the little forest bungalow, where ponies sent down by the general manager awaited.

Our car was odd, even by the standards of the day and already aged, appeared dependent on many odd pieces of wire for its continued existence. However, it went after a fashion, and we felt very superior as we hurtled along the road at about twenty miles an hour, flying past bullock carts and pedestrians in a most satisfying manner. The two rivers that had given us such trouble, both when I first came to India and when we left for Britain, were now bridged and we flew over them with no trouble, looking down on the places where we had sat in our carts being man-handled over the riverbeds and avoiding being ducked in the rushing water. We then mounted on our ponies for the last leg and barely noticed the distance as we rode along the plains and up the winding ghaut road, past the great waterfall, to the general manager's bungalow, where we were welcomed by drinks and hot baths. So much had changed for the better but despite the comfort afforded by modern developments, I quite missed the fun and adventure of the old days!

The war had brought a good deal of new knowledge about the treatment and prevention of malaria, but little had improved here. Those with fever were given quinine and sometimes recovered, sometimes not. We arrived in April, almost the worst month for malaria, and within a week had opened a dispensary on the verandah of Jim's office, from where I treated any coolies afflicted by the disease, with quinine. I also dressed wounds and burns and following the directions of the local Indian doctor who visited the estate once a week, dealt with other minor complaints. Thus, this dispensary of mine soon developed into an almost a full-time job, which kept me very busy for several months.

Doing this sort of work with no real knowledge or experience could be nerve-racking, but I drew comfort from the fact that without it, the poor folk who came to the dispensary would have been far worse off. I remember a small girl arriving one morning with a raging fever and when I took her temperature was aghast to see the mercury soar to 107! She lay in her father's arms, mouth open, lips parched, her breath coming in quick pants and I was almost afraid to touch the scorching little body for fear of harming her. At the time my knowledge was such that I couldn't determine whether it was malaria but taking a guess I gave her quinine and miraculously she began to recover and within a few weeks, was back on her feet. I gained notoriety from this cure, though God only knows, it owed more to the fact that she had malaria and responded to the quinine, than to anything extraordinary I had done for her.

Roads in parts of the estate were now better than before, at least where the elephants had left them alone, and one doughty individual at the other end of the district invested in a car. However, travelling even on the improved roads was no pleasure for anyone. The surfaces remained rough, to put it mildly, and since all roads were very narrow and winding, meeting a train of bullock carts loaded with tea or rice could become a major adventure and cause unlimited delay. All carts travelled in convoys as protection from elephants, and a convoy might well stretch from one corner of the estate to the next, and beyond. The bullocks were driven by means of a rope running through the soft membrane of their nostrils, combined with tail-twisting, shrewd kicks under their tails and shouts, none of which were designed to cope with an emergency such as the sudden appearance of a motor car. Terrified of cars, the bullocks would swing to one side or the other of the road, veering perilously close to a sheer drop of anything from 50 to 150 feet. There was no chance of ever overtaking them in a hurry! To pass one cart might take anything up to ten minutes or even more, amidst angry shouts from the cart-men and ineffectual rage on the part of the increasingly impatient driver. One cart safely passed, the next one had to be negotiated, by which time the bullocks, having heard the noise and fuss over the cart in front, were already in a state of terror and almost out of control. This state of affairs would hold good for each of the succeeding twenty or more vehicles. Given the amount of time wasted, it was quicker and certainly less trying to make the journey on horseback, and hence the possession of a car was regarded as more of a status symbol than a practical and comfortable mode of travel.

Around that time, we also seemed fated to suffer from the attention of elephants and found ourselves involved in a particularly awful incident. A friend was having a new bungalow built four miles away and during its construction was living in a less than comfortable grass shed. One evening, he sent a messenger over to Jim with an urgent request for information and having not received it by return, rode over the next morning to find out the reason. When it became clear that the messenger was missing, a search was launched along the river bank but the man was nowhere to be seen. Jim then suggested they explore a little-known shortcut and there, lodged in a tree, unconscious from a loss of blood, was the messenger.

From what we could gather, the man had been met by a solitary elephant as he climbed up the bank from the ford over the river. Rushing towards him, the elephant had knocked him down, driven its tusk through the fleshy part of the man's leg and then in order to shake him off had tossed its head, flinging the man into the branches of the tree. A makeshift ladder was constructed, and once retrieved, the injured man was carried on a litter by bearers to a little

Indian hospital some seven miles away. It seems hard to believe that a man could survive such an experience, but survive he did, and recovered sufficiently to return to work with only a limp to remind him of what must have been a terrible night.

Cloudland
1919

We only spent five months on that estate before Jim was moved to a much larger place, still within the unhealthy valley. During the war it had not been possible to replace the previous manager who was too ill to walk or ride around the estate. Oh, what a mess he left behind! Nearly half the estate had been abandoned and returned to the jungle and all the labour were infected with malaria.

In those days, many labourers on tea estates were held in lower regard than the masters' dogs and horses, and the plight of the people on this estate when we took over was pitiable. Jim sent a report to the Company outlining the problems with an added request for free rice to be issued to those who through sickness, were unable to earn enough to feed themselves. He received a reply to the effect that since this had never been deemed necessary in the past, the Company saw no reason why it should begin now. However, something had to be done, so Jim called a meeting of all the 'kangangies' or headmen and proposed that when the labour were issued their weekly ration of rice in 'minglies' – a measure used on the West coast of India, equivalent to two pounds – any surplus flicked off was used either to feed the sick or sold to buy alternative foodstuff for those unfit to eat rice. The Company agreed, much to the relief of those who had long struggled to feed themselves and their relatives on their none too generous rations.

We were then shocked to learn that no records had been kept on the many deaths on the estate; the disappearance of a worker's name from a rota being the only indication that they had either died or perhaps bolted back to their village in the plains. From that point on, we kept a strict tally and found to our horror that at the end of that year, 1919, the death rate, excluding that of non-workers, babies and the elderly, stood at 116 per thousand. The worst time of the year when most of the deaths occurred was the period from March to July. The weather during these months is warm and humid and ideal for mosquitoes, leading to outbreaks of malaria, which victims living in miserable little huts during the cold, wet conditions brought by the next season's monsoon rains, were unable to survive. Jim had three Indian assistants, two on the estate itself and one on a smaller estate attached to his, but unlike the white men with their better living conditions and hence greater resistance to the disease, they were too ill to work more often than not.

    Meanwhile, our friend who had now been living in his bungalow for several months, was facing problems from elephants who had taken offence to his new abode. Night after night, they surrounded his home, trumpeting loudly, and he had had to have a trench dug to keep them out of his garden. It transpired that his home had been built across an old elephant highway, and despite being apparently abandoned, the great beasts had not taken kindly to the obstacle set in its path. The pestering and noise continued unabated, and after a year of having his sleep disturbed, he decided to build another bungalow elsewhere. The very night after he had relocated the elephants moved in and by morning only the chimney remained standing. We were asked over to see it, intending to take photographs after staying the night, but when morning came even the chimney was gone and the whole place trampled flat as though the bungalow had never existed!

Adventures with Peramal

One Christmas, as there was no malaria to speak of on the estate and we were both well, Jim and I together with two friends decided to go out into the wilds; the men to shoot, and I to tag along and enjoy the countryside. Having sent men ahead to build grass huts for us to sleep in, we left at dawn, rode for a few miles, then marched, first through tea-fields, then uphill into jungle and grassland and by game tracks over the hills to our camp. But just as we topped a hill, our guides stopped and gasped in horror. There, by a small patch of trees was a flattened area on which three grass huts, constructed only the day before, had been reduced to a pile of debris. Beside the ruins were large footprints and elephant droppings which left no doubt as to who was to blame!

Instead of going in search of game as planned, and as we could not sleep out in the open at that time of year, we set to work rigging up shelters of some sort, and in case the elephants returned, collected enough wood to keep fires burning through the next few nights. After an early supper cooked by our kitchen coolie who had come with us, we lit a bonfire and retired to bed. Our new shelters, though far less comfortable than the huts were adequate, given that our main priority was to stalk and shoot game. As always, the first night in camp meant no sleep for me and thrilled by the sounds of the jungle, I lay awake enjoying the mingled trills of crickets, soft rustlings in the grass as some small creature crept by, and the cries of owls and nightjars. There was always a faint chance of hearing a tiger or a panther, and even the squealing and shuffling of elephants feeding, though fortunately those responsible for destroying our huts had long departed and we were left in peace.

At the break of dawn we set off accompanied by old Peramal, one of the best 'shikaris' or guides in the district. The weather was fine and cool, and tramping along game tracks on those rolling uplands was pure joy. Peramal marched ahead scanning the terrain for game. He was a quaint little character, barely five feet tall and thin to the point of emaciation, with rheumy eyes that despite looking incapable of seeing anything at a distance, could pick out game more quickly than anybody we knew. In fact, he would often point out a sambhur, bison, or elephant and describe it, when we with our field glasses were hardly able to see it.

Peramal had a catholic taste in clothes. On this occasion, he wore puttees wound round his legs above his bare feet, khaki shorts that were far too big, and a tailcoat made for a taller and much larger man for some long-ago dance, all fastened over his meagre frame with safety pins. As the day grew warmer, the balaclava sported on his grizzled head early in the morning was exchanged for a Y.A.D. cap; a most unlikely choice and a mystery as to where he had obtained it! Whenever we halted to scan for game, he would remove this cap and hand it, with a lordly gesture, to his young apprentice who would carefully examine it for lice; catching and cracking them between his fingernails, before returning it to Peramal.

At about nine o clock, we spotted and began to stalk, a small herd of bison grazing on a rise a mile or so away. In that part of the country, the direction of the wind had to be watched very carefully as it was liable to swing around the hills, and with this apparent change of direction, carry our scent to the quarry's sensitive nostrils. Finally, after a fairly long stalk, we lay down in the short grass just behind the brow of a small hill, where oblivious to our presence, the bison continued to graze whilst moving slowly towards us. Like Jim, both of our friends had served in France during the war and both suffered from nerves. The three men had tossed for first shot and Jim, who had won, would have waited quietly until the bull came close enough for a certain kill. However, lying in wait, one of the men began to fidget, until overcome with nervous impatience, he leapt up insisting that Jim shoot. In response, Jim took a snap shot at the bull which along with the herd was already galloping down the hillside towards a patch of jungle about 700 yards away. He hit him but failed to find the vital spot.

The Bos Gaurus or native bison of the South Indian uplands, is a fine animal. Mature bulls are black and heavily built with deep shoulders, light hindquarters and fine steel-grey tipped horns, whereas the cows and young bulls are dark chestnut in colour, and the calves a lighter, almost creamy shade. This herd had no calves, and the short time it took them to cover the distance between us and the jungle was some indication of the tremendous pace those heavy animals can travel.

Leaving me on the hillside, the men went down to where the herd had entered the jungle. Almost as soon as they disappeared from sight I heard a shot, and from my lofty position saw the big bull emerge and make his way slowly across the hillside. Clearly wounded, the poor brute then lay down in the long grass beneath a small tree. Knowing that he was invisible to the men, and noticing that they were about to unwittingly pass within a few feet of the wounded animal's tail, I yelled and waved my arms in warning, and when that failed I ran halfway down the hill. Thankfully, at the last moment I was able to make myself understood. A wounded bison can be highly dangerous, but so far this animal in its much-weakened state, had not tried to move. Jim advanced slowly, rifle at the ready, and from where I stood seemed almost on top of him before the poor creature heaved himself to his feet and charged. Surrounded by long grass, Jim was unable to see far ahead, and his first shot hit the bull's horn, splintering its tip. He was, however, luckier with his second. The bullet hit the bull's heart and its great body crashed to the ground.

Now that the bison was dead, it was left to old Peramal to arrange for the head and tongue to be removed whilst we made our way back to camp. As soon our load coolies heard of the kill, they immediately dashed off for their share and before darkness fell, their nearby camp was noisy with talk, song and the sound of meat being cooked in bubbling cans of kerosene oil. After a night of feasting the men then stayed up late, cutting the surplus meat into strips, ready to be hung out to dry in the sunshine and transformed into biltong.

Next morning, we were out again, tramping along game tracks that followed the line of elevation mid-way between where the grass grew long and coarse, and where it was short and sweet. We were able to see all round us and just when we were thinking of resting for a picnic lunch, we spotted a small herd of elephants on a nearby knoll, and between them and us, a sloth bear grubbing for roots. One of our friends was off at once after the bear, while the rest of us sat still and watched. As he stalked down towards it, his eyes glued on his quarry, rifle at the ready, our friend had to pass through a strip of long grass. Suddenly, there was a surge in the grass, a scamper of hoofs and a sambhur stag leapt out, almost at his feet. He shot wildly and thankfully missed! Sitting in the 'front row of the stalls', we then had the delight of watching the ensuing activity. The sambhur sprang across the hill and vanished round a shoulder, whilst the bear, slower in intelligence, took a fraction longer to sum up the situation then he too, hurried away into the long grass and out of sight of the hunter. We saw him again sometime later, still hurrying along a game track across the hill. The elephants meanwhile, had huddled themselves into a tight circle; calves in the centre watched over by the cows with rumps facing outwards, and two young bulls positioned at the flanks of the 'scrum'. At a slight distance, an unusually large bull boasting a pair of perfect tusks, stood guard, his head raised as if trying to discern the direction from which the shot had been fired and its threat to his family. Then, as if to demonstrate his power and to warn off any intruder, he dug his huge tusks into the ground and began picking up great sods of turf and tossing them over his shoulder. Mercifully, elephants are protected in the state of Travancore, so there was no question of shooting him.

It was a dull, damp day and before we had travelled more than a very few miles, the mist became so dense, that after a short rest, Peramal suggested we return to camp. Had it not been for Peramal, we would have been hopelessly lost, but well familiar with the terrain, our guide had his own small landmarks in the shape of stones on the tracks and other little peculiarities known only to him. He turned up later that evening, and whilst discussing the next day's plans, we watched fascinated as he sank a double 'peg' of cheap brandy. Part of his daily ritual and true to his eccentric character he somehow managed to pour the fiery liquor from a great height, straight down his throat, without ever putting the glass to his lips.

On the morning of our third day we set off in a different direction. The mist had cleared, and the sun sparkled on the wet grass. We soon spotted a small herd of bison grazing below us and because we had to take a detour had a long and arduous stalk, testing the wind and creeping through the grass, hoping they would neither see us nor catch our scent. I tried to keep my mind on the job in hand and enjoy it, instead of thinking about its inevitable conclusion to which I never became accustomed. As we drew near, I was once again struck by the grandeur of these animals. The bull with his enormous shoulders and looking tremendously powerful, stood a short distance from the herd, his head held high as he collected scents from the air.

One of the men raised his rifle and I found myself praying that he would miss, and the herd would dash over the hills, free and unharmed. But sadly, it was not to be. The shot rang out, the herd turned and fled, but the bull stood as if rooted to the spot. Swinging around, he then trotted off into a small depression, pursued by the three men and Peramal, with me trailing behind at a distance. Standing stock-still in the long grass, the bison appeared to be waiting for us and knowing that wounded bison are both highly aggressive and liable to stalk their stalkers, our two companions' nerves went to bits, and it was left to Peramal and Jim to put it out of its misery. Taking up their rifles they fired two shots, but it took a third from Jim to finally finish him off.

Our weary trek back to camp was made all the more exhausting by having to plough through long stalky grass, and we arrived desperate for tea, food and bed. However, before any of that, we had the treat of bathing camp-style. Standing on a board in a grass shelter and dousing oneself with hot water from an old kerosene tin must be one of the most refreshing methods of bathing and one guaranteed to make anyone feel like a new man or woman!

The following morning, the load coolies went on ahead to set up another camp, leaving us to roam the hills whilst heading west towards a bluff which fell from the rolling downs to the virgin forest inhabited by the Pandarams in the plains far below. Again, it was Jim's turn for the first shot and nearing the bluff, Peramal spotted a Nilgiri Tahr - a wild mountain goat indigenous to South India - standing on a precipice, some distance away.

Since tahr have near-telescopic vision, it was certain to be a very short stalk and a very long shot. This little buck was the sentinel, using his wonderful eyesight and his sensitive nose to guard the herd grazing between the rocks below. As we got nearer, it became obvious that he had been alerted to our presence. Jim immediately stopped in his tracks and as he rose, the tahr turned to face him. Jim fired and with one leap in the air the animal disappeared over the cliff. We hurried over to discover that having cleared the rocks, the little stag had plunged over one thousand feet to the forest below. There seemed no obvious way down, but two of the coolies eventually found a track, and after a long descent and following directions yelled from above, the men managed to reach the forest floor. Standing at the top, we then heard cheerful calls to confirm that after an hour's search and by some miracle, the animal's shattered body had been found.

Our new camp proved unlucky. We had brought food supplies in the shape of live chickens, bread and rice, and that night jackals raided the camp, broke through the wall of the hut in which the chickens were kept, and carried off our last couple of birds as well as much of the rice. This left us very short of food and as we were a long way from the nearest estate, we decided to head for home. It was a sunny day with little wind and long before mid-day, feeling very hungry and terribly thirsty, we stopped for a snack by a small stream. The bearers drank from the stream, whilst believing it to be contaminated, we refrained. Back then, like all Europeans, we never drank water without boiling it first, and limited by the small amount held in our bottles, remained thirsty. It was only later, when living right in the jungle, that I learned it was perfectly safe to drink water in the wild as long as it did not run close to any human habitation.

We were not long in continuing our march but after a short while noticed that old Peramal, for the first time in his life, had lagged behind. We waited, and when he caught up, Peramal shamefacedly handed over Jim's rifle which he had always considered his special privilege to carry and announced: "Dorai, I am an old man, and no longer any use since my legs do not walk well." He kept up gamely, but it was obvious that the old man was beyond weary. The trek through the long grass made the hot afternoon seem even hotter, and we emerged on the riverbank streaming with sweat, barely able to face a further uphill trail of four miles to a friend's bungalow on the estate. By the time we arrived we were exhausted and so hungry that we emptied our host's larder! Peramal meanwhile, was taken off by his young apprentice to his house, less than a hundred yards up the road, and the other men were sent over the hill to our own bungalow. Having rested and sated our hunger we invited our host to spend the night with us in our bungalow, and together we set off on the five-mile journey home. As always, I loved riding through the dark over the grassy hills, with their soft undulations outlined beneath the starry sky. Too tired to talk, the only sounds were the clatter of our horses' hooves, the occasional cry of an owl and once, the clear, wild 'bell' of a sambhur, not far away.

Battling Malaria and Encounters with Bears

We had been away for five days and in our absence, Jim's work had accumulated. It was December, a healthy time of the year, and with no serious cases of illness amongst our labour we once again settled into our usual routine. January and February were lovely months, cool and fine, and seldom indoors, I began to spend more of my spare time in the garden. We had a new garden coolie, Mundayan, who, engaged in September 1919, remained one of our most valued servants until we left India in July 1948. Despite his initial lack of experience, he was a natural and before long the garden began to take shape.

Then March arrived, bringing warmer and more humid weather and with it; the start of our troubles. Reports began to come in of fever and ague and I took on the job of visiting the sick in their lines. We still knew next to nothing about malaria and could only give the sufferers aspirin for their ague and huge doses of quinine for their fever. As the weeks passed, the number of cases increased; babies were born dead or died soon after birth. Frightened people tried to bolt back to their villages and there was no way of telling how many of those poor souls died either on the way or shortly after arrival.

We worked hard, doing whatever we could with the limited knowledge at our disposal, but during those months our hearts would sink every time we heard the death 'tom-toms' that seemed to beat all day and night. That was our first experience of malaria as a killer and a terrible time for us both. It was not until July that the number of cases began to drop, but we then faced with the problem of workers, who anaemic and lacking in energy, struggled to cope with their jobs in the tea-fields. Jim had malaria on and off, whilst by some miracle, I managed to stay free of it. Medical supplies were limited but using what could be sourced from the central hospital, everyone's health slowly improved. Deaths became fewer though stillbirths and death amongst young babies continued for some time.

Some years earlier, the general manager had managed to persuade the Company to sanction the opening of the valley to tea, on the assurance that the area was free of malaria. Despite being both unfounded and ridiculous, his assertion was taken seriously and it was almost as much as the man's job was worth to admit to being afflicted. Every attack was therefore described as a 'chill on the liver' or anything else they might invent, but never malaria! He also held firm his misguided belief that any labourers diagnosed with malaria had contracted it in the plains; an impossible scenario.

Meanwhile, the Company was losing enormous sums of money, not only through losses in tea crops, but also in the loss of money advanced to the coolies. At the time, it was customary for new labourers to be advanced a sum of money partly to pay off their debts and partly to send home to support the families they had left behind. This was then deducted and repaid from their earnings which being low, took a long time. However, if they were laid low or died from malaria, it was never recovered, and in a bad year the Company could lose as much as £2,000.

The malaria season of 1920, already particularly severe, ended with another tragedy. We received a call from a neighbour urging us to come over. On arrival, we discovered that our friend K had shot himself early that morning and had been found by his poor wife. K had been extremely ill with malaria and it appeared that legal and financial problems had pushed him over the edge. Jim sent news to both the owners of the estate and police in order that arrangements could be made for the funeral, whilst I took K's wife who was numb with shock, and their three small children back to our bungalow. Realising how unbearable it would be for her ever to return home, we decided it would be kinder to pack up everything there and then, and once sorted and listed, Jim had all their belongings transported by bullock carts down to our bungalow. The little family stayed with us for some months, and thanks to the endless kindness of our three assistants who spent their evenings playing with the children in the garden, they soon recovered their cheerfulness. Plans were then made for the family to be sent to Britain, and to pay for their passage, all their possessions bar the absolute necessities, had to be sold. Fortunately, the district rallied to buy nearly everything, and the family left India for good.

Another malaria season came and went; not as bad as the last one, but bad enough. We were both tired and often felt that malaria was winning the battle. Despite my not being afflicted, I was not feeling at all well, and after suffering severe pain following some particularly heavy riding, collapsed. Jim decided to take me to hospital in Colombo and I shall never forget that drive, bumping and slithering along roads deep in mud from the continuous monsoon rains. The last few corners of the ghaut road were especially nerve-racking since great bamboos and telegraph wires, pulled down by elephants, kept getting caught by the canvas hood of the car. Having navigated our way through the heat and dust of the frightful plain roads, we arrived at a small village just as it was getting dark. At this point, our driver announced that without adequate lights we could go no further till the morning. Luckily, Jim managed to buy two hurricane lanterns from the villagers which we lashed to the car's headlamps and aided by their dim flickering light we continued on our way, more slowly than ever. It was eighty-five miles to Madura where we had arranged to spend the night with a friend, and they felt like the longest and most agonising eighty-five miles I had ever travelled! The hurricane lanterns were too weak to show up the potholes in the road and we seemed to fall into each and every one of them. Then, on the outskirts of a small village and with a screech of brakes, the car came to a sudden stop. Jim discovered that as a result of our feeble lights, our driver had mistaken the trunk of a tree for the road, and our vehicle had jammed between two great roots. Fortunately, Jim and the driver managed to extricate the car with the help of a few curious villagers, who looking like mummies, turned up wrapped from head to foot in grubby white cloth!

We eventually entered Madura at about four o'clock in the morning, whereupon our driver had to navigate streets strewn with the sleeping people, dogs, donkeys and cattle, as well as men who had escaped the heat of their homes and come outside to sit on their mats on the road. Aroused by the violent blowing of our horn and much vocal vituperation, the sleepers reluctantly dragged themselves out of the way, then almost before we had passed, had rolled themselves up in their drapes and fallen back asleep. It was nearly five when we arrived at our friend's house and oh, what exquisite relief after that nightmarish drive, to be still and stretch out in bed! The final leg of the trip to hospital was comparatively comfortable and after a nine-week stay followed by a few days of recuperation at an aunt's house in Newara Eliya, I was ready to face the long drive home. As the car sped along, I could well recall the previous, agonising journey but this time, ensconced on the backseat buffered by cushions, was spared the worst as we hopped over bumps and slithered in and out of ruts.

Shortly after my return, Jim and I had just mounted his new motorcycle to visit a friend in an elephant-ridden part of the country, when we were stopped by a man running towards us. In a state of high alarm he announced that two men had been badly burned in a blasting accident and needed our help. I shall never forget the sight that awaited us! The men, carried by their workmates from the quarry, lay in growing agony on blankets on the ground whilst their rescuers fanned their bodies and sprinkled them with cold lime water. They must have been going through hell! Jim and I rushed to a small village nearby, and after buying all the castor oil we could find, mixed it with flour to make an oily paste which we applied to the burns. Having hired a bullock cart to take them to hospital and unable to do more, we set off for the weekend. On the Monday, we headed straight to the hospital to inquire after their condition. Sadly, the man with lesser burns had died from an internal injury, but the other, though desperately ill and badly scarred, was expected to recover and indeed, many weeks later, came to see us, ready to start work.

We were now entering another malaria season, and as the weather became warmer and more humid, the number of reported cases accelerated. Before long two of our assistants became ill and one in particular gave us a real fright. Smitten with ague whilst out in the field, he had staggered into the factory and thrown himself onto a pile of new blankets waiting to be issued to the coolies. Much to our alarm, his body quickly became covered in huge, inexplicable blisters which grew bigger by the minute. It was a terrifying sight, but just as we were sending for the doctor who lived miles away, the tea-maker arrived and explained that the blankets on which the dorai had lain had been accidentally soaked in acetic acid. We were naturally greatly relieved to discover the cause, but almost as soon as our two assistants began to recover I received an S.O.S from the third assistant who happened to be a cousin of mine. His shakily written note stated: "I have a temperature of 106°F! Please come." So, off I went, and on arrival discovered that whilst confined in bed for a day and a half, he had been fed by his equally ill housekeeper, and furthermore, had been told by the local apothecary that no one could be expected to survive if their temperature rose above 105°F! His spirits instantly lifted when he realised I was far less shocked by his temperature than the fact he had been living on badly fried eggs of a doubtful age by his housekeeper!

I promised to bring him up to our bungalow the next morning, and having made him comfortable, set off for home on a narrow road flanked by a verge piled high with 'yards' of firewood. It was getting dark and as I was walking along, listening to sounds of the jungle and enjoying the coolness and peace of the evening, one of the woodpiles got up and ambled off the road and into the tea-field! A sloth bear! Encounters with wild animals are not unexpected in jungle country, but it still came as a shock and I confess that hurrying home, I was glad to get safely indoors. We rarely saw bears, since they tend to favour the grassy hills where the wild ginger and the little wild dates grow, but on treks to and from the cardamom estates, we sometimes came across them. Neither of us was keen on shooting, so we did not carry a rifle. There was however, one evening when we might have been glad of a weapon, had things turned out differently.

The journey to the cardamom estates was usually undertaken in one go, but on that occasion, we decided to do the first nine miles in the afternoon and spend the night on a grassy ridge with a particularly gorgeous view and the possibility of seeing some game. We set up our camp, had tea, and were sitting at the door of our tent enjoying the scenery, when out of a small patch of jungle came two sloth bears, the larger of which was probably male. Delighted, since this was exactly what we had hoped for, we watched them for some time, grubbing on the hillside for ginger and other succulent roots in the short grass. Jim then decided that they were coming too close for comfort. Bears have poor eyesight and hearing, and their power of scenting danger is not what it might be. Thus, easily startled and inclined to panic, they are very likely to attack by rearing up on their hind legs and striking out with their large, strong claws. Being unarmed, Jim had no option but to stand up and attempt to scare them away by shouting and clapping his hands. The smaller bear fled in an instant, but adopting a threatening attitude, the male stood his ground and looking around angrily, rose on his hind legs. Fortunately, when hearing us clap again he slowly ambled off, but not without rearing up once more and several backward glances.

When Jim heard about the bear on the road, he told me that a female bear had been sighted that morning in a field some distance away, frightening many of the women. It was of course impossible to tell whether it was the same bear, but mine had seemed harmless enough. However, a few days later a female bear again appeared amongst the pluckers, this time far more truculent and unwilling to be driven off. As a result, the pluckers refused to work that field and Jim decided to go after her and shoot her. I helped him stalk the bear to a patch of short grass, but the light was fading, and Jim couldn't get close enough for a clean shot. So, rather than risk leaving the animal wounded and in pain he advised that we return home.

We had not been walking for long when we heard a noise coming from behind us, but surrounded by tall grass, could see nothing. Our first thought was that the 'old lady' was stalking us, and to scare her off raised our voices to make as much noise as possible. It made no difference, and with no other option we struggled on, cursing both the grass that impeded our progress and the small prickly date palms that tore at our legs at every turn. In my hurry, I grew clumsy, repeatedly tripping and falling, and was relieved when we finally emerged in a small newly planted clearing from which we made good pace to the road. It was only then that we discovered we had been followed not by the bear, but by two bull elephants, though we had to wait until the next day for an explanation as to why they had failed to catch up with us.

    The district had been troubled for some time by an old, solitary or rogue elephant who had befriended a young bull spurned by its herd. Both harboured a grudge against people and indeed, anything that annoyed them. Our servants, from the elevated viewpoint of the bungalow, had spotted the elephants in the tall grass and bearing lanterns, had bravely come down to meet us, welcoming us as if we had returned from the dead! Retracing our tracks in the morning, we discovered that during their pursuit the disgruntled elephants had stopped to pull up and trample to a pulp every bit of grass or little date palm that bore our scent, and thus distracted, had allowed us to get away. Those two elephants continued to roam the district for several more years making a thorough nuisance of themselves. Meanwhile, the bear responsible for scaring the pluckers was eventually stalked by Jim into a patch of eeta and humanely shot at close range.

Consecration of our New Church
1920

When we first moved to the district, the only church was a tiny mud-walled building that had been built by a few of the Indian-Christians on an estate not far from ours. It was far too small to accommodate the Europeans, let alone the Indians, and after many meetings and much talk, it was decided to build a new one. The chosen location was on our estate, which was fairly central, and Jim was given the job of overseeing its construction. The site was a flat rocky area on top of a small hill, with a magnificent view up a narrow valley to the hills beyond. It was easily reached by a footpath which could be made into a road for cars. Plans were prepared and approved, the foundations were chiselled seven inches into solid rock, and beautifully dressed blue-grey granite was ordered for the walls from a nearby quarry. In due course, the Bishop of Travancore was asked to come up and lay the foundation stone, which was suitably engraved. The Travancore Government then presented us with two fine rosewood trees which provided enough timber for rafters, reapers, doors and windows. It was going to be lovely and we were very proud of it.

However, just as it was nearing completion, I had a horrible thought: shouldn't a church face east? Ours faced north: Whatever were we to do? This was dreadful! Our old bishop had retired, so we immediately sought advice from his replacement, explaining that the building had been built into solid rock. His reply was encouraging, and it was an enormous relief to hear that although it was a pity about its aspect, it was perfectly alright as it was.

Prior to being appointed, our bishop had been in charge of the college in Tinnevelly, and amongst the labour the most respected person in that district. People would bring their quarrels to him, and after taking them 'before the Lord', he would advise them what to do. They willingly accepted his decisions and coming from a race whose one delight was litigation, that was recommendation indeed! We were lucky enough to have him as our guest when he came to consecrate our church, and one of the best and most saintly of men; he was a joy to have around.

To ensure that the first service in the church was a truly wonderful and inclusive experience, the Company's head clerk, a teamaker, and I, representing the Tamils, Malayalams and British respectively, got together and between us chose chants for the Venite, the Te Deum, and the Benedictus as well as hymns and psalms known to all three sectors. I shall never forget that service in our new and gaily decorated church. All of the Indian women sat on mats on the floor on one side of the aisle: the Tamil women in vividly-coloured saris with bright flowers in their hair, and the Malayalams in snowy-white saris. On the other side sat the men, all clad in white. We Europeans were given chairs and benches. The bishop preached an inspiring sermon in Tamil, as Tamils were in the majority, and when it came to singing, we fairly let ourselves go! Everyone sang the same tunes and chants in their own languages, and we made a truly joyful noise before the Lord, even if that noise was not exactly great music! After the service, Indian children crowded around the church doors, each hankering for a flower from the decorations, then scampered off; the Tamils tucking flowers into their hair and the others clutching them in their hands.

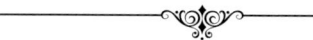

More Malaria, a Family Reunion and the Curse of Muniandy

It was then back to work and dealing with other pressing issues. Within the boundaries of our estate was a large swamp on which squatters had planted rice and erected a grass shack on stilts. Constantly inflicted by malaria, they all looked half-dead, with skinny bodies and enormously enlarged spleens. Not only were they killing themselves by living in such a place, but unknown to us at the time, were a reservoir of parasites for mosquitos to carry to our labour's quarters nearby. The Company ordered Jim to evict them, but was prepared to allow them to return to harvest their rice if it ever matured. I don't remember where they went, but they departed for a while. However, before long they were back. Jim again evicted the poor souls, only to have them return. It was a situation repeated over several years, giving rise to a curious legend which undeservedly tarnished Jim's reputation.

Sorry though he was for the squatters, he had to do his job, and frustrated by their refusal to take his orders seriously spoke to them severely, and in anger used the word 'nasamapochi' which roughly translates as 'you are done for'. Again, the squatters were housed elsewhere, and not long afterwards, due to continual attacks of malaria and their persistent return to the unhealthy swamp, two men and one of their children died. We did what we could for them, but their only hope of survival was to get back to their village on the West coast.

Our malaria season was upon us again, far worse than the previous year. The death tom-toms seemed to beat day and night, and although with care and attention we were able to save many people, the toll was frightful. Jim was ill himself, and despite injections and huge oral doses of quinine he frequently went down with rigors. I too, was ill, though not with malaria, and altogether life was pretty grim. Roads were improving all the time and my next journey to Colombo and hospital, though no picnic, was less agonising than the last. Again, the car came right up to the bungalow, but this one had lights. Escorted by my cousin, I left Jim behind and after a day and night on the train, and then a ferry crossing, spent a night in a mission house in Colombo. I was admitted to hospital the following morning. Jim wangled a little leave to meet me when I came out and after a few days of rest which he sorely needed, we returned to the estate.

Having eventually been granted our application for Home leave, and after handing the estate over to a locum, we left for England just as the malaria season was drawing to a close and in time for the children's summer holidays. They had of course grown beyond all recognition but were still our own blessed babes, and we looked forward to getting to know them again over the next six months. We stayed with my parents and slowly, very slowly, began to recover our strength; Jim after many bouts of malaria and me from my stay in hospital.

An aunt then lent us a house in Swiss Cottage from which one of our favourite excursions was to Regents Park Zoo. The children made many friends among the keepers who much to their delight allowed them to feed the seals and pet the kinkajou. We discovered that monkeys preferred fruit to nuts, while deer and antelope became quite excited by cabbage leaves and lettuce, and so a local greengrocer kindly saved any produce which would not last the weekend for us to feed to the animals on Sundays.

During this holiday, Jim was called up to the city for an interview with the chairman of the Company. Many questions were asked as to the reason for the heavy death toll on the estate and the losses on advances, to each of which Jim gave the same answer: malaria. It did not go down well, but had to be said, and from experience, Jim knew what he was talking about. I think his frankness all but lost him his job but not quite, and so, at the beginning of 1923, we set forth again for India, sadly parting from our children.

On our return, field and factory work kept Jim busy'whilst I, with no household duties beyond giving orders to my quite efficient boy', concentrated on the little dispensary and my garden. Each morning I would walk the short distance to the dispensary to issue drugs made up in bulk each week by the visiting doctor, dress wounds or burns, and generally try to make the lives of the labour, especially the women and children, more bearable. By now, a change of heart in London enabled us to buy meat for those who needed it and provide soup for the sick. We were also able to get milk, sago, arrowroot and extra rice for those convalescing, which again, made the labour's living conditions slightly less grim. Occasionally, I rode over to the other division of the estate to a dispensary in the charge of an individual who called himself an apothecary. He was not much use but better than no one at all.

Amongst his other work, Jim was having a good deal of bother on the small estate across the river attached to ours. During our absence, the locum had put up a row of lines to house extra labour and although deemed suitable, there had been a lot of sickness on a previous, temporary settlement. This site faced a small hill supposedly inhabited by a particularly malignant deity, Muniandy. It was an odd little hill on which tea grew halfway up and above the tea, scrub and coarse grass, topped by a bright green cap of marshy grass and rushes. The coolies swore that lights could be seen on this green cap at night, which they attributed to the Muniandy's spirit. As a result, no self-respecting Indian would go anywhere near the place after dark, nor indeed live in a place that looked out on that hill. The building had cost a deal of money, and it seemed a shame that the rooms should not be occupied. Jim therefore had a meeting with the kanganies and asked whether the coolies would feel better if the windows and doors that faced the hill were blocked and replaced with new doors and windows facing the other way, which incidentally, was onto a rather high bank. After some consideration, the kanganies said they thought that would be all right, and with the job done, the coolies went back quite cheerfully. However, not long after they had been re-occupied, the lines were deserted again. Muniandy had discovered the trick and was coming to the doors and windows on the other side. Accepting that nothing would ever dispel such fear and superstition, the rooms were abandoned and to satisfy all concerned, a new set built, well-hidden from that hill. We were later told that the hill's bad name came from the fact that a set of lines had been built on its other side, some years before, and in a particularly bad malaria season, more than half the inhabitants had died.

The Arrival of Colonel C, Cholera and the Hydrodam

Our general manager retired and a great friend of Jim's was installed in his place. Whether this had anything to do with it I do not know, but almost immediately, we heard that the Company had engaged a malarial expert named Col C. to visit the estates in our valley and advise on antimalarial measures. This was good news indeed, and in anticipation of his arrival we set up a small laboratory, and shelves for his equipment on our verandah. We then began to hear unfavourable accounts of his reputation from another firm with estates in our valley, and from rubber plantations to the west of our hills. Nevertheless, having made up our minds to support this initiative and to learn all that we could, we were prepared to carry out his instructions, however mad they might sound.

Col C. finally arrived accompanied by his sister and a willing slave. We welcomed them, showed them what we had arranged, and settled down to learn from them. I think our expert had had some unfortunate experiences with people who were impatient of change, impervious to new ideas, and frivolous in their approach to antimalarial work. Be that as it may, after the first twenty-four hours during which the law was laid down before us in concrete blocks, our guest became more human, especially when he found us not only anxious to learn and co-operate in every way, but also determined to find a way to control malaria, whatever the cost.

Jim had his job to do, but I dropped everything and became Col C's shadow. I went with him to catch larvae and hatch them in pans, watched him classify and dissect mosquitos, then stain and examine blood smears. Officially, he had been given four days to examine our place and make his report, but on the fourth day asked if we would object to his team staying on and using our small laboratory while they worked through the whole valley. We happily agreed on condition that he consider me an extra, full-time assistant. Thus, began what was probably the most interesting and instructive six weeks of my life, after which I was able to classify mosquitos, had done a little dissecting, and received lessons in the staining and examination of blood smears.

By ironic good fortune, a neighbour developed a severe attack of malaria. His blood showed all the stages of parasites and we owe much of our success with blood examination to our poor sick friend, a good-tempered man, who did not mind having his blood taken fairly frequently. The samples he provided showed how the malarial parasites changed as they matured and this supply of perfect specimens, coupled with guidance offered by our resident expert, gave us the best possible practice. We felt that we were beginning to tackle malaria from the right angle, and at last making a reasonable effort to combat this devilish disease which had long been our nightmare.

Col. C, now our valued friend, showed us how to chart and maintain changes in temperature, humidity and other conditions, thus giving us 'slide rule' instructions to determine when to begin anti-malarial measures, before the season began. He also taught us how to check the effectiveness of the various measures undertaken in streams and swamps. We felt confident that there was a good chance of improving the labour's health and the children's survival, if we could carry out his instructions to the letter. It required a great deal of work and a lot of supervision which would fall to me, but any effort was well worthwhile if we were to succeed. Col C filed his report in which, aghast at the estate's high death toll, he fully endorsed Jim's accounts of the valley and its malaria, and we in turn began to prepare anti- malarial measures to be implemented early in February the following year.

It was soon after Col. C's departure, that we were faced with one of those emergencies that catch one unawares and require great courage and energy to combat. A family of coolies arrived on the estate from the plains, and all seemed well when they registered at the office. However, that very night, we received a report from our little apothecary that two of them were very sick. The local doctor was called, stayed but a few minutes, and after telling the apothecary that it was cholera, gave him instructions and departed in a hurry. Jim and I went down to find the apothecary frightened to death and so we stayed with that tragic little family all through the night. We did what little we could to ease their suffering, then watched them die one after the other, by the dim light of hurricane lanterns, in a crowded little room. Out of the family of a father, mother and five children, only a small boy of seven, blinded by smallpox in infancy, and a six month old baby survived, so it was little wonder that panic spread quickly through the other rooms in that row of dwellings.

The next morning, Jim left me amongst those now terrified people and went up to the house where he immersed himself, clothes and all, in a bath filled with disinfectant, then once changed, walked to the little village by the factory to buy all the strong liquor he could find. Returning to the lines, he ordered that every soul over the age of nine was given strong drink to stem the panic.

While they slept off their liquor, two men less panic-stricken than the rest, helped build a huge bonfire onto which we piled the entire population's clothes and blankets, along with weeds and undergrowth from the surrounding area. We then applied heavily disinfected limewash to all of the rooms both inside and out and sprayed the ground wherever infected material might have dropped, until finally able to hand things over to the apothecary, we staggered home exhausted, to baths of disinfectant and bed.

As soon as we woke, we went back to the lines and were very relieved to hear there had been no further cases. New clothes and blankets were bought for all those who had lost everything they owned, and that by the grace of God, was the end of what might have developed into a major epidemic. By the time the workers had recovered, the whole place was clean and with no more deaths, their panic disappeared; but oh, what a scare it had given us!

We subsequently heard that the doctor had given himself an anticholera injection as soon as he got home and taken to his bed. It was a terrible thing to do, and unable to live it down, he shortly resigned and moved to pastures new. Appalling though his action was, it must be remembered that he was Indian and may well have had experience of cholera, seen its devastating effect, or inherited an inborn fear of it. Unfortunately, the poor fellow just didn't have the courage to face it, and we sincerely hoped his replacement was made of sterner stuff.

Since our experts had visited in September, we had plenty of time to prepare for our all-out attack on malaria, planned for the spring of 1924. The little laboratory became permanent and we set about stocking it with test tubes, pans for breeding mosquitoes and glass slides on which to take blood smears, alongside bottles for catching larvae and a spray for treating the grassy edges of the streams where the mosquito larvae fed. I also borrowed a microscope of sorts from the small local hospital. It was not a very good instrument, but it allowed me to practice examining blood smears so that if and when required, I would be more able to identify parasites.

Cases of malaria that cropped up, as they did off and on at all times of the year, were dealt with, thus reducing the number of parasites that the mosquitos could trap when the bad season arrived. Everything was ready; but what would the next season bring forth?

One of the things our expert particularly condemned was the labour's water supply, which came from open wells where mosquitoes could breed. We covered the largest and that used by the high castes, with a concrete lid and gauze-covered opening, and inserted two taps from which the water could be drawn. Jim then installed a piped water supply to all the other sets of rooms. This enabled him to treat all open water within half a mile of all dwellings with oil, and thus deprive female mosquitoes of anywhere to lay their eggs.

It was fun building a small dam across a stream way below the bungalow and even more exciting to oversee the installation of a 'Hydrodam'; a hydraulic ram pump, which powered solely by the force of water flowing down a drive pipe, is capable of lifting water to an elevation of 150 metres. In our case, it would effectively fill a large tank with enough water to serve everyone's needs. We started the ram, held our breaths, and behold it worked! Ours was the first in this part of the country and what a wonderful machine it was! Requiring little or no attention and involving little or no cost, it delivered adequate supplies of water to the labour for many years.

There was just one thing left to organise: a regular round of oiling which became my responsibility. It entailed a great deal of work and vigilance, but we hoped it would be well worth it.

A Trip to Calcutta and the Ganges

In December 1923, a young cousin came to visit, and we decided to take a trip to Behar to spend Christmas with my sister and her family. Opting for the comparative comfort of the car, we planned to leave at the beginning of the month, visit relatives on the way, then return in January. We left the estate early one morning for Madura and after spending a night with friends, took the train to Calcutta where we stayed for almost a week with an aunt and uncle at the college in Howrah.

Calcutta was crowded and dirty, with many terribly thin and miserable children and mangy dogs roaming the streets. We were driven around the city and the surrounding countryside in my uncle's car, with every outing beginning on the particularly congested Port Street, which like every other, was jammed with trams, buses, rickshaws, gharries, bullock carts, bicycles, pedestrians, dogs, cattle, hens and all manner of livestock. Drivers had to be ready to brake at any moment to allow animals to pass or to avoid collision with other vehicles, and I was amazed by how the great car manoeuvred its way through the noisy chaos. Amidst the din of the taxi drivers' constant sounding of horns and the rickshaws' and gharries' bells, drivers and pedestrians had to shout at the tops of their voices to be heard. Dogs barked, goats bleated, and poultry, finding themselves under the wheel of a vehicle or in close proximity to fighting mongrels, fled with tremendous cackling. Meanwhile, protected by their holy status, the cows and little sacred bulls, wandered peacefully and freely wherever they wished. Indians are seldom in a hurry and have no apparent objection to noise, whereas the Europeans, ever- impatient and usually in a rush, fuss and fume, and by chafing at the thousand and one things that get in their way, end up delaying their progress! A week in Calcutta was more than enough. I hated everything about it, especially the curious sense of despair amongst the Indians on the street, and the air of cynical blindness and self-satisfaction amongst the car drivers, white and Indian alike. Our relatives were very kind, but I was thankful when the time came for our departure for Behar.

We reached Makamaghat on the Ganges in the early morning where we boarded a ferry steamer along with a crowd of Indians dressed only in thin white cotton. They must have been frozen, for even in our warm clothing, we felt thoroughly chilled. The Ganges that day was without a ripple, and we found ourselves entranced by the dream-like quality of the dawn haze and the reflections of the little fishing craft in the still muddy water. The crossing took about an hour and as the wind grew keener, we clutched our collars tightly around our necks as we hurried towards the train waiting on the opposite bank. Sitting in the warmth of our first-class carriage, we then watched in amazement as Indians plunged themselves, fully clothed, into the icy water and emerged dripping and shivering in the bitter wind. The Holy Ganges is believed to wash away all sins and at certain times of the year tens of thousands of pilgrims congregate on the river's banks, camping in the most primitive conditions, to bathe and drink its water, but even so, I can't imagine how anyone could bear to immerse themselves on such a cold day!

Our train trundled slowly through the flat countryside, passing small villages with little patches of cultivation and 'tanks' or village ponds of greasy-looking water. We eventually came to a stop at the small station of Muzaffarpur where we were met by my sister and brother-in-law, just as evening was drawing in. Since they lived some distance away, arrangements had been made for us all to stay in a relative's beautiful home on the outskirts of the village. Unlike anything I had experienced in the south, all the Europeans here lived in very large bungalows, served by tribes of servants, ready to jump to attention. Both my cousin and I initially found this quite embarrassing, but soon warmed to all of these servants, mostly men, on account of their friendly and pleasant manner. However, our household aside, the local Indians were generally far less amenable than those we knew at home and showed little interest in the Europeans in their midst. We often passed small villages when walking the dogs, but seldom received a greeting or indeed, acknowledgment of any sort. It was as though we were invisible; a queer feeling altogether and one to which I found it hard to become accustomed.

One of the most memorable moments of our visit was the first time I saw the 'snows'. Early one morning my brother-in-law summoned us quickly outside. Throwing on our dressing gowns we ran into the garden, and in the cool light of dawn had a clear view of the Himalayas soaring majestically in the North. It was a breath-taking sight, and as the dark hollows turned a shell-pink and lavender in the sunlight, the mighty range looked as though it were suspended above the haze of dust of the plains where we stood. Depending on the light, the mountains looked different each morning; sometimes white and pale blue with grey and black shadows, and sometimes with no definite outline, as imponderable as clouds and as liable to float away and dissolve into mist.

Although my first sight of the Himalayas is the clearest, every glimpse of their beauty never failed to thrill me.

My sister and brother-in-law went out of their way to introduce us to their friends and show us around their estate. We were also introduced to pig-sticking; a sport in which a pig is driven out of the cane and speared by men mounted on horses. One morning, we watched a pig escape into the shelter of the cane after being struck by several spears. The plucky brute, now the very personification of rage, then emerged once more and having miraculously managed to cast off the spears, charged at his tormentors, and showing no sign of fear, met his death gallantly. Always a rebel in such situations, I had great sympathy, not only for the pig, but also, the Indians who unlike the well-padded riders and their equally armoured mounts, were expected to drive the infuriated animal out of the cane without any form of protective clothing whatsoever!

My sympathy was similarly roused on an occasion when we were hunting jungle cock along the banks of a dried-up stream. My brother-in-law had already shot several birds, when we came upon a family of peafowl feeding in a grassy patch. Up they flew, the cock displaying his full plumage, from the electric-blue crest on his head to the exquisite and gloriously long tail feather that streamed out behind him. My brother-in-law fired and down he fell, crumpled and dead, to the ground. I love the jungle and its inhabitants too much to enjoy any kind of shooting unnecessary for either food, or in self-defence.

After Christmas we began to think of returning south. My sister Kathleen had two children, and although I enjoyed their company, being with them made me homesick for my own. Each of the children had their own attendant, the boy his bearer and the girl her ayah; adoring slaves ready to fulfil the children's slightest wish. Riding their small ponies, racing about the large garden and playing under the shady trees, such children had an ideal existence. What a pity it is, that they remember so little of their early childhoods when they return to Britain and school.

At last our holiday was over, and on a cloudy, dusty day, we took the local train to the Ganges, where after endless delays and difficulties caused by a dispute between the railway officials and the captain of the ferry, we managed to board the mainline train on the opposite bank just before it steamed away. Since there was no restaurant car and no food to be bought on the way, we were forced to travel on empty bellies from Makamaghat to Calcutta, but despite all, could hardly wait to get home. We then had a rather amusing experience. Being first in, we had established ourselves in the two lower berths of a four-berth compartment. Along the way, we were joined by two women; one a gentle creature, the other a loud-voiced, fussy individual who complained bitterly about having to climb onto the upper bunk. I feigned sleep, hoping that she would go to bed and cease her grumbling, but not to be put off, she leaned over me and in her strident voice, announced: "I am always sick on trains and if made to sleep on the top berth, will be sick in your face." Lying still, my memory flew back to Fraulein B on the German ship. The threat was then repeated in a louder and more menacing tone, and rather than chance my luck, I capitulated and agreed to the swap.

This good lady proceeded, not to be sick, as I feared, but to keep us awake all night. At every station, she leapt up and crouching by the door, shouted: "Hut jao", translated as "Go away!", along with other Urdu epithets I did not understand. Weary and deafened, we were very thankful when, a few stations from Calcutta, she and her meek companion left us.

The train journey to Madras was long but cool, through great tracts of uninhabited terrain interrupted now and then by the odd small mud hut surrounded by a patch of land, too poorly cultivated and by all appearances, utterly inadequate to feed anybody. It was a great relief to finally arrive back in Madras among our Tamil folk. No longer a novelty, we drove directly from the station to the bungalow, accepting all the rattling and bumping as a matter of course. The rain-filled hollows seemed irresistible to our driver, who drove through the middle of as many as possible, showering both the car and his passengers with mud. However, given the option to travel at a tremendous rate of 25mph, instead of 5mph in a bullock cart, we were prepared to put up with anything!

The remaining weeks of my cousin's stay were spent visiting our friends in various parts of the district. She was a very attractive young woman and many of the local bachelors fell in love with her. On her last night, no fewer than a dozen turned up for her farewell party. Camp cots were strewn all over the wide verandah, and we danced to music from the gramophone in our big sitting room until the small hours. We could only guess how many proposals of marriage she had that night and could not help laughing, as one after another, her dancing partners went out into the garden, smiling and cheerful, only to return a few minutes later looking woebegone and depressed! After a little sleep, we left in a hired car to catch the overnight train to Ceylon where my cousin would board a ship to Australia. One of the lovelorn lads joined us, evidently hoping that he would have more luck without the distraction of competitors. He hung around, looking alternatively cheerful and despairing, as his hopes rose and fell. My cousin however, resisted his charms and set sail, heart intact and eager for more adventures.

Snakes in the Hydrodam, Rainstorms and Floods

Having played for long enough, I settled down to helping Jim prepare for the coming malaria season. We were then let down by our Hydrodam. As it was the first of its kind in that part of India, many people, including an engineer from a neighbouring tea estate came to see it. Jim duly took him to the top of a hill to listen to the steady beat of the pumping action that drove the water uphill to the tank. The ram had been working without a hitch for weeks and Jim was calmly extolling its virtues when the beat became irregular, then stopped. They hurried down to see what had happened and after some investigation, found that a pair of mating snakes had been carried down the big pipe that delivered water to the ram and become wedged in the valve! Once removed, the water again flowed freely through filters into pipes feeding the taps in the lines.

The permanent supply of fresh, clean water accessible to all was the first step of our anti-malaria campaign, and by February, the scheme was in full working order. The next step involved oiling all other sources of water to render it unfit for mosquito larvae to breed. I was put in charge of a small team of Indians whose job it was to spray oil on every drop of water within half a mile of any dwellings, every ten days. The team worked continuously and as often as possible, every yard of that oiling round was visited by one of us and a search made for living larvae in everything that looked too clean. We were determined to make the scheme work and no trouble was too great to obtain that end. March, April and May passed with unbelievably few cases of malaria and when the rains came in June, we stopped spraying. The scheme's success was beyond our wildest dreams and our efforts convinced the labour that all our larvae catching and searching their houses with torches for mosquitoes had all been worthwhile.

Then with July, came a truly terrible week of torrential rain, gales and floods. It poured and it blew like no other S.W. monsoon, and on the 9th of July alone, nine inches of rain fell in twenty-four hours. Water levels rose to unprecedented heights, and down by the factory, the once peaceful stream had become a raging river that spilled over the top of the high concrete bridge. Jim and I watched anxiously as great rushing waves, muddy with soil from the hills, battered the bridge's piers and then to our horror, spotted the enormous body of a fully grown elephant. It had presumably fallen into the river where the bank had subsided somewhere up- river and if driven against one of the piers, already strained to breaking-point, the bridge would have been swept away. Mercifully, rolling and twisting in the tumbling water, it slipped between two piers and floated away downstream. The water on the bridge itself was knee-deep and piled high with driftwood and debris, but we managed to get across and fight our way through the storm back to the bungalow.

That afternoon, as I stood on the verandah, the sky cleared for a moment and I spotted two sambhur gallop across a small hill, obviously highly agitated and in a hurry. A further fifteen inches of rain proceeded to fall and the next day we found ourselves completely cut off from both the factory and the rest of the estate. The rumble of landslides could be heard above the noise of the wind and rain, but Jim and I braved the weather and walked out to a tea field overlooking the Periyar river. It was an extraordinary sight. Far higher than the previous day, and carrying trees and debris of all kinds, the water was now swirling around the jungle vegetation well up on the banks. The hillside, not far from where we were standing, suddenly appeared to shudder and rumble and before our very eyes, two acres of the tea plantation slid slowly towards the river. It took two more days and eighteen more inches of rain before the sky cleared and the rivers began to moderate. I stood on the verandah and looked out over the valley to where I had seen those two sambhur and wondered what had become of them. The once green hillside facing our bungalow was gone; transformed into a gaping, reddish- brown scar, a muddy abyss, over which two large trees hung by their roots.

Twenty-four hours after the rain stopped, we were able to cross the stream at the foot of our hill. Despite being piled high with tons of mud, trees and bushes, the stout little concrete bridge had survived its terrible battering, but we soon discovered that the four-day storm had washed away practically every culvert as well as much of the road on either side. Any trees on the riverbank that had somehow survived were festooned with wreckage, and all that remained of another bridge were steel girders, twisted and bent by the force of rushing water. The Periyar river had surged through the factory's lower storey, leaving heaps of silt in its wake, and carried off most of the firewood for the driers, stored in a nearby shed. News began to arrive from estates further up the valley that landslide had destroyed sections of the road, and given that it was our main access to both the plains and the railway, gangs of coolies were dispatched to assess and repair the damage.

Our gang was first to arrive and what a mess we found! Less than a mile from our factory, trees, bamboos and huge rocks had obliterated the road making it impassable, and at first sight, it appeared that some parts would need to be completely rebuilt. Other gangs joined us, armed with digging and cutting tools, and with great will and effort, managed to cut a narrow path to allow us to access and assess the next section hit by the landslide. It soon became apparent that it would take weeks of work and thousands of workers to make the path fit to carry wheeled traffic, even bullock carts.

Away from the noise of the workers, the jungle was unnaturally still and the air, saturated and breathless. Even the birds were silent. On we trudged, the sound of our footsteps reverberating loudly beneath battered and dripping trees, until we were brought to a halt by something lying in our path. Drawing closer, we discovered it to be a human skeleton and deduced that some poor soul cut off by landslides during the storm, had died all alone in the wind and the rain, then his body picked clean by jackals and vultures. It was a tragic sight, but just then, a gleam of sunshine appeared between the clouds, lighting up the trees and undergrowth where a Malabar whistling thrush burst into glorious song; a candle and choir for the unknown dead. With that first glimpse of sunlight, the unearthly stillness was broken: the jungle sprang into life, cicadas began their strident screeching, and birdsong resounded from the trees.

When we eventually reached the top of the ghaut road, we were then faced with a chasm, carved by the torrent of water, too deep and wide to be negotiated without a bridge. Looking around, we spotted a pile of teak logs, which by luck, were long and strong enough to bridge the gap, so Jim decided to commandeer a few, much to the consternation of the forest guard. Once appeased by Jim's willingness to sign a guarantee not to damage the logs, the guard hung about for the fun of watching our attempts to place them. Exceedingly heavy, wet and slippery, they would have been immoveable without the aid of two of the Forestry department's elephants kept especially for such tasks. By the time the chasm had been bridged, it was getting late, and unable to go further that night, we headed back, collecting gangs of workers along the way. Everyone had had enough for one day and we were all thankful to return home, for drinks, baths and food.

The next day Jim and I were joined by neighbouring planters, and leaving the gangs to carry on, went straight to the frontier at the top of the ghaut to see what damage had been done to the road on the other side. Many sections had been swept away entirely, and it was obvious that it would be a very long time before transport would be able to flow freely again. Arrangements were made with village headmen for loads of rice and other foodstuffs to be carried on bearers' heads, as far as the frontier, where collected by coolies, they would then be distributed amongst labourers working on various estates. News began to percolate through from estates at the other end of the district, many of which had been hit much harder than ours. On the western side, a road workers' settlement had been swept away, lost without trace, and in another district, bungalows and even factories had been destroyed, coolies' settlements buried under landslides, and many acres of tea had disappeared. There were terrible reports of hillsides sliding into rivers, rushing full flood to the plains, carrying bodies, trees, bushes, and vehicles out to sea. Ships were said to have sent messages ashore asking if there had been an earthquake or a battle. One district had clocked up the world's highest recorded rainfall; 32 inches in 24 hours followed by 28 the next, totalling 60 inches in 48 hours! Small wonder that the land slipped away, given the natural underground drainage's inability to cope with that vast amount of water.

The roads were slowly cleared, bridges were rebuilt and life on the estate returned to normal. The badly damaged big bridge was renovated using dressed stone instead of steel pillars, teak girders, and a concrete platform. It was fascinating to watch the two elephants hired to lift the beams into position. The cow was taken by her mahout to carry the beams to the bridge. Each beam had a hole in one end, through which a length of thick rope was passed. The elephant picked up one end of this rope, placed it between her teeth, then pulled the beam behind her along the narrow estate path. The log had a tendency to slip under her feet but with usual elephant sagacity and without disturbing her progress, she kept it straight with gentle sideways kicks every few steps. Arriving at the water's edge, she used her head and feet to push the beam across to the bull who, waiting to receive it midway between the buttress and the central pier, caught it just before it tipped and floated away. To see him then lift it high in the air on his tusks and carefully place it in position on the central pier was a revelation.

Elephants are creatures of habit with a seemingly, instinctive sense of time. Each day at four o'clock, the cow from the bank, and the bull from the middle of the steam converged upon a sandy spit. Once there, both lay down on their sides, filled their trunks and sprayed themselves with water. After a thorough scrubbing down, they lifted the mahouts upon their backs, collected their chains and ropes, and shuffled off down the road.

The Lull after the Storm and an Attack at Sea

Now came a period of comparative peace. As the general health of the labour improved, they became more cheerful and co-operative; particularly the youngsters, who brought insects of every size and description for us to examine for malarial parasites. I spent hours meticulously following all the given instructions, and with practice, began to feel more confident when I examined blood slides taken from ex-malarial cases and from anybody who was sick, but despite the occasional success, never became proficient at it. However, it soon became clear that the infections were caused, not by the anopheles mosquito as we had thought, but by some other vector.

It was during this lull that I took the opportunity to pay a quick visit to Britain to see the children during their summer holidays. I had been asked to take a friend's little boy who was to stay with relatives and start school. Life on the tea estates was very quiet, and when we arrived at the London terminus, poor little Robert was so overwhelmed by the crowds and hustle and bustle, that he clung to me, begging to be taken back to India. His relatives met us at the station, and I had to watch that homesick, miserable and bewildered little boy being led off by people who to him, were complete strangers. I wondered whether Robert would later remember that day as one of the worst in his life, but my joy in seeing my own children overshadowed any worries.

We spent a wonderful holiday staying in a former convent in St. Jacut, in Brittany, marred only at the end, by Monica being laid low by a severe attack of appendicitis. Bill, now called Ted at his own request, was sent back to London to start school whilst Monica was admitted to a small hospital in Dinan for an emergency operation. Thankfully, she made a quick recovery and we travelled back to England together, just in time for me to catch my ship back to India.

On the return journey I shared a cabin with three other women, one of whom distrusted anyone in authority but happy to confide in me, revealed that she kept all her money, about £250 in notes, in the bag strung around her neck. It was quite common for stewards to be sent to cabins to shut the port-holes if rough weather was expected, so I was not unduly worried when one night, I awoke to see a man in ours. However, just as I was dozing off, I suddenly felt a body leaning over me and hands slipped gently round my throat. Too horrified to scream, I dug my nails as deep as I could into his arm, whereupon he jerked away and was gone. In the morning, I was told that our cabin and table stewards had been arrested pending further enquiries but since I had had a fairly clear view of the intruder in the light from the passage outside, I was able to assure the Captain that neither of those arrested, bore him any resemblance. Both men were released, and in gratitude, our cabin steward slept outside our door for the remainder of the voyage. Meanwhile, the foolish woman was persuaded to entrust her money to the purser. I was unable to recognize the culprit at a parade of the ship's personnel; he had been a small man with a Charlie Chaplin moustache, and there were at least four men who fitted that description. This was unfortunate, as later on, several women in first-class lost jewellery and money, and the thief was never traced.

A huge crowd of coolies had gathered on the roadside to welcome me back to the estate; the women setting up shrill ululations as the men placed marigold garlands around my neck. During my absence, a party of V.I.P.s had visited the estate, and highly impressed with the garden, had advised the general manager to allow us an extra gardener. Over the years, we had collected and planted, then catalogued the botanical names and dates of 120 varieties of trees, shrubs and creepers, which in addition to the wide selection of flowers and grasses that covered our two and half acres, created a perfect paradise. Having invested so much time and effort on the garden, we were naturally delighted by this initiative which in due course, led to it becoming a showpiece.

It was Christmas time; the weather was fine and having mastered malaria, we no longer feared the forthcoming season. Life was good and all was well. But we were too optimistic. At the end of March, in hot and humid weather, we had a weekend party and about a month later, heard that one, and then another, of our guests had become very ill; both with malaria. Jim and I were the next to be struck, followed by a mild but quite definite outbreak of new cases around the bungalow.

This was very worrying and as soon as we were on our feet again, Jim and I searched the streams and swamps for faulty oiling, without any success. We then scoured every inch of ground within half a mile of our bungalow, which seemed to be the centre of the trouble. It was a tremendously tiring job in the hot, thundery weather, but I eventually discovered a tiny pocket of water, no bigger than a washbasin, hidden amongst the tea bushes, teeming with anopheline larvae. We oiled the pool and with no new outbreaks, believed we had solved the problem. However, there must have been somebody living close by who had malarial parasites in his or her blood, from whom the mosquitos had obtained their supply. We examined all the Indian staff living in nearby quarters, found the culprit and treated him.

My own attack of malaria had been the most severe yet, and it took me a while to recover. I relapsed continuously, and my already keen sympathy with malarial sufferers intensified. Our success in stamping out malaria had brought our district notoriety, and before long, we had the honour of a visit from Mr Malcolm Watson. Famous around the estates for collecting spleen rates and taking cine pictures of anything of interest, he was most complimentary and wrote a glowing account of our work and its results.

With less to do, I began to explore the wilds of the surrounding countryside. Rambling the grassy hills alone, and with just a couple of hard-boiled eggs and bread in my pockets, became my greatest joy. I was often able to watch some wild creature for quite some time without their being aware of my presence: deer, monkeys or birds, but seldom anything that could be described as dangerous. Now and again, I saw a family of elephants and once, a female panther and her two cubs, some distance below me. Not far from our bungalow was a small patch of jungle with some very large trees. One evening whilst sitting on a rock enjoying the view, I heard a ponderous flapping overhead, and into a tree on my right flew a pair of giant hornbills; prehistoric looking creatures with black, white and yellow plumage and enormous and unwieldy, flame-coloured bills. Clumsy and awkward, they are large enough to dwarf any tree upon which they alight. In this instance, the female chose a branch rather low down, whilst her mate chose a dead branch above her, and together, they broke into a duet akin to the sound of large stones being thrown into a wooden box. This continued for a few minutes, with her looking at him as he gazed into space. Suddenly he broke off, and lowering his huge orange-yellow beak, so like a drunkard's nose, smirked at her. Yes, 'smirked' is the only word for it, and he looked so utterly comic that I could not help but laugh!

Sometime later, I heard strange sounds coming from high up in that tree, and looking up, noticed a single hornbill, looking decidedly worn. Near him, the female had walled herself into a hollow of the tree with a sort of cement, made I believe, of the bird's own droppings. Unable to get out, the hen was entirely dependent on the male for food while she incubated her eggs. From that point forth, I visited the tree regularly, and was lucky enough to see the hen very shortly after she had been released. Looking as though she had been partially plucked, her breast was bare and mottled, and her feathers, what was left of them, drooped and had lost their colour. Three young birds sat on a branch close by and I later delighted in watching them flapping their wings madly, and with necks out-stretched to balance the weight of their enormous beaks, they attempted their first flight.

Precious memories, such as this, remained with me for the rest of my life, shining like jewels amongst more sombre recollections of all the sickness, death and misery with which we long wrestled. We endured many hard times, but there was always a thread of joy to be found in helping people in need and making their lives just a little bit easier. We were slowly making a difference, there was no doubt in that, but although conditions were improving, they were still far from good. The labour still lived in very small, overcrowded and airless rooms, without any form of sanitation, but at least they could now get help when sick, and perhaps, being visited and fed by somebody in whom they had confidence, feel that their lives mattered.

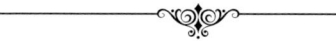

Jungle Treks

It was a healthy time of year and because we had more time to relax, we agreed to a request from a friend in Madura to arrange a fully catered camp, shikaris, and shooting for him, two of his friends and their wives, in the hills beyond the Periyar dam. Being V.I.P.s, the Travancore Government consented to the construction of grass huts for his guests at a place called Salt Lick Creek. The site was prepared and spacious huts erected with delightful rooms lined with beautifully patterned and plaited beta leaves. We then booked a shikari named Raman and arranged for the transportation of food for ourselves and our bearers to the camp.

Being V.I.P.s with the Simon Commission, as well as minor political figures, and because feeling against Europeans was running high, these people had to have protection wherever they travelled in India. So, when our friend brought them to the frontier post at Thekkady and drove them to the launch which would take us across the lake, they were accompanied by a detective. However, by a smart piece of manoeuvring, we managed to give the poor man the slip, and sped over the lake, free of all worries and ready to enjoy camp life to the full!

The trip on the lake was one of our favourites, though we were seldom able to indulge in such things. It had been formed when the construction of a dam across the Periyar river had flooded a series of heavily wooded valleys. The tops of the hills rose above water level, creating numerous islands divided by narrow waterways and in the shallows, the protruding 'ghosts' of the forest trees, dry, and whitened by weather, were beautifully reflected in the lake's mirror-like surface. Now and again, we saw a cormorant with wings outspread, sunning itself, or a 'snake bird' perched on the branch of a dead tree, ready to dive for fish.

Having crossed the lake, we made our way westward up a narrow arm to Salt Lick Creek, then accompanied by bearers carrying food, beds and cooking pots, wound our way, snake- like, for two miles along a rough track lined with tall elephant grass and scrubby trees. The Munnans, a hill tribe expert in building huts from grass and eeta, had created a luxurious camp. The huts, warm, weatherproof and fully furnished, accommodated a dining area, kitchens, bedrooms and servants' quarters.

Madge   Jim

Madge and Jim's wedding, Munnar 1911

Rathmore School Scotland

Alice Bewley, George Bewley, Madge, Jim, Bill and Monica on furlough at Pevensey

Cattle Cart

Munnar racecourse and gymkhana

Moving to Cloudland

Monica and Madge, first Austin car

Sambhur Camp

Tea on Suruli Falls, Monica, Jim, Madge

Hampton Hut

Madge and Margaret on Sher Khan jungle trail

As mentioned, the two V.I.P.s had brought along their wives. I had imagined being stuck at camp, playing host to society ladies in high-heeled shoes and pretty frocks, whilst they pottered about and took photographs. How wrong I was! One was an experienced stalker, more than capable of trekking through difficult terrain, whilst the other, though unaccustomed to camp life, happily joined in the day's activity, ignoring blisters and aching muscles, until she was as tough as the rest of us. I remember well our guests' delight on waking the first morning to discover that instead of riding elephants they would be tramping on foot over the hills and along the game tracks. Countryfolk, born and bred, they were tired of the ultra-luxury that had surrounded them in other parts of India.

After a few days in the camp provided by the Travancore Government, we decided to venture further afield, this time camping rough, so that one of our party could hunt Nilgiri goats. We set off at early dawn with a few bearers carrying our bedding and enough food for two days. Having deposited their loads, they then returned to the first camp, leaving us to build our own lean-to and do our own cooking.

On the way, we spotted a herd of bison, and since there were no good heads among them, would have left them alone had one of the bearers not mentioned they were short of food. Jim reluctantly consented to shoot a beast for the pot and after taking a young bull the rest of the herd galloped off. Stampeding bison are an awesome sight, and as they swept by in the near distance, one of the wives filmed them with her cine camera and was rewarded by unforgettable footage that few people would have had the pluck to procure.

Our first night in our row of lean-to shelters was peaceful and uneventful, but on the second, I awoke to find something crawling over me and became aware of a sickly-sweet smell. Switching on my torch, I discovered that we had been invaded by a sort of 'daddy-longlegs'; curious creatures, resembling scarlet beads on long spindly legs. They were everywhere, and the strange distinctive smell was emanating from the crushed bodies beneath us. There were far too many to remove, and so we had little option but to put up with them. None of us slept much that night, and to this day, I can still remember that very odd, sickly-sweet smell.

After one more night at the more comfortable camp, it was time to return to civilization. Packing up involved a great deal of shouting and mild squabbling amongst our carriers, with the toughest and heftiest trying to grab the lightest and easiest loads. Our guests had brought a special fluid which had been used to cure the skin of the first bison shot, but when attempting to bundle it up for transportation, we found to our amusement, that its folds had set like cement. Had the Indians been left to treat both that and the other the skins with salt and wood ash, as was their custom, they might have been rather highly scented but softer and far more pliable.

With all our gear stowed on the launch, we sped across the lake, each of us harbouring memories of early morning walks along game tracks and patiently waiting for dawn to pit our wits against those of the wild jungle animals. The outcome, however, was a pile of dead bodies and in my opinion, no trophy could ever warrant the destruction of such beautiful creatures in their natural habitat. We were greeted on the wharf by the detective, looking very relieved to have his charges back all in one piece. All of us were sorry to leave, particularly our guests. Up until then, they had only met Indians with an axe to grind against anyone in the government, whereas with us they were simply regarded as the Dorai's friends and therefore treated with respect.

A new tea district was being opened up in a range of hills to the southeast, and accompanied by our friend K, I was invited over to make a malarial survey of two small areas. We drove as far as we could, then piling into bullock carts made our way across the fields to the foot of a steep ghaut road, little more than a track, where K had arranged a dhooly for me. A dhooly indeed! I was insulted; if he could walk up, then so could I! K was determined to show me my limitations, whilst I was equally determined to prove that I was as good a 'man' as he, and so, determined to out-walk each other, we climbed that steep and rocky path faster than either of us would have done alone! The scrubby jungle of the foothills gave way to rocky grassland through which we walked a further six miles through dust and searing heat, towards the treeline. Reaching the top was like entering a different world. The air was cool and filled with the sounds of running water and birdsong and it was lovely to dangle our legs in the stream as we sat with our picnic in the shade of a small wooden bridge. Having won each other's respect, we tacitly decided to slow down and enjoy our new surroundings as we trekked the last two miles along a shady path, soft with moss and jungle leaves.

Our hosts were delighted to see us, as theirs was a lonely life with few people to talk to. We rested until after ten, then went to the swamps to collect mosquito larvae. The next day, I walked to an area about four miles away, had lunch with the manager, and after conducting a malarial survey and catching more larvae, was ready to return to the bungalow. When he gallantly offered to escort me, I assured him I would enjoy the walk back through the jungle, and had no need of protection. He then tried to warn me about the wild animals, insisting that there were man-eating tigers in these jungles. I did not believe his stories, but realising that the poor man was lonely and wanted to enjoy company for as long as possible, I consented. What a lovely path it was and as we walked along, the evening came alive with the calls of countless birds and insects. Pink balsams flourished at the edges of every small stream, and in the undergrowth bloomed a lovely pale blue Baleria, alongside pink Impatiens Grandis or giant balsam, Magenta Osbeckia, and purple Oldenlandia. Just before we left the forest I heard the call of a Malabar squirrel; a beautiful, clear, ringing sound that never fails to send shivers up my spine.

When we finally reached the young tea surrounding the Cloudland bungalow, I had only about half a mile to walk to where my host and hostess were waiting for me. We stayed one more day and by the time we left I had fallen in love with a new and enchanting part of the hill country. Little did I know that it would become our home for many years.

Local Hill Tribes

During that period, Jim represented our district at the annual meeting of the Sri-Mullam, or Parliament of the State of Travancore; a duty which involved travelling south to the capital Trivandrum, to discuss the needs and concerns of the tea planters. It was whilst there, that he met a young journalist anxious to visit places in India not included in the usual tourist itinerary. Jim offered to bring him back to our estate and arrange a trip into the jungle below our hills to the west, where he might catch sight of the native Pandarams. He also proposed a trip to the other side of the Periyar Dam, where the journalist could take cine-photographs of the Oorali and Mannan hill tribes living on the banks of the lake.

Young John jumped at the chance and since Jim was unable to free himself from an accumulation of office work, arrangements were made for our assistant Dennis and I to at least show him where the Pandarams lived, even if we failed to see them. We set off early one morning with the usual string of bearers carrying food and bedding. It was quite a spectacular descent of several hundred feet to the forest floor, dim under its heavy jungle cover. I, of course, was in my glory, for any chance of exploring my beloved jungle was pure joy, and John, his servant and I were greatly entertained by our bearers enlarging on the dangers and difficulties we were certain to encounter.

Once we had negotiated the cliff face, the going was easier and because of the density of tree cover, with little or no undergrowth, we were able to see quite far into the distance. We walked along silently in single file, and barely conscious of the rest of the party, I focused on admiring my surroundings and the few sounds that could he heard above my own footsteps.

John's movements however, were altogether clumsier, and I began to fear that the Pandarams, with their keen eyesight and hearing and knowledge of the jungle, would not allow themselves to be seen.

What happened that night, albeit tremendously exciting, was entirely my fault and could have been prevented. The only one in the party who supposedly knew the jungle, I should have avoided camping on that delightful spit of sand by the edge of the stream. We were without tents, sleeping instead under mosquito nets propped up with sticks, and the site seemed ideal with its good supply of running water and a perfect bathing place below the camp itself. As a small excuse for my stupidity, there were no signs of elephants anywhere.

After setting up camp, we went for an exploratory stroll during which we found some Pandaram tracks. They could actually have been within a few feet of us, but such were their powers of concealment, they remained invisible. After eating our supper in the dusk, I enjoyed a heavenly bathe, naked, in the rushing, sandy bottomed stream; then everyone crept under their nets and silence fell on the camp. Suddenly, there was a crashing sound. Fearing the worst, I immediately sat up and to my horror, recognized the squeals of elephants, none too pleased at the presence of trespassers on their spit of sand.

By then, everyone was wide awake and realising how vulnerable we were, the camp burst into violent activity. Piling out of their blankets, the coolies frantically tried to scare the elephants away, shouting and yelling as they raked up the ashes and rekindled our tiny fire with sticks and logs until it was ablaze. This went on all night and though the elephants kept their distance, they continued to show their disapproval by squealing, scuffling, breaking branches and generally milling around, making as much noise as possible. None of us slept that night, and John's servant having already been scared by our men on the way down, was especially relieved when morning came, and the elephants wandered off into the dimness of the forest.

After breakfast, we went on a ramble and keeping by the stream, walked towards a familiar path that led up the cliffs some miles ahead. There was no sign of Pandarams; hardly surprising, given the commotion of the previous night, but we nevertheless, had a wonderful day. There are few animals in this sort of jungle and not many birds either, but it is always a delight to watch sunlight flickering through the tree cover and listen to the sound of the insects.

Around lunchtime, we came across a hanging branch of gorgeous red and white flowers, and wanting a closer look, I scrambled over a small stream. Only legumes grow in such places and I had no knowledge of this particular species. As I approached, I became more and more puzzled, then suddenly, what I had assumed to be a cluster of flowers, exploded and out flew a cloud of red and white insects. Though very similar, they were definitely not butterflies, and unfortunately, I was never able to discover their identity. We later saw some cabbage whites or the Indian equivalent, flying in a steady stream like a fluttering white ribbon, not far above the ground. As we watched, we noticed that when they reached a certain spot, the butterflies rose into the air as if to avoid an invisible barrier, then swinging sharply to one side, continued their flight. When this stream had gone, another followed in its wake and to our astonishment, behaved in exactly the same way!

Our second night in the open passed peacefully, without any interference from elephants or any other jungle dwellers. We might not have accomplished our mission, but nevertheless, had experienced three memorable days in the jungle.

By the time we got home, Jim had caught up with his work and was free to join us on a visit to our local hill tribes, and the famous Periyar Dam. We hired a motor launch to take us the nine miles from Thekkady to the sluice gates of the dam, boarding on the bank of a small arm of the lake at a place where an outlet tunnel had been blasted through the hill to carry water down to the plains in British India. Sailing through the channel, we passed buffalo, descendants of domesticated beasts and now semi-wild, wallowing in the small marshy flats, and in the sparse clusters of trees, marsh birds in abundance. Alongside the Malabar Racket and Tailed Drongo, was another little drongo commonly known as the 'king crow', which pugnacious in nature and swift in flight, made a habit of attacking and routing larger and clumsier crows.

The lake widened, bringing us just beyond the dam to two small settlements of hill tribes: Ooralis, some of whom were descendants of those we had previously helped, and Mannans. Ooralis are a dying race, and even then only a few small settlements remained in the Periyar Valley, mostly on the banks of the lake. Like the Mannans they suffered from both malaria and hookworm and most of the children were extremely thin and listless, with huge protuberant bellies. Despite living in close proximity, there was little interaction between the two tribes and in fact, they despised the other, each considering itself a higher caste.

The Mannans usually build their huts close to the water's edge and because of their curious affinity with, and power over elephants, had no need to protect their nearby pockets of cultivated land. There are many stories of how a single Mannan had taken control over wild elephants interfering with hunters in the jungle. I only saw one instance of this, and it impressed me deeply. Jim and a friend had been fishing in the River Tanikudi whilst I scoured the bank for wildflowers, and on our way back to camp that evening, spotted a solitary elephant feeding on wild ginger in a swampy patch, uncomfortably near our grass huts. We all shouted and clapped our hands in an attempt to convince him that he would be more comfortable elsewhere, but he completely ignored us and continued grazing. Meanwhile, our Mannan guide stood by, smiling in a superior manner until exasperated, we asked whether he could persuade the elephant to move away. He turned to face the elephant and called "Oo-ay" in a loud clear voice. The elephant raised his head. "Ani, Mela po," "Elephant go up," he called, and with that, the great beast turned around and lumbered slowly up the hill with never a backward glance!

The Ooralis, on the other hand, feared elephants. This settlement typically consisted of lean- to huts, occupied only in daylight, and other small huts erected in the branches of large trees where they slept at night. An amicable chap, the head man happily consented to John taking photographs of the women climbing the ladders to their night huts, and even climb up himself to take shots inside. These friendly and kindly people provided us with a unique experience, and we wished we could have done more for both them and the Mannans. However, short of resettling them elsewhere, far from the deadly malaria of the lake, there was nothing we could do but accept that they were best off living the life to which they were accustomed and indeed, happy. Escorted by some of the men and a few skinny children, we walked down the bank to our craft and were soon on our way home; John with a unique set of shots of his travels in India, and Jim and I were refreshed by contact with people who were so very important to us.

Just as we neared the narrowing of the waterway, one of us noticed a flurry at the water's edge, and standing on a small ridge, was a magnificent sambhur stag. Sailing closer, we then spotted a pack of wild dogs tearing apart a doe. If John were to capture this unique sight, and since the light was fading, we had to be quick, so we drove the boat ashore, leaving him positioned behind an anthill, with about ten minutes to get his shots. The dozen or so dogs had reluctantly skulked off, but we had hardly left, when sitting a little way offshore we noticed that they were back and becoming agitated. One or two were jumping in the air, sniffing the breeze, while others stood up on their hind legs, the better to see what was happening. Knowing their character, their fearlessness and natural resentment at being deprived of their meal, we couldn't risk leaving John any longer and hurried to collect him.

Sadly, John later wrote that the two rolls of film had somehow been spoiled when processed in Bombay, and we shared his heartbreak at the loss of such irreplaceable records of the hill tribes and scenes of the Periyar dam.

Cochin, Friends and Chance Encounters

During that period, when malaria was no longer a worry and the estate was jogging along nicely, we were now and again able to get away and enjoy ourselves. Jim was chosen as the district's delegate at a planters' meeting in Ootacamund, so I decided to go along and combine it with a holiday. These meetings were always very gay affairs, with dances at the Club, gymkhanas, rugger and tennis matches, and I actually bought some new clothes, quite unsuitable for life in our district, but fun to have nonetheless! On our way back, we visited the Island of Cochin in the western backwaters. It was a delightful place and home to a prosperous group of British and Swedish businessmen who engaged in west coast trade, worked hard, played hard, enjoying sailing and tennis clubs, as well as big bungalows overlooking the backwaters or sea.

In addition to the Indians, British and Swedes, Cochin was home to a community of 'White Jews', who after the fall of Jerusalem in 70 A.D had fled Israel, and driven from every country en route, had arrived on the west coast of India and been given leave of stay on the island. Over time, their descendants formed a prosperous community of the 'Black Jews', but the more staunchly religious White Jews remained very much a closed community, and to maintain racial purity, inter-marriage was prohibited, resulting in genetic flaws and sterility.

Their synagogue, floored with priceless blue and white tiles, is a most interesting place. We were shown two ancient parchment scrolls containing the scriptures, purported to have been brought from Israel centuries ago and therefore highly valued by the Jewish community. There is also a famous clocktower, but we were mystified as to how the clock worked since its components appeared to be tied together with string and odd pieces of wire. Wound up in the manner of a cuckoo clock, with a long and much-mended length of rope, it is a fantastic piece of mechanical ingenuity; somewhat typical of the East, where things are operated using the most surprising materials, or the lack of them!

This coast is also famous for its so-called Chinese fishing nets. These enormous, clumsy looking erections, resembling giant shrimping nets, are suspended over the water by a complicated series of poles and ropes. Each net is balanced by weights, enabling the fisherman to lower it into the water, and after an interval, raise it, with the odd fish flapping about. It seemed a lot of bother, and the contraption over-complicated for such a poor return, but far from unusual in the East, where no one is ever in a hurry.

I have so far mentioned a few acquaintances, but we had many very dear friends amongst the widely scattered community of tea planters. Before the 1914/18 war, and even afterwards on our return from the UK and before cars had replaced horses, we used to ride far and wide to visit them, often staying the weekend. We discovered what marvellous friends we had when up against it and valued their loyalty when we were in the doldrums and feeling that all our efforts to eradicate malaria were not appreciated by those in authority.

One of our first friends was 'Old Man', more often known as 'Daddy'. During a period when the Indian labourer was considered no more than an animal, he looked after his workers and their families, supplying them with free milk, free medical attention and stud bulls for those who owned, or would like to own cattle. A staunch Roman Catholic, he was also enormously supportive of efforts made by priests and nuns to improve the living conditions of Travancore's poor, who at the time, suffered a level of poverty almost impossible to comprehend today.

He always displayed the same easy-going temperament and we were both very fond of him. His inordinate thirst made him somewhat of a nuisance at parties, but even when very drunk, he was never unpleasant, and no matter how late the hour, he could rely on his faithful nag to get him home and an old servant to put him to bed.

Daddy was known as the most generous and kindly of men and as a consequence, when he later came into a very large fortune, was often visited by people in financial difficulty. Always self-effacing, he perhaps began to believe that anyone who visited him only did so in order to ask for help. He lived in a very remote part of the country and we had not seen him for several years, so when business took us within a few miles of his home, we decided to pay him a visit. He was delighted to see us, and with his usual hospitality, dined and wined us lavishly. As we sat on his verandah preparing to leave, he made some excuse to go inside, and calling Jim into the bungalow, our dear friend asked if he needed help. Jim was touched and when he assured Daddy that we had come for no other reason than simply to see him, he was so overcome that his eyes filled with tears. He was reluctant to see us go, and we parted with the sad realisation that he was seldom visited by anyone who wanted nothing more than his company.

There was Frankie, a good friend of Jim's before we were married, and whom we saw only occasionally since he lived quite far away. He was a quiet man with a twinkle in his eye and a hidden sense of humour, whilst his wife, a big, generous woman, loved a good story and by exaggerating the facts to add sparkle, made a first-class job of telling it unless Frankie was there to rein her in!

Then there was Reggie, a small man who played the banjo delightfully and made model ships in his spare time. He was not strong, and until he got himself a wife, was often ill. He gave very enjoyable parties at which his 'boy' Julien, pulled out all the stops by providing food fit for the gods, and decorating the bungalow until it looked like a fairyland.

E.C.S, another old friend of Jim's, remained one of our best friends until he died. Sadly, he had ended up in quite the wrong job. He should have been a research scientist, or a linguist translating the foreign literature into English, but due to his father's sudden death, was forced at a very early age to support his mother and sister. He accepted a tea planting apprenticeship, the only job on offer, and because those two women depended on him throughout his life, was never able to fulfil his own ambitions. Ill luck dogged his footsteps; his attempt at marriage was a wretched failure and later, his attempt to provide a home to a young niece proved equally unsuccessful. He was a man in a thousand, who, unable to unburden himself to his friends, was very often misjudged.

Our nearest neighbours included Mac, Marjorie and their four children; very dear and much- valued friends, of whom we saw a great deal. Mac suffered from a gastric ulcer and was often in good deal of pain. One day, on a stroll with Marjorie, I enquired after Mac. "Oh" she replied airily, "He's feeling rather ill, but I expect he'll be better soon. His ulcer has burst, and he is passing a lot of blood." Utterly aghast, I insisted on returning at once to the bungalow, whereupon I contacted Jim who sent for Mac's assistant. He in turn, was ordered to send a telegram reporting Mac's condition to his firm's headquarters, and another, to Dr Somervell - of Everest fame - in Neyvor, asking him to come up immediately. Meanwhile, Marjorie and I scurried about gathering everything he might need to operate, including dragging out a heavy wooden table and sterilizing all the surgical instruments in the little local hospital. Having temporarily rallied, and adamant that he wasn't going to have any doctor fuss over him, Mac then ordered all arrangements to be cancelled!

Marjorie duly set off to the post office to dispatch a telegram to Dr Somervell cancelling his visit. Fortunately, Jim met her on the way and managed to stop her, though almost by force.

After travelling all night, Dr Somervell arrived looking wild-eyed and flushed, but took in the situation at a glance. The male nurse who accompanied him was ordered to get everything ready as quickly as possible, and using a spinal anaesthetic, he operated on Mac in the open verandah of his bungalow, with rain streaming down outside. The doctor told us afterwards that he had seldom seen a man in such a mess and were it not for our prompt action, he might have died. Still worried about Mac, he stayed over, having left very strict orders with the nurse that Mac should only be given fluids. However, during the night, Mac awoke and persuaded Marjorie to bring him toasted cheese. Dear Marjorie, always ready to please him, had waited till the nurse's back was turned, and was in the middle of preparing the snack, when alerted by the smell, Dr Somervell managed to catch her just in time. The consequence would have been fatal, but assured that a lesson had been learned, Dr Somervell left that day. Mac seemed fairly comfortable, then the very next morning, Marjorie sent a message asking us to come over since he had relapsed. On arrival, we found that poor Mac had been racked for several hours with hiccoughs which after his operation, was agony. There was nothing anyone could do, but the hiccoughs eventually subsided, and Mac made an uneventful though slow recovery.

Back then, we had but a few intimate Indian friends, but were close to the Bedis, a Bikh family, whom we liked immensely. Colonel Bedi was assistant agent to the Governor General of the State of Madras, and because he rented a bungalow not far from us during the hottest season, we saw quite a lot of him, his wife and their three children: Dhumi a boy, and two girls, Moini and Shilla. We sadly lost touch when they moved away.

There was also Mr. Conjako-Conjako, with whom we had made friends in rather an odd way, and who called in to see us whenever he came through our district. Sometime after his visit, way back in 1923, Sir Malcolm Watson sent a letter asking us to make a malarial survey in a particular valley in Travancore. Apparently, an ideal breeding ground for malarial mosquitoes, it had neither mosquitos nor malaria and Sir Malcolm wanted to find out the reason why. Jim applied for a few days' leave and we set about searching streams and seepage patches for mosquito larvae, taking samples of water from streams to be sent to Madras for analysis. We also measured the spleen rates in as many children as possible, especially those living in villages close to malarious looking streams and swamps and scoured houses and cattle sheds for adult mosquitos.

At one of these villages, we were watched with interest by a local Travancorean, who after providing us with information regarding levels of malaria in the district, invited us to join him for coffee. The valley was almost at sea level, and because the climate was hot and humid, his house had been constructed with all the rooms open to fresh air. Outside the living room was a wide balcony, through which projected a palm tree, with the seats under its shade providing a cool and inviting resting place with views over rubber trees to the hills beyond. In the course of our conversation, he told us that he and his family were tormented by mosquitos and asked for our help. Walking round the surrounding area, we soon discovered larvae breeding in the hollows of rocks, in the well, and in holes of the trunks of felled banana trees, but although a nuisance, none of the hatching mosquitoes were anophelines and therefore not dangerous.

On our way out, Mr Conjako-Conjako took great pride in showing us his collection of highly coloured prints of all the reigning monarchs of Europe, past and present, which adorned the walls of his living room, and was quite shocked that we had neither met any, nor indeed, knew who they were!

That malarial survey gave us cause for thought, but we left none the wiser. Given the valley's streams, humidity and warmth, the place should have been highly malarious, yet all the small children whose spleens we had tested were perfectly healthy. Moreover, the samples of the water sent to Madras were apparently normal, with nothing to explain the absence of breeding anopheline.

Once back home, I busied myself with preparations for a forthcoming concert and it was always a tremendous thrill to drive my baby Austin through several miles of jungle road to rehearsals at our friends W and D's bungalow. There was little danger from elephants at that time of year, and despite being alone, I was able to enjoy myself without feeling anxious. Reaching the section with a steep, winding hill, I would switch off the engine and one night, when freewheeling in silence, my headlights picked out a three-quarter grown sloth bear, looking just like a big, black, long-haired puppy, with his fat, clumsy body and paws he had yet to grow into. Weaving from side to side, he attempted to escape the dazzle by scrambling up a bank, but as he neared the top it collapsed under his weight, and down he fell amidst a deluge of earth and small stones. Frightened by the headlights, he squeezed himself against the bank where he remained frozen until after a minute or two, I released the brake and went on my way.

On another moonlit night, as I was freewheeling down the same road, with a stiff breeze masking the sound of my car, I came across a sambhur doe standing on the grassy verge. I switched off the headlights and after her first spasm of fear, watched as she bent to lick her large-eyed fawn who, newly born, was still unsteady on his spindly legs. Finally, after quite a long time, during which I sat completely still, she began to shoulder him slowly off the road and down into the jungle shadows.

Chance encounters whilst driving my baby Austin were not confined to wildlife. Travelling to the West coast through the rubber district on the edge of the backwater, I was held up by a bullock cart beside which a woman was walking, wringing her hands and weeping bitterly.

She was clearly very distressed, so I drew up to see if I could be of any assistance. Both the cart driver and the woman were Malayalams and I spoke only Tamil, but I managed to glean that the woman was begging for a lift into Kottayam where her daughter was very ill in hospital. Having walked a fair distance, she was weary and footsore so, with no idea why the cart was unwilling to take her, and as I was heading for the town, I offered to give her a lift.

Although a little nervous at first, she soon got used to the swift motion of the car and relaxed. I was given her family's history, or so I assumed, since I only understood about one word in twenty, and made sympathetic noises as she wept over tragedies and shared her laughter at more joyful events. After driving some twenty-five miles along a lovely tree-lined road amidst the intoxicating scent of pepper vines, we reached the rest-house where I was to meet Jim. My passenger, however, was reluctant to get out of the car and in eager anticipation, indicated that her sister's house was only a short distance up the road. Realising that she was dying to drive right up to the door in a private car, albeit a very small one, to show off to her sister's family, I laughed and pulled up with somewhat of a flourish in front of a small thatched hut. She was thus able to climb out in full view of the street, but to further ensure that her grand arrival had been missed by no one, insisted on bidding me a very loud and garrulous farewell!

A Plague, Thieves and a Move to High Wavys
1938

There was a large deep pool at the bottom of the estate made by landslides during the flood of 1920, where we used to have great bathing parties. It was a lovely place, set in a bend on the river, and because the trees on its banks hid all signs of human habitation, we might have been miles away in impenetrable forest. During afternoon showers, which came down like rods of ice, we kept warm by diving into the water and staying there until the rain passed. While bathing, we were often watched by monkeys and scolded by black Wanderoos who would show their disapproval by throwing down twigs and jungle fruit. Other more occasional onlookers, including the Malabar Grey Hornbill, would sit and watch our antics then burst into song that sounded like jeering laughter.

Once whilst walking by the bathing pool, our friend Denis and I noticed a pair of Brahminy Kites fishing from one of the rocks near the edge of the main stream. Hidden out of sight in the long grass we watched them catch a small fish, but before they could eat it, a small Indian Pariah Kite swooped down and took it away, leaving them looking bewildered and mewing pathetically. Within minutes, they resumed their fishing, only to have their catch grabbed from under their beaks as before. Again, they mewed and looked surprised and offended, but made no effort to protect their meal. We left them to it, wondering how long it went on, and whether in the end, the Pariah Kite became satiated, or the others got fed up providing meals for him!

Our life in this district where we had achieved so much and been very happy was drawing to a close, though we did not know it at the time. In the meanwhile, we were looking forward to our furlough in Britain, the best we ever had, staying at D's parents' home in Somerset. Not long married, D had given us some of his wedding cake, packed in a neat little parcel, to give to his parents at Port Said; a simple plan that was anything but! After being rowed ashore from our ship, we were stopped by an official and asked to declare the contents of our neat little parcel. When told it was a piece of wedding cake, he became both suspicious and annoyed, and then distinctly agitated when he heard we had come from Columbo. "Why?" he asked, "bring cake from Colombo when good cake can be found in Port Said?" We tried to explain that this was very special cake, made for the marriage of the son of the friends we were meeting. He insisted we open the parcel to show him. Our reluctance to do this confirmed his suspicions and he became rather truculent. We were just about to open it when D's parents arrived, and with a few sentences in their fluent Arabic, a smile and a laugh, all was well. We all bowed to each other and parted the best of friends. After spending an enjoyable hour or two with D's parents, we returned to the quay whereupon the recently suspicious official popped out of his cubby hole, and greeting us like old friends cried out: "No more cake?" Then roaring with laughter, he bid us farewell.

Once settled in the lovely old house in Somerset, we looked forward to spending time with our children, who by then were young adults. Ted, now working, visited whenever he could, and Monica, who had just finished school, stayed for the duration. She then planned to return with us for a holiday in India before training as a nurse at Great Ormond Street Hospital. This was our first winter furlough in Britain since 1913, and we enjoyed it tremendously. We had the use of a second-hand car and drove and tramped all over the beautiful countryside, exploring many of the caves both in the nearby Coombes and at Wookey Hole and Cheddar.

Time flew and one streaming wet day in May, we set sail for India once more. It was fun having Monica on board and to witness that magical moment of her arrival, and the ecstatic, almost overwhelming, welcome from the labour. She loved both the tea estate and the jungle and threw herself into helping me work with the anti-malarial squad and looking after the sick. However, after being shaken by her first encounter, it took her some time to become accustomed to the leeches!

Shortly after our return in June we found ourselves in the midst of a plague scare. Dead rats had been found in a house at the frontier post, six miles away, and the report on bodies sent away for testing, confirmed the presence of bacilli. Everyone got into a flap and all residents, as well as anyone entering the district, were inoculated. However, as time went on we began to wonder whether the scare was justified. For instance, Denis' wife Mary caught a female rat in a trap and three days later, found three tiny hairless bodies in the toe of one of her shoes. Orders had been issued that all dead rats, whatever their age or the circumstances in which they had been found, had to be sent away for examination, so the bodies of the baby rats were duly sent off. Imagine our surprise when the report came back stating they had tested positive for plague! I suspect that the laboratory had never returned a negative report, perhaps on the premise that it was better to be safe than sorry, but those inoculations made us all feel thoroughly wretched, and it took many months for me and many others to fully recover from the side-effects. No new cases of plague occurred in the district and life returned to normal. Months afterwards, we were told that the dead rats that sparked the scare, had been thrown into the window of one of the frontier officials by an enemy, in an attempt to frighten him away, but we would never know the truth of this story.

In August that year, 1932, we left our home, our work and the people whose welfare had been our key concern and responsibility for over thirteen years. During that period, people's health had improved enormously. Malaria had been reduced to a few cases imported from the plains, or in one or two people living near the river. Deaths had dropped from 116 per thousand to 13 per thousand, and it was hard to find any very thin, pot-bellied children within the boundaries of the estate.

However, we were now without a job: a bolt from the blue that brought a tremendous change to our lives. Facing an unknown future, Jim went off to a planters' meeting in Bangalore in search of a job, leaving Monica and I to pack up our belongings whilst staying with various friends. Fortunately, Jim returned with news that our old assistant and very dear friend had offered him the management of one of the smaller estates; a job that entailed an experiment in tea manufacture and opening more land to tea. It was not, however, all plain sailing. Having completed our packing, we drove by car to the village where we met our bullock carts and encountered our first snag. All our boxes had to be opened, and the contents made up into fifty-pound bundles to be carried by load coolies up the ghaut. A few bundles were lashed on poles, but most of our treasures were stashed into sacks, and it says much for the carriers that the only thing lost from that heterogeneous collection was Jim's tailcoat!

The carriers were all Kalar-Thevars, the thief-caste, and as such, were under constant police supervision. However, neither then, nor at any other time except for the tailcoat, did we ever lose goods in their care. We liked and trusted these people and many years later had an old Kalar-Thevar coolie who carried our mail and large sums of money along a twelve to fourteen-mile strip, six days a week, without ever losing any of it. Bandits then began to operate the road and one day, set upon our tapaal coolie, who happened to have a large number of envelopes containing money sent by the masons and carpenters to the postmaster to be transferred into money orders, then forwarded to their families. The bag was seized and the coolie ran off to report the theft. The next day, the stolen bag was discovered with the letters intact but all the money missing. Deeming it too dangerous for a single man to carry such large sums, our then agent in the plains, Kolar Rowther, enlisted large squads of coolies, all of the thief-caste, to accompany him. Each man was given a sack of rice to carry, but no one knew which sack contained the hidden bag of cash.

Leeches and Other More Amenable Locals

Our new, temporary home was a tiny three roomed building but we got most of our stuff into it, and made it look as homely as possible. Luckily, the weather was fine, which made the move easier. It was a beautiful setting, but everything was new and strange and we initially found the readjustment difficult, and in the absence of a clerk and a typewriter, Monica and I had to spend quite a lot of time in the office helping Jim with spadework. Once settled, we slowly became acquainted with the staff and labour. The only doctor lived four miles away through the jungle and when required, I began to apply dressings to the women and children. Though anxious not to rush things or antagonise the doctor, I was nevertheless determined to take charge of a modest dispensary, located in a tiny office across the road from our bungalow, as soon as possible.

We had arrived after the rains in September, when the jungle flora is at its best. Swamps glowed with wild balsams in many shades of red and pink, the forest floors were carpeted with a nettle-like plant bearing masses of tiny smoky-blue flowers, and deep within the jungle, wild begonias appeared in areas spared by almost impenetrable thickets of eeta and thorny cane. Those sparse clear areas were also home to leeches, more numerous and hungrier than any I had ever encountered!

Christmas came and went and I made the most of Monica's company. We went bird-watching and were tormented by leeches; we collected butterflies for the South Kensington Museum and were tormented by leeches; we explored the surrounding countryside and climbed many of the hills and were tormented by leeches. Leeches ruled our lives!

We also became involved with two little mouse deer. The doe had been caught in the weeding field, and the stag was brought to us with a broken leg after being attacked by a dog. Splints were put on his leg and both deer then moved to an outhouse where we were kept busy feeding them every three hours, day and night. Sweet little things, they were still very young when they arrived, and looked so appealing with their huge limpid eyes, their ever-twitching ears, and soft wet noses. We named them Mite and Midget. Mite's leg set without trouble and seemed quite straight, which was something of a victory, given our rather amateurish method of applying splints. They became so tame that Monica and I could open and shut boxes stored in the outhouse, drop tin plates, or make any sort of strange noise without them worrying in the slightest. However, it was interesting to note that whenever we made a noise that sounded like the rustle of an animal in grass, their survival instincts came into play, and both would instantly dive for shelter and lie low, absolutely still.

Although Monica joined most of our trips around the countryside and helped in the office and dispensary, she was not at all well and in a great deal of pain, so I decided to take her to the nearest hospital in Madura, some ninety-five miles away. We left the estate just as it was getting light, walked the long rough road to the plains, and after bumping across fields in a bullock cart, were very relieved to see our taxi from Madura waiting for us on the main road. The cheery young driver, in an effort to impress us, drove with fury, his finger continuously on the horn as we sped past bullock carts, cattle, goats and pedestrians, and by the time we arrived we were all but deaf and had splitting headaches.

Admitted that evening, we were given accommodation in the hospital's European ward where we were seen by Dr Bobs, a slim woman with greying hair and gentle voice, who would become a close and lifelong friend. During the next few days while Monica was having tests, I spent much of my time in the hospital's laboratory observing pathological work undertaken by two Indians, Dr Zeline and Annammal, a technician, as well as accompanying Dr Hilda on ward rounds to collect blood and other samples for examination. Having no doctor on our estate, I wanted to be capable of at least a little pathological work, in addition to the malarial work, at which we were becoming quite proficient.

Once Monica was well enough, we returned to the estate, where amidst our daily duties, we had the joy of seeing our jungles in all their spring glory. Most of the year, the only colour to be found in the jungle is in patches penetrated by the sun, mainly in swamps or along the edges of streams. However, in spring, when the leaves of deciduous trees are yet to open, the ground is carpeted with flowers, creating a dazzling patchwork of colour. It is quite exquisite but alas, short-lived. There had been nothing like it in our previous district, and I was so glad that Monica had been able to see it before she left.

I missed Monica sorely after she left for London in April, but we were so busy that I didn't have time to be sad. Jim was organising the construction of our new bungalow and a new factory in addition to his usual duties, and although excellent, his staff were fairly new to estate work and needed a considerable amount of training. I helped him all I could, still making handwritten copies of estate accounts etc. whilst dealing with sick employees. I was also in charge of the vegetable garden we had planted nearby. One day, our former head gardener who had worked for years on the old estate, suddenly turned up and to my surprise and delight, announced that he would like to work for us. I had to point out that we had no garden and would need to create one from scratch, but undeterred, our ever-faithful Mundayan insisted on staying, and until the new bungalow was ready, was a willing and very welcome helper on the vegetable patch.

After the day's work was done, Jim and I often went for a stroll around the tea fields and the strips of jungle that had been left unfelled as windbreaks, between the field boundaries. Occasionally, we saw birds and animals that we did not recognise; the most exciting and unusual of which was the Pyrotrogon Fasciatus Malabaratim or Malabar Trogan. We first saw him fairly late one evening, sitting on a branch, just on the edge of a long stretch of jungle, with his wonderful cherry-red breast gleaming in the sunlight, then watched his curious fluttering as he flew from his perch, all the while keeping up a strange call that sounded like jingling bells. We had never seen such a bird and hurried home to identify him in our book of Indian birds. Another lovely bird we saw for the first time, in the dense jungle undergrowth, was the Hodgson's Rose Finch; a small variety of finch, with no particular features except for its beautiful rose colouring.

We also took great delight in watching more common birds. First and our favourite, the whistling thrush, then the various babblers and in particular, the Deccan Scimitar Babbler, whose lovely call sounds rather like a thin trickle of water pouring into a small silver ewer. There were Golden Orioles, and the vividly coloured Minevets - the males orange, and the females yellow- as well as giant hornbills, kites, eagles and owls, and of course, the Paradise Flycatcher. We were too high in the hills for the famous 'brain fever' or the 'broken pekoe'; both cuckoos with maddening, repetitious and monotonous calls, but we heard them when we went down into the jungle, lower down the hill.

During the months after Monica's departure, there were many cases of malaria among the labour, and I myself was having a series of attacks. Jim had to run the dispensary on the days when I was laid-up, although I was usually able to undertake the staining and examination of the blood slides, and the copying of the estate reports and accounts. In between my bouts of fever, we continued to search the streams for mosquito larvae, as well as the cattle sheds for adult insects, but these expeditions and every other around the estate, were made miserable by leeches! In despair, we managed to evolve a fairly leech-proof leg covering which reduced the number of bites although we seldom escaped entirely. We found that if we wore thick closely woven lisle stockings over thick hand knitted woollen stockings, the leeches could penetrate the first layer but not the second. Wide garters made from tubes of cotton filled with rough salt were tied around our legs to deter leeches from invading at ground level, whilst those attached to bushes, we attacked with sticks hung with little bags of salt. Those that managed to elude us, hid themselves away and were only discovered when we got back to the bungalow, or when they dropped off naturally, having gorged themselves and left some unexpected part of our bodies streaming with blood!

One of our favourite walks led to the ridge of Metla Mullay, at the end of which lay a deep rocky gorge and a magnificent view over the plains to the Travancore hills beyond. Sitting eating our picnics, we would regularly spot Nilgiri goats scrambling over the surrounding cliffs, and far away in the north, the tiny forms of wild elephants feeding in the valley. Mist and drizzle would sometimes fill the valley for weeks on end, but only on the jungle slopes of Metla Mullay and never on its dry grassy face. This curious phenomenon created wonderful effects at sunset, and lit by the glow, the rolling mist turned a deep red and the hill looked as if it were on fire. Remote, empty and silent, bar the sounds from the jungle, it was a place of perfect peace. As usual, we were tormented by leeches, until reaching the grassland, where the sambhur flies took over. By the side of the track was a clearing where game could sleep in the daytime, free from attack. The soft, muddy ground was covered in prints and hollows where sambhur and bison had lain, and the trunks of the trees, shiny and marked, where the animals had rubbed their bodies, and in the case of the deer, the velvet from their antlers. The atmosphere was like that of a well-used sitting room, recently vacated by guests who had gathered for a quiet party.

We eventually moved into the new bungalow at the end of May. It was roomier, more comfortable and once filled with our treasures, soon began to feel like home. Shortly after we had settled in, Dr Bobs paid us a visit, and having greatly enjoyed our jungle walks and exploring the hills around the estate, she returned to Madura feeling perfectly rested. Prior to meeting us, she had spent her holidays at Kodaikanal, the official missionary resort; a lovely place, perfect for missionaries, but not for medical missionaries. During one of her stays, she received no fewer than two hundred calls for medical advice, whereas with us, there was no one to bother her, and apart from sometimes lending a hand at the dispensary, she had a complete break from medicine. Such was her love for our place, that she decided to have a small grass hut constructed on a site that had already been cut for another build then abandoned - on the side of a jungle-covered hill. Delighted, we immediately agreed to have it ready in time for her next holiday.

After she left, we experienced an increase in malaria cases, which was something of a surprise, given our altitude, and in my diary entry of April 25th, 1933, I noted: "Examined several more blood slides; all positive B.T. We are beginning to wonder whether some are not indigenous infections. I shall have to go larvae and mosquito hunting tomorrow." I too, was getting intermittent, debilitating attacks of malaria and was exasperated at the amount of time wasted lying in bed when there was so much to do. It seemed ridiculous that I should succumb now, having weathered years on Munji, surrounded by people dying of the disease.

The next day, we conducted an extensive larvae hunt in the row of coolie lines, emptying all rooms of impedimenta and searching walls and thatch for mosquitos. Any samples taken from both the lines and mosquito traps placed in the cattle sheds nearby were innocuous. However, as we were within seven miles of the malarious villages where many of the coolies came from, it was highly possible that those infected had visited family or friends or gone down for shopping and stayed the night. They all assured me that they hadn't, but I often had my doubts.

The previous manager, who knew nothing of malaria, had been in the habit of issuing every feverish coolie with a bottle of some sort of patented pills, and as I was frequently asked for supplies, I began to wonder whether they had some value. Then, just in time, I discovered the reason for their popularity. One day, while having a clean-up, I came across some strange blue sticky stuff behind a set of lines, and when I asked what it was a small boy said it came from the pills that the other dorai had given them for malaria. It transpired that the pills had been issued in little blue screw-topped bottles, which perfect for keeping things in, were highly coveted by the labour! In this instance, his mother had thrown them out and used the bottle for her father's opium pills.

He offered to show me other places where pills had been thrown away and from then on, I made sure everyone took their medicine.

Meanwhile, Jacob, our head conductor and one of Jim's most trusted employees had married and on his return from his village, brought his new wife Amirtham to see us. I immediately warmed to this young woman, whose face had been badly pitted by smallpox, and to this day, consider both she and Jacob our good friends. Living on our isolated estate, the Indian members of our community who didn't work for us, and especially the wives of the Indian staff, became very bored, so I decided to start a sewing class twice a week in the bungalow. Amirtham joined immediately, and the most regular and able member, was soon helping her classmates. As time went on, her skills surpassed mine. She learned how to use my machine and began making shirts for Jacob, then later, when her babies arrived made clothes for them too. There will be many references to these two as my story unfolds, since they were both in their own way exceptional people. Had they not had the good fortune to be schooled by the Mission in Madura, they would have lived out their lives, on the edge of starvation, in their respective villages; Jacob sweeping the village streets, Amirtham bearing children and working in the fields, each for a pittance.

Bobs, a Seaside Excursion and Building the New Factory

The monsoon broke in gales, rain, and chilly driving mist. At our present elevation of 5,200 feet above sea level we had not made the sort of plans for its arrival as we had on the Munji estate, but nevertheless, there was enough malaria for us to welcome it. We hoped that it would improve matters and sure enough it did. As people's health improved, I handed over routine dispensary work to Jacob, whilst Jim arranged for Harty, his medical officer, to make occasional visits and deal with emergencies. We then left for Madura to see Dr Bobs, who in response to the constant relapses that were making my life a misery, had suggested a stiff course of anti-malarial treatment.

Life in her delightful house was good, and despite taking many revolting drugs, I was able to join Jim in the hospital lab to learn more about the examination of diseases other than malaria. We joined in Sunday evening hymn singing and on other evenings, were taken for drives to a charming little 'tepkulam', or small lake, where we would sit in the car enjoying the peace and beauty of the place. My health improved daily, allowing me to participate in more activities with renewed energy. There was a nurses' feast one evening, where we sat on the roof, cross-legged, playing games and eating off banana leaves with our fingers. The nurses and Indian doctors found Jim's efforts to get a tidy amount of rice and curry into his mouth highly amusing, and their peals of laughter rang out as they teased him. It was impossible to be formal with those happy young women and wearing a sari lent to me by Dr Bobs - Bobs to her friends - I felt just like one of them.

Bobs was determined that I should have a breath of sea air before returning to the hills, so we rented a small bungalow at Mandapam near the ferry port to Ceylon and Adam's Bridge, which in December 1964 would be destroyed by a tidal wave killing many people. It was fun to walk on the West side of a narrow peninsula, where battered by the strong southwest wind, we watched huge waves roaring up the beach, then crossing to the more sheltered east side where the water was completely calm.

We also hired a fishing boat, one of the odd craft found in this part of the world, with timbers sewn together with cord, and sails primitive in the extreme. Once away from the lee of the land, it was rough and blustery and it was fascinating to watch the sailors dismantling, then raising the sail at a different angle as we tacked against the wind. On the way back we hit a coral reef, causing every bit of gear on board to shoot to the bottom of the boat. The sailors shouted, waved their arms about and got in each other's way, and in the process of trying to push off from the reef, a pole got stuck in a cleft of the coral rock. It was quite alarming, but no one seemed too bothered and when we struck the reef again, three of the sailors hopped into the water, which was only about two feet deep, and with much shouting and gesticulating, shoved her free once more. We arrived back at the jetty without any further incident and the boat seemed to be none the worse for wear. Thanks to my dark skin, I achieved a deep tan, but poor Jim, Kay and Bobs all suffered terrible sunburn. Nevertheless, having bathed, relaxed and drunk in the clean sea air, we all felt the better for our lovely three days' break.

The day after we got back to the hospital, Jim had to return to the estate. I however stayed a few days more, spending every morning in the laboratory, and the afternoons watching Bobs at work in the operating theatre. The more I learned, the more I admired what she and the doctors and nurses were doing for their patients. There were the five little girls with spinal T.B, who without admission to hospital, would have lived miserable lives lying in rags in some airless mud hut in a rural village. Despite being there for several years, lying flat on their backs, they were never bored and indeed were amongst the happiest people in the hospital. Another place of pilgrimage was the nursery, a place of surprising gaiety, given that it was filled with children aged between one and six, who suffered every complaint in the book and various unknown illnesses besides. The kind and patient nurses did everything they could to ensure that the children had fun. Bobs was regarded as a playmate, and as soon as she appeared was greeted by a clamour of noise as the children, especially those unable to join the wave of little brown bodies that swarmed around her, shouted at the tops of their voices, vying for her undivided attention.

One particular women's ward was another place of joy. The patients, predominantly wives of the town's Muslims, suffered from various ailments, most of which related to their confined and lonely lives. Husbands would bring their wives to the hospital, saying they were very sick, and Bobs would order a spell in hospital 'for observation'. On arrival, the women were treated for worms, examined for anaemia, or malaria, and prescribed medicines accordingly. It was only then, that the real cure began. They were not allowed to be seen by any male, of course, but within the hospital that was easy. Able to move about freely, they could visit patients and watch the nurses going about their daily work. Bobs also organised parties on the roof, where together with nurses and doctors and amidst much laughter, the women enjoyed music, childish games and feasts. In short, they had a really good time! A few weeks spent in hospital undergoing such 'treatment' turned bored, frustrated women into almost happy individuals, and indeed, Bobs told me that some of her ex-patients made a habit of staging an attack of the 'vapours' or some such trouble, just to get a bit of fun in their lives! If asked what Bobs gave in full measure to the Indian women in her care, I would say it was laughter. By making the women laugh, she would break the ice and ice broken by Bobs was never given the chance to re-form.

After another week in hospital, I was considered well enough to make the long journey home. Now August, the monsoon in the hills was two-thirds over and the country was very wet. I was greeted by streaming rain, high winds, and a thick enveloping mist and because conditions were ideal, there seemed to be leeches standing erect on every dead leaf on the path. Jim had sent down a dhooly and although I usually scorned such things, I was glad to sit in it for part of the long hot climb up the hill. Despite its newness, our bungalow felt so welcoming and homely, that it was hard to recall the months spent in that tiny place near the dispensary.

By then the construction of the factory was well under way. Building in these hills was quite a problem and as Jim had no contractor, he did that part of the work himself. The estate provided stone for the buildings and timber for doors, whilst that for the windows, rafters and reapers was cut from the nearby jungle. Everything else, including cement and fastenings for windows and doors, had to be carried on men's heads up the long steep hill from the plains. It was delightful to hear them chanting as they worked, but these fellows had to be tough. Capable of carrying weights of up to seventy-five pounds over a distance of seven miles, from 500 to 5,000 feet above sea level, they laboured for five and sometimes six days a week, clad only in a thin cotton 'dhotis', which offered no protection against the elements. At that time of year, those with the unenviable task of transporting ten-foot lengths of corrugated iron also needed to muster all their strength and agility to battle the strong winds that caught the sheets like sails, almost lifting them off the ground.

Jim had just returned for lunch one day when we heard a noise at the edge of the jungle, and then watched a sambhur hind emerge, followed by a small pack of wild dogs. We stayed out of sight hoping she would succeed in giving them the slip. After lunch, we walked down to a small vegetable garden belonging to one of the coolies and spotted a sambhur fawn, presumably separated from the hind, cowering beneath the plantain trees. The fawn had been well trained to stay still, for he lay like a soft brown shadow even when we approached. Reluctantly, we drove the fawn into a nearby strip of jungle to prevent the coolie from killing him for meat, and in the hope that the mother, with her wonderful powers of scent, would eventually return for him.

As the rains decreased, the weather became colder and work at the dispensary was reduced to delivering medicines for coughs and colds. There were not very many children on this small estate so I decided to make them warm garments from the rough blankets issued to the labourers for work in the field. Most of them wore them day and night until they were unspeakably filthy, but no doubt they were even warmer that way!

An Earthquake, a Leopard and a Cardamom Plantation

Early in the morning, at around 3am in January, we were awakened by a deep rumbling, followed by an earth tremor. It was nothing of any consequence, and lasted only a few seconds, but arriving at the dispensary, I was met by a worried throng. Had I felt the earthquake and what had caused it? When everybody had simmered down, I managed to find out what had happened. In their small quarters, the coolies were in the habit of piling all their brass cooking pots in a corner of their rooms. The tremor had caused these piles to collapse with such a devastating clatter that everyone had imagined the situation to be much worse than it was, but were calmed when I told them that in our part of India, earthquakes were never as bad as those in the North.

When we received our newspapers, as usual three or four days' late, we heard of the terrible earthquake that had hit Behar, where my sister was living. After an anxious wait, we finally learned that her bungalow had been completely destroyed. My brother-in-law and their young daughter had escaped but were cut off for some time by fissures and piles of sand, whilst my sister in hospital, had been pinned to her bed by the collapse of a wall and large wooden cupboard. She was lucky to survive, since other wards had been reduced to rubble.

Nature was thoroughly upset that month, for on the 24th we had a cyclone with terrific wind and torrential rain. From the verandah, we watched as raging water filled the drains and gullies and had to rush out to empty our overflowing rain gauge. Then, later that evening, whilst sitting by the fire listening to the turmoil outside, we heard an ominous creak followed by a loud ripping noise as water began to stream into the room. We hurriedly dragged the carpet into our bedroom, and despite moving the furniture as far as possible from the cascade, it stood in swilling water for two days. Paddling outside to assess the damage, we could see nothing but mist and lashing rain, but greeted the next morning by a truly terrifying wind, discovered our new wireless mast thrashing about and several corrugated iron sheets ripped from the sitting room roof. A little later, a man who had been camping some miles down the valley, came up to our bungalow. He and his coolies had been washed out of their tent and everything had blown away. Apart from the sitting room, the rest of the bungalow was thankfully weatherproof, so we managed to get them all fed and warmed. Out guest stayed the night and by next morning, the storm was over.

We saw very few white people. A few of our friends visited when we first arrived, but the difficult journey frightened them off, and only one ever returned! However, with more than enough to keep us occupied, our lives were full and interesting and we became accustomed to being on our own. As the weather grew warmer, bringing April thunderstorms, we began to prepare for the return of malaria, but before we became too busy, our friends Denis and his wife came to spend a holiday with us.

One day, Jim and D went for a stroll along the jungle ridge to the grassland, where Jim hoped to see ibex. They had just the one rifle between them, for they were unlikely to see any other game, and were not expected back until midday. However, at around ten o'clock, a man came running to say that the visiting dorai had shot a tiger and would we come with the camera. I quickly collected some sandwiches, drinks and my faithful battered camera, and on the way was given a vivid description of the enormous animal that D had shot. Arriving at the scene we discovered that it was not a tiger but a black leopard; a really magnificent animal, measuring seven foot three inches from nose to tail. Then, as we sat with our picnic, waiting for men to help carry the leopard back to the estate, we heard what had happened. It was an unusual story. The two men had walked along the ridge, keeping a look out for ibex. None were to be seen which had surprised Jim, as they were usually to be found in large numbers in this area. He was very disappointed on D's behalf, so suggested they made a final search from a little rocky shoulder running at right angles to the main ridge. As they approached, Jim noticed a black shape in a patch of grass, moving slowly towards them. A black leopard! Jim had no weapon, and Denis only a light rifle. Jim quietly touched D's shoulder and as he pointed in its direction, the leopard emerged from the grass and spotted the men. They had fully expected it to bound away to safety, but instead, and much to their alarm, charged directly towards them. As soon as the animal was within range, D positioned his rifle, waited a moment, then fired. The leopard somersaulted, staggered to its feet and collapsed on a flat rock close by. Jim advised D to wait awhile before approaching. The leopard was still alive but obviously badly wounded and thus, very dangerous. Then, suddenly, the leopard silently sprang towards them, with jaws open wide. D fired, missed, and fired again, and the

leopard fell dead within a few feet of them. It had been a nasty moment for Jim since he was unarmed and had no knowledge of how D would react in such an emergency.

On closer examination, we saw that D's first shot had hit the leopard in the mouth, breaking his jaw, which accounted for his open mouth, and silence as he charged. The coolies lashed the body to a pole and we returned to the estate where the animal was skinned and butchered. He was in fairly good condition but with an empty stomach, which perhaps explained his extraordinary lack of fear of the men and led him to attack. The skin was packed in salt and sent to the internationally famous taxidermist Ingen van Ingen, in Mysore to be cured. Amidst great rejoicing, every last scrap of the leopard was distributed among the coolies, who believed that a man who eats the meat of a leopard or tiger takes on some of the beast's fierceness and courage.

There was another, very different, incident during Mary and Denis's stay. One evening, when out for a jungle stroll, our two dogs disappeared down a bank and after a scuffle, emerged with the body of a big red mongoose. The mongoose, like the skunk, has the ability to eject a highly malodorous fluid, not apparently objectionable to dogs, but intolerable to humans. Nevertheless, I thought our guests would be interested to see it, and as I was not far from home, held my nose and took my evil smelling quarry back to the bungalow. I called to our friends from the garden to come for a look, but disgusted by the odour, they quickly retreated indoors. My effort to expand my friends' knowledge was unappreciated, I had the mongoose buried under a tree in the garden, and we all went out for a walk. However, on waking the next morning, I became aware of a frightful smell, followed by groans of horror from Jim and our guests, and quickly realised what had happened. I had made the mistake of leaving the dogs out all night, and having dug up the mongoose, they had triumphantly deposited its body on the verandah!

This was the time of the year when leeches were only to be found in damp places near streams. However, in their place were flies: elephant flies, sambhur flies, and many other little flies whose names we didn't know, that attacked us whenever we left the shelter of the trees. Walking behind Jim, I have seen his back completely covered with flies, trying and often succeeding, in penetrating his shirt! It was also the time of year of intense heat on the plains, so we finished preparing a grass hut on the hill, to allow Dr Bobs and one of her nurses to enjoy our cool, hill air during a fortnight's stay. We had planted flowers around the hut to make it look welcoming and since Jim's second name is Hampton, Bobs decided to name it the 'Hampton Hut'. After a night spent in the bungalow, we escorted them up to their new abode which backed onto a steep jungle slope and with heavenly views over the valley on three sides, looked particularly lovely that morning. Settling into a primitive, lazy lifestyle was wonderfully relaxing for them both, especially Bobs, whose love of the jungle and its sounds was almost equal to my own. Each evening they lit a bonfire and we often joined them for dinner. Entertainment was provided by Kay, who accompanied by her banjo, sang songs learnt in childhood from her old Negro 'mammy'. Listening to her soft velvety voice as we sat by the glowing fire, with the dark skeleton of an old forest tree silhouetted against the sky and the lights of the labourers' huts twinkling in the valley below, felt almost unworldly, and when we eventually tore ourselves away, Jim and I would walk back home still under the spell of it all.

The weekly sewing classes continued in our bungalow, with Jacob's wife Amirtham coming regularly with her knitting and sewing. She was refreshing company, full of humour and down-to-earth common sense, with none of the distressing humility prevalent in Indians of her caste, and we became close friends. There was also great excitement when one day, a friend flew over our valley to take aerial photos of the lay of the land which we had bought for growing cardamom. Many of the coolies had never seen an aeroplane, and the fact that one of the Dorai's friends was up there, added to the thrill.

Having completed his survey, Pat also decided to purchase land for cardamom, albeit on a grander scale, comprising thousands, rather than a few hundred acres. He, Harty, Jim and I discussed our plans until the early hours, at the end of which, Pat suggested that we go into partnership. We decided to survey the land on foot, and rising early the next morning, spent the day scrambling up and down steep, stony hillsides whilst ripping our hands in the process. The day ended with us literally sliding down one boundary, crossing a rocky river and then being stung by a particularly poisonous type of nettle. It then began to rain, and as soon as we hit the path we were covered in leeches from head to toe. I found them in my hair, neck and even, under my arms. By the time we reached the bungalow, we were about as bitten and dirty as could be. My bath was quite pink with blood, and still bleeding after tea, I went to the dispensary decorated with blobs of cotton wool!

Our new factory was now finished and Jim was kept fully occupied by experiments in tea manufacture. Any work on our land devolved to me, but Jim engaged a young man called Samuel to oversee the clearing of the jungle. Mercifully, cardamoms grow fast under forest shade, so only the thick undergrowth and none of the big trees had to be removed. The overseer was accommodated in a grass hut whilst a house was being built, temporary lines were made for the labourers, and whenever possible, Jim and I went down to teach them how to trace roads and demarcate boundaries. As a 'sleeping partner', Harty helped us buy the land and then left the work to us! It proved a very satisfactory arrangement, especially for him, since in years to come, the little place we named Kardana, meaning 'jungly place', became a thriving estate and tourist attraction. Across the valley, opposite our bungalow, stood a ridge that we had named Windy Ridge. On a wild, southwest monsoon day, it was quite impossible to stand either on the ridge or in the gap that ran through it, and the tea field on the high section was so battered by continuous gales that the plants died. The area reverted to jungle and tough woody scrub, but a variety of bamboo grass managed to survive, and in the course of years, covered the top with green.

During the monsoon, Dr Hilda from the women's hospital in Madura, came up for a holiday. Tired of heat and sunshine, she longed for a spell somewhere cool and cloudy. It was however, a wish granted with vengeance! Her arrival coincided with a truly dreadful spell of gales and rain, and our little recorder in the garden showed just fifteen minutes of sunshine in the fortnight she spent with us. To make things worse, there were leeches everywhere, and in the wet misty weather even our most careful methods of protection did little more than reduce the number of bites. Our guest's dog Swanee, being old and slow, suffered the most, and while trying to bite them off, got one up her nose and there it stuck, refusing to drop off. Since depriving Swanee of water proved unsuccessful, we then allowed her to drink and eventually, as hoped, it popped its sucking end out towards the water. However, it slid from our fingers as soon as we caught hold of it and because Swanee always jerked back at the critical moment, further attempts with tweezers and scissors likewise failed. As a last resort, we packed Swanee's nose with salt for four or five days, nearly driving her mad in the process, and then working together, one to hold the dog, one using a wet pad to entice the leech, and one with a pair of tweezers, eventually managed to remove it.

Madura

I had been experiencing recurrent bouts of malaria, and since Jacob was capable of dealing with the coolies' coughs and colds, I decided to accompany Dr Hilda back to Madura. This time I would be given a concentrated course of treatment which, although very unpleasant, would be well worthwhile if it put an end to my continual relapsing.

Madura is a Brahmin city, with extensive bazaars offering a surprising variety of wares if one knows where to look. In the intervals between my spells of treatment and visits to the laboratory for practice with the microscope, I enjoyed afternoons poking around the dark and mysterious cave-like shops. At every entrance, proprietors sat cross-legged and alert, like spiders waiting for flies. After making a small purchase, I would sit in the cool, dark interior, savouring the spicy smells and watch fascinated, as the ritual of buying and selling came into play. Poor people were served quickly, but whenever prosperous Brahmins came along, a boy would be sent out to buy a bottle of the syrupy soft drink so loved by Indians. The great men would be invited to sit down on a mat and relax over their drinks, then only after they had been consumed and appreciative belches made, was the subject of the purchase mentioned. On one occasion, I saw two men of substance enter a shop, receive the usual welcome, then mention that they wished to sample the shopkeeper's sweets. They tasted a few, then finding them not to their liking, tried some other kind. The shopkeeper grew ever more flustered, and they must have eaten at least half a pound of sweets before finally and in a lordly manner, bought a small amount of the least expensive. When I empathized with the poor, harassed shopkeeper, he simply smiled rather wanly and said that at least, he had had the credit of presenting a gift to a Brahmin, which is always good. He begrudged neither the time wasted nor felt as aggrieved as I would have done. It was a lesson in cheerful patience!

My favourite shops were those that sold fabrics for women's saris. Ablaze with colour, the interiors were stacked high with silks and muslins of black, white and gold, as well as every shade of red, blue and green, all edged and sometimes woven throughout, with heavy gold or silver thread. The shopkeeper would run to and fro, fetching and patiently unfolding ream upon ream whilst customers, mainly wealthy men, debated the rival merits of perhaps a scarlet heavily edged with gold, or a black with a pattern of gold all over it. Since any embroidery was always of pure gold or silver, the cost of some saris could be very high indeed. The men always seemed to do this kind of shopping in groups, arguing about what would suit their wives without any consultation with the women. Imagine the scene: Four or five stout and opulent men with their sacred cords and shaved heads, sitting amidst the fumes of joss-sticks, literally buried in mountains of exquisite materials, whist outside temple bells jingled and elephants shuffled by!

Most of the silk shops were situated within the walls of the temple walls on Temple Square, flanked by monumental gopurams, or entrance towers. We were lucky to have been taken there by friends, so knew the layout, but for strangers visiting the temple there was always the danger of straying into holy places where only priests and Brahmins were allowed. I have been there alone on crowded feast days, and far from meeting resentment, received almost embarrassing friendliness; perhaps because I spoke Tamil. Except for missionaries, many people were prepared, to their shame, to live and work in South India without making any effort to learn the language, or indeed, anything about the people. In Madurai at least, missionaries were welcomed everywhere and since the women's hospital had helped many of the priest's wives and children, they were loved by all.

In the central hall of the temple stands a special pool of evil-smelling water, often covered with green slime, into which locals descend to wash and even drink, in the belief that it will unburden them of their sins. Highly unhygienic, it is open to all but as far as the deities are concerned, Europeans are allowed far more access than many of the low-caste Indians, who can only worship at a distance. There is one small peep-hole through which they can see the golden dome that covers the abode of Meenakshi, the deity to whom the south part of the temple is dedicated. The north belongs to her consort, Shiva, but reigning over all is Kali, the most feared goddess of doom. Three times the size of the others, fierce of face and with her shining black, muscular body, she looks capable of anything. In times of sickness and outbreaks of epidemics, Kali is the goddess to whom the devout make their offerings, and after being dabbed with pats of ghee or melted butter, she is surrounded by the most astonishing rancid aroma, making her even more terrifying.

The poor, thin folk who crowd around Kali seem far more needy than those around any other deity, and it was distressing to see them paying outrageous prices for offerings bought from stalls within the Meenakshi Gate in the belief that they had greater potency than those purchased outside. Other deities in the temple, including Subramanian and Ganesh, the elephant god, were adorned with garlands of small chrysanthemums, jasmine or intensely sweet roses, again sold to impoverished worshippers at an enormous profit. It was ironic to see wealthy bankers and businessmen roll up in large and expensive cars, then prostrate themselves before these deities in earnest and without any hint of self-consciousness, clad only in dhotis and sacred cords.

One day, I was taken by Olive, one of the sisters in the hospital, to watch the procession of Subramanian's annual visit to Minakshi. The din was tremendous, with the sound of the priests' trumpets and tom-toms, punctuated at intervals by the rise of shrill calls and ululations from devotees, and as they drew near the crowd all but disappeared into the clouds of dust raised by their many feet. The procession was led by two priests blowing conch shells, followed by the deity's small litter covered with jasmine and chrysanthemum flowers and carried by four stalwart men. Olive told me that the daughter of one of the leading priests had been discharged from hospital only a few days before, and as the procession drew level the priest in question recognised Olive. Surprised and delighted to see her, he held up his hands to stop the procession. Then placing his palms together in greeting, asked if we would like to see Subramanian; an invitation which of course we gladly accepted. The bearers were ordered to lower the litter and there, in a bed of flowers, stood a tiny jet-black figure facing an equally tiny mirror. We had expected something far more impressive! This godling, off to visit Minakshi in her enormous temple, was about five inches long, and so roughly carved that it required some imagination to recognise a human figure at all. The priest informed us that Subramanian was so vain that he would never consent to travel away from home unless he had a mirror in his litter in which he could admire himself en route.

We spent some time hearing about this god, but nobody seemed to object to the delay, or find it in any way objectionable to have their deity shown off to foreigners and unbelievers. Naturally, Olive being a sister at their beloved hospital had something to do with it, but there must have been many in the crowd who hailing from distant villages, knew nothing of that. The long weary miles between outlying villages and the city could only be undertaken by those in good health, or those driven by religious fervour. Anyone infirm could not have attempted the journey, and few villagers could afford even the most primitive form of transport. At that time, six or even four pence a day was all a villager could expect for his or her labour. Every person capable of any sort of work was expected to pull their weight, or starve, and it was hard to comprehend how these villagers managed to survive such dire poverty.

My concentrated malaria treatment came to an end, and fully recovered, I decided to travel home by bus. By virtue of my white face, I was given a seat at the front beside a smartly dressed young man who eyed me with obvious misgiving. After much shouting, swinging of starting handles, and pushing from behind, our vehicle roared into life. Everyone cheered, our driver leapt into his seat, and we were off. My neighbour made a tentative remark in English, to which I replied politely. Realising that I was someone on whom he could practice his English, his face lit up and he launched into a detailed story of his life, stumbling over some words and asking for correction when he made mistakes. The issue of my entertainment during the long drive was solved! As we bumped and lurched along, the heat increased, both from the sun outside and from what seemed to be a red-hot engine under our feet. I was beginning to have serious doubts as to our safety when we drew up at a coffee shop in Usilampatti, a large village some twenty miles from Madura. My friend disappeared into the shop which, incidentally, sold almost every sort of drink except coffee, and I got down from my seat to stretch my legs, and cool off. I talked to some of the inevitable crowd that had gathered to gaze at me. Because of my white face it was assumed I spoke only English, so I was not understood at first; my overtures being met with embarrassed stares. Suddenly a small boy, always the most intelligent member of any crowd, shouted, "She's speaking Tamil." At once every face lit up, smiles broke out, my questions were answered and even my jokes were understood.

The children were so skinny that none looked as if they had ever had a full meal in their lives. The two to five-year olds looked the worst. Having had to relinquish their mothers' milk, probably in favour of a new baby, they were having difficulty in adjusting to the family's far from adequate diet. In these desperately poor regions of India, mothers continued to breastfeed their babies, often for years, until the next one arrived and I actually saw a woman feeding a new-born from one breast and a four-year-old from the other. Food is scarce and incredibly poor in quality and variety. Many families survive on only one meal a day, taken in the evening, of either rice, or a variety of millet called 'ragi' or 'kaepe', seasoned with salt.

The water in which the ragi is boiled constitutes breakfast, and any leftovers are wrapped in an old cloth to be eaten at mid-day. Children unable to digest this diet are fed only the water in which the food is cooked. Any scraggy chickens the family may possess run loose, scavenging for food around the village. Their eggs are never eaten, but instead, sold or more likely set under a hen to hatch. The chicks are then sold to finance the family's needs in the way of salt, cooking pots, matches, raw sugar, coconut oil for cooking, dried fish as a treat, and when absolutely necessary, clothes. For these transactions, the nearest big village must be reached on foot, and whatever is offered for their goods accepted. This is usually far below their value, but the villagers have neither the time nor energy to go elsewhere. In addition, any time spent bartering reduces both time in the fields and the pittance they receive for their labour. Poverty such as this is incomprehensible to anyone who has not experienced it, and even we, who saw much of it, could not properly appreciate its implications.

Mission hospitals will treat anybody free of charge, and offer the best of medical and surgical care, but if the mother is ill, or the father or baby is sick, the family can rarely take advantage of what is on offer. Either the healthy members of the family cannot spare the time from the fields to escort the sick to hospital, or the hospital is too far away to be reached by a sick person on foot. Hence, those without means to pay for transport, remain in the village, and live or die according to God's will. It is virtually impossible to get Indian doctors or nurses to come to these remote areas since work in the cities is more lucrative, and even if they did, the sick would probably refuse to leave their families for fear and dread of the unknown.

On one of my visits to the Madura hospital, a cart entered the compound carrying a woman with the most tremendous abdominal tumour anyone had ever seen. She was literally hidden behind it. Nurses and orderlies were called, and with great difficulty she was carried into the building. After making her as comfortable as possible, we managed to extract her history. Apparently, this tumour had been growing for a while, making her life a misery. Unable to work, her loss would not deprive the family of income, and since her husband could not take her to hospital, she pluckily decided to go on her own. Incapable of walking, she began her terrible journey shuffling along the hot dusty road on her bottom; a feat so excruciatingly slow and painful, that she must have felt like giving up long before she reached the main road, some three miles away. Having reached the road, she sat crying for help from every passer-by, without success. She spent the night on the verge and in the early morning, a farmer going into Madura managed to heave her vast bulk onto his cart, but that journey along the rutted road, exposed to the sun and dust, must have been purgatory. Deposited in the city, starving and desperate, she sat on the kerb asking for directions to the hospital, and luckily, a man whose wife was a patient came to her aid, and helped by others, lifted her into a jutka. After due care and attention and three meals a day, she became happier, healthier and most importantly, fit for surgery. The operation, performed under a local anaesthetic, involved tapping and draining the fluid from her enormous growth, and she laughed in amazement then wept tears of joy as she watched her tumour shrink. It then took just one more operation for her to make a full recovery.

Let me now return to my tale of my journey home by bus! When the polite young man emerged from the interior of the coffee shop, he was chewing 'vethali' or 'pan'; a mixture of areca nut, cardamom, tobacco and lime wrapped in a vine leaf. Tamils are passionately fond of it, but it involves much blood-red expectoration. My companion chatted away and asking my pardon each time, a well-aimed jet from his mouth would be directed across me to the road beyond. I bore this for a while, then taking advantage of a stop to pick up passengers, suggested that to make things more convenient for him and less alarming for me, we changed places! After some eighty miles, I left the bus and boarded a bullock cart which bumped its way along a track to the foot of our hills where an old white horse, belonging to Harty, was waiting to carry me to the top.

Trouble

Jacob had managed well during my absence and there had been little sickness among the labour. Harty, meanwhile, had been moved to another district, so Jim was in charge of both estates which though enjoyable, kept him terribly busy. The running of Kardana was now left almost entirely to me, and I was soon helping young Samuel to trace roads, make nurseries, clear undergrowth and generally open up the place ready to plant cardamom. Monica was doing well at Great Ormond Street Hospital and the results of her final exams were imminent. To our great joy, we soon received a cable from Mother, with the simple message: "Monica passed". The very next day, and much to our surprise, we had a letter from the postmaster offering his deep sympathy on the death of our dear daughter, and later on, received several notes of condolence from Indians to whom the postmaster had spread the sad news! We had quite a job convincing our sympathisers that Monica was alive and well.

My daily work in the dispensary was usually uneventful, but occasionally there were cases which worried me or emergencies to be attended to in a hurry. I was always deeply touched by the coolies' trust in me, when God knows, they had little cause for it. However, I did what I could, and they knew that I really cared about their welfare. One day, whilst dispensing drugs, I was greeted by a cheery old man in a spotless white dhoti, who asked if he might watch what I was doing. I invited him in and he watched the proceedings with great interest. There were often very sick children who needed attention, but that day there were very few, with only the usual coughs, colds and scabies. Every child needing medicine was given a 'dose' of sugar to suck. This was so popular that stout healthy youngsters would often appear and with long faces and mournful expressions recite a heartrending catalogue of ills suffered during the night, for which they insisted, the only cure was sugar! We had a rule that no child could have sugar unless they had received some kind of treatment, but they still thought it worth a try. Keeping up the pantomime, I would gravely take their pulses, examine their tongues and feel their spleens, and then announce my verdict: "Your sickness is caused by dirt, so you may have your sugar medicine if you wash your face and hands in that basin over there". This would often lead to a mob of grimy young toughs clustering around the basin, and after much splashing and chasing the carbolic soap across the floor, a sea of shining, clean faces would gather at the dispensary table, eagerly looking for sugar. Now and again, one of the children would cheat and present themselves at the table without washing. This was the signal for a mock beating, which was the climax of the entertainment. When the culprit was brought before me, I would place a hand, palm outwards over the child's and clap it loudly with my other hand, arousing shrieks of laughter.

Whilst cleaning up the mess and sterilising my equipment, I heard a voice asking if I was a doctor, and when I told him I was not, he asked why I did this. I replied that there were sick people on the estate and there was no one else to attend to them. "You have a gentleman?" He enquired, "Yes." I replied, "My husband manages the estate." "Then I see him when I come back. I am the father of Mr. G's agent. I go to see Mr. G's estate. I walk there because I am strong-strong." He emphasised that last point by banging his chest with his fist, but I nevertheless warned him that the journey downhill through leech infested jungle would be long and rough, and advised him to take protection of some sort. He had someone to carry his food and drink, but both men were barefoot and I could ill-imagine how the pair born in the plains, would negotiate that steep, rocky, zig-zagging track, and told him so. The old man looked indignant, and after repeating that he was "strong-strong", asked how old I thought he was. He looked around sixty, but to be tactful, I suggested fifty. Roaring with laughter he said he was sixty and very strong, and in turn, guessed that I was fifty-five, when in fact I was only forty-two! Then, having reiterated how strong he was and ignoring my advice, he and his follower trudged off.

After mentioning my encounter to Jim that evening, I then forgot all about him until two days' later, when riding back from the neighbouring estate High Wavys, we saw the old man sitting exhausted in blood-stained clothes on a rock by the roadside. I greeted him and because he was clearly in no state to manage the long walk to his village in the plains, I promised to send bedding down to one of our high-caste staff's houses, where he could rest for the night. Looking mutinous, he pointed to our house and declaring it too big for just two people, announced that would stay with us. We were surprised, since we presumed that his caste would prohibit him from eating with us. This was indeed the case, but one easily resolved by letting his servant milk one of our cows into one of his own pots, and by providing him with oranges and bananas with their skins intact. After warming himself by the fire he ate alone in our spare room, but later, when our dinner was announced, asked if we would object to him watching since he had never seen how English people eat! His curiosity satisfied, we all adjourned to the sitting room where much to his delight we listened to Indian music on the radio until it was time for bed. The next morning, he again ate in his room, and before he left insisted that we took a photograph of him sitting in Jim's armchair reading a newspaper. It was a peculiar request, given that he could neither read nor speak English, but it made an impressive picture which we later sent on to him.

The story however, did not end there. Perhaps the old man or his family had thought he had found a pair of softies, because a few days later he sent Jim a letter with an enclosed signed receipt, in lieu of a loan of five hundred rupees! Jim immediately wrote back advising that he never lent money and warning that it was very dangerous to send a receipt for money that he had not received. We never heard from the old man again. His letter, of course, had been penned by a professional letter writer, and Jim's reply read to him by the same man. He was evidently deeply offended; a pity, since we had enjoyed our time with him.

Shortly afterwards we received news that my sister was very ill, and since it was agreed that Bobs would help her, she came down from Behar to Madura. During Kathleen's treatment, her young daughter Margaret stayed with me at High Wavys and once settled, the child reveled in her life in the jungle. Our windows looked out over forests to the plains 4,000 feet below and in addition to sightings of birds and the occasional monkey, we often heard the calls of sambhur and muntjac. Elephants usually stayed clear, but one moonlight night a family passed through our garden. There were several adults who quietly lumbered on without deviating from their course, but one inquisitive youngster broke away, and approaching the verandah, pushed his head through the window just outside our bedroom. I saw his silhouette, then watched when startled by our scent, he hastily rejoined his little herd. Perhaps not surprisingly, her North Indian ayah was convinced that she and Margaret were going to be attacked by some wild beast on every walk they took, and so, to make things easier, I decided to send the ayah to care for my sister. However, before any of that had been arranged, I had a terrifying experience.

We were trying out some pills which were supposed to be an especially good prophylactic against malaria, so I had given orders that each morning all coolies were to stay in their lines until I arrived at the dispensary. Having collected syringes and needles, along with a tin of these special pills, I set off as usual, but on my approach to a narrow bit of jungle, about midway between our bungalow and the lines, I was met by our 'boy' shivering all over. Assuming he was having an attack of malaria, I put out my hand to take his pulse. He instantly grabbed it, then pulled out a knife. Waving it madly, he cut my chin and after knocking me to the ground, fell upon me, striking both my side and my throat! After a struggle, I managed to disarm him, whereupon he fled up uphill. I was losing a lot of blood and unable to follow him, but I ran down to the dispensary and told the men to run to the bungalow in case the man had gone there with the intention of attacking Margaret and her ayah. I then collected dressings from the dispensary and limped home, followed by a crowd of weeping women. Meanwhile, and in a state of panic, the men had told Jim that the 'ammal' the mistress of the house, had had her throat cut! Luckily, Jim was quickly reassured by the sight of me walking up the road, and by the arrival of the doctor soon afterwards to nervously examine and dress my wounds. My attacker's weapon was one of our table knives which had been honed until razor-sharp. By good fortune, he had struck the ground whilst trying to stab my side, bending the knife. As a consequence, the cuts to my throat were superficial, and because the knife was bent, I had managed to wrestle it from him by the blade, though my hand was deeply cut in the process.

Jim sent a runner to the nearest police station, about fourteen miles away down in the plains, then some of the coolies to search for the culprit, who, named after his father, happened to be the son of my parents' old servant. Towards evening the men returned with my cowering attacker and in due course, three policemen arrived. The bull-necked sub inspector had such a hateful cruel face that I felt sorry for the poor wretched captive, and my fears were confirmed when after accompanying Savrimuthu to the factory where he was held overnight, Jim reported that he had been brutally beaten. The following morning, Savrimuthu was marched down to the plains, and two days later we were summoned to court, presumably to exhibit my injuries. Except for a few scratches on my neck, the wound on my chin and of course, my bandaged right hand, I was none the worse for wear.

Rising at 3am the following day, we walked down the hill to a waiting car, and after changing at an Indian Club from khaki shirts and shorts into clothes more worthy of H.M. Court, attended the hearing at ten. On the way I had my wounds listed at the Government hospital and the doctor responsible was called as a witness. I felt quite embarrassed, as it was quite evident that it would have been easier all round had I been a corpse and not an exhibit with ideas of my own. It was a terrible day in many ways and made me realise how justice can be manipulated by a policeman wanting to make a good case and by a lawyer who, while taking a defendant's money, can do his client more harm than good by the clever use of words. As the inquiry went on it became clear that everybody, including the defending lawyer, was intent on getting a conviction. The prosecution tried to persuade me to say that I saw a man in the tea field who must have seen everything, and I had to be on full alert to ensure that I was not tricked into saying something that could in any way be misconstrued. I truly believe that these 'vakils', as lawyers are called in India, are more astute in twisting words and their meaning than any lawyer in England. I was cross-examined by Savrimuthu's vakil who managed to put his questions in such a way that whatever I said seemed to incriminate the accused. The accused meanwhile, trusted his vakil to defend him, but without any English, remained unaware that this was not the case. After refusing to answer some of his questions and stressing that Savrimuthu had been such a satisfactory servant that his salary had recently been raised, I suggested that the man had experienced a brainstorm by way of explaining the attack. I felt very depressed when we were finally free to go and wondered how judges in India were ever able to arrive at the truth.

There was no time, however, to dwell on my experience in court as we had to get back to the estate and Margaret. Three miles from the foot of our hill, the car came to a halt and after a quick inspection we discovered we had run out of petrol! There was no point in waiting for a messenger to bring fuel from the nearest town four miles away, so we left the driver and set off for the long walk home; three miles on the plain, then seven miles up the hill. It was quite dark by the time we got to the rough hill road, and with no torch we made slow progress. As we neared the top, we promised ourselves a lovely long drink, a cold beer for Jim, and a whisky soda for me, but by the time we dragged our weary bones up the verandah steps, all we wanted was tea, and plenty of it!

Jim ordered a sword stick for me and offered to arrange an escort for when I was alone on the estate. I carried the sword stick for a long time, often used for digging up weeds up or cutting specimens from jungle plants, but an escort I refused, for fear it would make the coolies think I didn't trust them and also because being followed about would have driven me mad! There were times when my heart did an acrobatic tumble when I was accosted by anybody from behind, but that soon wore off. I could not feel nervous among those friendly people and was soon as happy as ever to wander the jungle.

By chance, whilst looking for a replacement for Savrimuthu, Francis turned up. At the time he was serving another family but had saved me from the drunken boy in the jungle many years previously. I greeted him and asked what had brought him to see us, since no longer young, the journey up the hill must have taxed his strength. He told me that he had read about my attack in the paper and had decided to come and take care of me! I was tremendously touched; he was such a tiny person with such a big heart and there was nobody I would rather have run my home. He stayed with us until he died four years later.

The Trail of Sher Khan, the Trial of Savrimuthu and the Jewels of Madura

I can readily cite the hazards imposed by leeches, swinging stinging caterpillars and nettles found in the deeper gorges, but in all my forty years in or near jungles, I never felt in danger from wildlife. This may not be the case of jungles elsewhere, but despite there being plenty of tiger, leopard and bison about, they got out of one's way as fast as possible. The only potentially dangerous beasts were the pig and possibly bear, if one came upon them unexpectedly, but since the latter are hard of hearing and nearly blind, if you make plenty of noise you'll be safe. Travancore's numerous populations of elephants undoubtedly posed a danger to cars driving along dark roads, but as a rule, if left alone, they too ignored humans. Jim had for many years given up shooting and I had never shot an animal, and despite being unarmed we had always been able to travel freely about the jungles and patnas. It was only after coming to these leech-infested hills that I was advised to take somebody with me if going off track; not as protection from wild beasts, but to go for help or carry me out should I sprain my ankle or be unable to walk for any reason. If left to their mercy, leeches are able to suck all the blood from a human in a very short time; a situation famously illustrated by the story of a soldier who, wounded in battle in the old days of conflict in Ceylon, hid in the jungle and was later found dead, completely devoid of blood!

Usually accompanied by the dogs I saw very little game during my walks around the estate, but sometimes I left them behind and was rewarded by a glimpse into the domestic life of some wild animal. One evening, when Jim and I were without our dogs, we came across two golden-throated martens playing on the bend of the road. Unaware of our presence, they gambolled and rolled over and over; their small weasel-like bodies flowing from one lovely posture to another. We watched them frolic; their bright golden throats gleaming in the sunshine, then slowly backed away with one more lovely picture to add to our gallery of jungle memories.

At Kardana, our little cardamom estate, the foundations were being cut for a set of lines for the labour close to a little ravine in which we intended to dig a well. The ravine was dry for much of the year, but we expected to find water fairly close to the surface. Jim had brought down a team of experienced well-diggers and as we stood watching the first foundation stones being laid we heard exclamations of surprise, followed by a man running towards us carrying of all things, a live fish! Apparently, whilst digging, they had noticed movement about two feet down in the damp, sandy soil and found several mud fish similar to those in the tanks in the plains. How they had survived so far beneath the surface in a virtually dry ravine for months at a time was a mystery. We therefore considered their existence a good omen, and indeed, that particular well supplied all the water required by the labour as long as they were there.

Margaret was now without her ayah and with me all the time. My sister had made a partial recovery at the hospital, but unfit to make the demanding journey up to our bungalow, was going back to her husband in North India. The ayah, a Behar, was homesick for her own people, and so had been sent down to Madura to help my sister on the journey. We were due Home leave in spring, as were my sister and brother-in-law, so we had offered to keep Margaret and hand her over in England. Now truly entrenched in jungle life, my niece was a delightful companion. She named a lovely flat-topped rock on which we used to picnic the 'Council Rock', and to this day one of the roads she helped me trace on Kardana, is still known as 'Margaret's Road'.

One day, after heavy rainfall during the night, we went for a walk along Windy Ridge and nearing the top I spotted clear tiger tracks on the soft, damp earth. In the evenings I had been reading her Rudyard Kipling's Mowgli stories, and so, pointing to the tracks, suggested that Sher Khan had passed this way during the night. She was very excited and even more so when we saw another set of tracks, very uneven and much smaller, alongside the first. They obviously belonged to a cub who had been running with its mother, jumping and running here and there. Margaret, however, was certain that they had been made by Bagheera, and jumped for joy when I told her to follow them. Sher Khan's trail which instantly became 'Margaret's trail' led us right along the top of the ridge, and at one point to her discovery of a little mound of soil where the cub had relieved himself and being a cat had tidily covered it over. We then lost sight of the tracks, the cub having run up a big rock and down the other side, but found them once more disappearing into the thick jungle. I called a halt and disgusted at my cowardice, Margaret hardly spoke to me all the way home. I eventually made her realise that no tiger would appreciate being followed into his jungle bedroom after he had been hunting all night, and might get angry and smack us. I went on to explain that a tiger's smack would be like a kick from a horse, which capable of hurting us, would certainly kill the dogs. The realisation that her beloved dog might have been in danger convinced her, so I was forgiven.

The time then came for Jim and I to eventually be called to Madura to appear as witnesses in the case against Savrimuthu. We would stay with Bobs, but instead of our usual driver we were given a much younger and far more casual character who persisted in driving at a rapid pace, with one hand on the wheel and the other either on the horn, or more alarmingly, searching his rather long hair and flicking whatever he found in his locks in the general direction of the road.

The Court of Sessions was held in the old Palace, one of the finest public buildings in India, with huge pillars surrounding the inner courtyard, and beautiful internal architecture. We reported in at about 8.30 a.m. and our case was taken at once. I hated the whole affair and was somewhat aghast by how the proceedings reminded me of the court scene in Alice in Wonderland, and the resemblance of two of the assessors to the dormouse and the lizard. The Indian judge, in whom we had complete confidence, was a very able man, but the prisoner was defended by that rogue vakil who had called upon the same witnesses as before. There was no jury, just seven assessors, all of whom were villagers. They soon became bored and drowsy amidst the endless stream of words, and I was struck by the problem of holding court and getting justice when the language used was the flowery high-caste Tamil used by the gentry, and beyond the understanding of villagers.

Finally, after hours of statements from witnesses on both sides and cross-examination by the vakil, the judge turned to the assessors and along with a long discourse, announced that it was now their duty to weigh up all they had heard from the prosecution and defence. When the translator boomed out what the judge had said, the assessors came to with a start, looking bewildered and a little nervous. Eventually, after much hurried whispering, their spokesman in a vague and apologetic tone uttered "Not guilty, Swami" then sat down again with a loud sigh of relief. The judge looked as if he would have liked to have laughed, but instead replied: "In view of what you have heard today, I am at a loss to explain your findings. I therefore pronounce the prisoner guilty of murderous assault; the sentence for which should be ten years' hard labour. However, in view of the good character reference given by his employer, I make it four years only."

Again, my attempts to have Savrimuthu certified and sent to an asylum where he would have had to be released, were a failure. Then again, I knew nothing about asylums in India, and he may very well have been no better off. My heart was sore for him. He was brought into the courtroom by the guards, looking glum, frightened and rather grubby, not at all like the Savrimuthu I knew. Catching sight of us, he then beamed and tried to salaam with both hands, making me feel worse than ever. The sub-inspector who considered himself responsible for running the case and whom I detested more and more, came up to Jim outside the court and had the audacity to ask for a lift back to his village the following day. Jim reluctantly agreed, but the inspector was far from impressed when told to be ready at 5.30am!

Meanwhile, the Rani of Nabba, who was staying with Bobs, had arranged to show her the temple's jewels; no easy task since it required the presence of seven priests with seven keys as a security measure. The Rani, though not in purdah, was undergoing one of Bobs' famous cures. Her husband was a political prisoner, confined to their house and garden in Kodaikanal, and feeling bored and fed up, she had come to the hospital in Madura to enjoy a few days of freedom. The visit was arranged for that afternoon and accepting the invitation to go along, I packed my camera in the hope of being allowed to photograph these famous and rarely seen treasures.

The jewels were set out on a table in one of the halls of the temple, lit by a shaft of light from an aperture high up in the roof and to my delight, I was permitted to take photos provided I gave the priests copies. What a heterogeneous mixture it was to be sure! Pieces of great value, perhaps priceless, lay nestled alongside absolute trash, and everything was dirty beyond belief. There were little goblets made from "the biggest pearls in the world," but whether real or not, those pearls, rotten in parts and with large gaps, were far from perfect. Other pieces were similarly disappointing, perhaps as a result of original gems being sold off to pay for the upkeep of the temple. The pearls covering the short, padded reins of the goddess were again of poor-quality, and although her breastplate was still adorned with pearls and rubies, the emeralds that had once decorated its fringe had been unconvincingly replaced with cheap green glass. A magnificent gold cobra had likewise suffered the insult of having an emerald fringe on his hood removed in favour of glass. We were then shown the somewhat gaudy carriages in which the goddess travels abroad but found their embellishment of brass, glass and jewels were almost hidden by layers of grime and the accumulation of sacred pink powder with which she is bombarded on her outings. I suppose that this powder which is never removed, enhances her holiness in the eyes of believers, but to my mind detracted from her beauty, especially when compared to that of her cleaner rivals! A carpet of such fine craftsmanship that had been sent, closely escorted, to be admired by Queen Victoria, had fared better. I recall it being a truly beautiful piece, with a red ground covered in a highly intricate pattern encrusted with pearls.

As arranged, we picked up the police sub-inspector early the next morning, whereupon we were reneged with all the trouble he had taken over the case, to the extent that I had difficulty in controlling my temper and biting my tongue. "Anyway," he exulted, "we won our case, no?" Smirking, he then turned to Jim and continued: "I have now won your case. You will be grateful to me and I will accept some presents from you. I desire a well-bred bull-terrier dog, and I wish to be given a case of beer. My children are of school age, so maybe you would arrange for their education too?" Jim is a mild man, but this was too much. He told the man in no uncertain terms that he had done his duty, for which he had been paid a salary, and would get nothing more from him.

Animal Rescues and the Rise of Sagunam

On the final leg of our journey, along the rough path in a bullock cart, we saw a Muslim leading a pathetically thin and absolute wreck of bay mare covered with harness galls. Jim was on the lookout for a pony for me to ride to and from Kardana, and since the mare looked as though she had good breeding somewhere in her pedigree, he stopped the cart and asked the man if he was willing to sell her. He looked surprised, then said he wanted a hundred rupees for her. Jim rode her up the road and after finding her capable of carrying his weight and her paces good, agreed on the price, which would be paid when the mare was delivered to the estate. I thought of that sad little creature as we rattled along in the cart and looked forward to getting her fat and her coat shining, probably for the first time in her life. When she arrived, we called her Melindy – 'melinge' being Tamil for thin which was later shortened to Lindy. Once settled, she soon lost her nervousness, became my pride and joy, and as sure-footed as a goat, carried many people up our steep hill in the years to come. To get her in condition I let her eat her fill, but after a while her tummy was huge, and Jim accused me of giving her too much grass. It didn't bother me, and having done nothing about it was as surprised as everyone else when one day, the man who looked after her, announced that she had produced a foal! Margaret was especially thrilled with her baby horse, a pretty little chestnut with a white blaze down his face, whom she named Timothy.

I was finding less time for dispensary work now that I was looking after Margaret, but relieved to find Jacob increasingly useful. He was steady and reliable, used the stock mixtures that I made up for him sensibly and for the right complaints, and was good at applying dressings. If in doubt, he sought advice and although the children received less sympathy for imaginary complaints and far less sugar, no one suffered. Meanwhile, Amirtham visited regularly, spending afternoons knitting or sewing, whilst I was giving Margaret her lessons.

Jacob and Amirtham's personalities, coupled with their mission schooling, made them a very fine pair. Sargunam, a young man who came to Jim straight from school to train as a tea-maker, was likewise very amicable and, keen to learn, quickly picked up the job. However, the man who operated our two Petter engines considered himself far superior to Sargunam, especially with regard to his knowledge of the machinery and his higher caste. It was inevitable that they would clash and one day, refusing to work with Sargunam, the engine driver had stayed at home, presumably until the younger man was turned out. In response, Jim went down to the factory at once and gave Sargunam a lesson on running the engines. Both alert and intelligent, the apprentice had already gleaned much of the process and between them they got the engine going. Jim then told the engine driver, a truculent and unpleasant character, that he could take a month's pay in lieu of notice, and go. From then on, Jim and Sargunam took charge of cleaning and stripping the engines. For several years thereafter, Sargunam was our sole engine driver, and having acquired the expertise, kept the engines and machines in perfect running order until promoted to a higher position elsewhere.

It was now nearly time for our Home furlough and we looked forward very much to seeing our two children, and also my mother who was now alone following the death of my beloved father in 1932. An old friend of Jim's would look after Cloudland while we were away; an ideal solution, given his knowledge of malaria and experience of dispensary work. There was a good deal of malaria about and before we left we were asked to visit an estate belonging to Mr G to assess whether the many people laid low with high fevers had contracted the disease. The estate was in the valley, a long walk down a rough steep trail through the jungle. We slid and slithered down that awful zig-zagging path, and after negotiating 105 zigs in all, eventually arrived at noon. Going through the lines we found many sick folk, all suffering from malaria, but none so badly that they were likely to die. The cause of their poor condition was lack of food; the working men having taken the lion's share, leaving the sick to do without. We dosed the patients, left some aspirin and quinine and told them that food would be delivered the next day, if they sent up carriers in the morning. We kept in touch, replenishing medicines as required, but one man with a particularly serious bout had to be carried up to our dispensary where he was given a bed and left in our care. As mentioned, there were many different malarial infections at this time and it transpired that he was suffering a severe attack of malignant Tertian. I sent some slides of his blood to the hospital in Madura where they were kept as specimens for students to study. How he survived, I'll never know.

Just before we left for England, I happened to be strolling behind the thatched hut used by Mr G when he was on the estate and came across a miserably thin but obviously well-bred Airedale dog lying beside an emaciated bitch amidst vomit and bones. We discovered that there had been a third dog, which had died, and because there had been a leopard about, they had been tied up to prevent them from running away. We obviously couldn't leave them, so Jim and I decided to take them with us. Once freed, the dog, whose name was Snip, remained where he was after a pathetic attempt to stand, whilst the bitch, named Sita, seemed reasonably strong. We therefore hired two men to carry Snip up the steep path on a litter of sorts and an extra man to carry Sita, in case she floundered. Sita was an uninteresting animal, with very little character, but good tempered and amiable, whereas Snip, despite his emaciated state, had a beautiful head with lovely speaking eyes. I doubted whether we would be able to save him, but he joined Scrapings and Biddy as one of Margaret's entourage, and was prepared to be nursed in her hospital and take on the role of a horse or indeed anything else that took her fancy! Almost two months later, Mr G passed through Cloudland on his way to his estate and took Snip and Sita back with him.

We were all sad to see Snip go, especially Margaret who was already dreading being separated from Biddy and Scrapings when we left for Home in a few weeks' time. I kept assuring her that she would feel better when she got on board, with children to play with and the prospect of meeting her family to look forward to. However, some days out at sea, I returned to the cabin to find her in tears. "Oh, Aunt Madge," she sobbed, "you said I'd feel better and not miss the dogs so much, but I feel worse, since I'll never see them again!" I found her hard to comfort, since without any children to play with, those dogs had been her only friends and playmates for many months. She had put them to bed, fed them, let them out in the morning and after being together all day they had sat and watched her have her bath and supper. She adored them, but fortunately as the voyage went on her yearning faded, and she began to look forward to being reunited with her parents and the brother and sister she had all but forgotten.

Ours was a great reunion too, and after delivering Margaret to her parents, Jim and I, Mother and Monica talked far into the night. Time with our children was precious but sadly limited. We managed to see Monica during her time off from the hospital and stayed in rooms in Norwich to see Ted when he finished work. Monica was nearing the end of her training, and before she started her midwifery course welcomed our suggestion that she came out to stay with us for a while. Delighted, we booked her passage and had the joy of seeing her receive her medal before we all set sail for India.

Kolar Rowther, Ooty, Mysore and the Surili Falls

Six months pass very quickly when one is on furlough, and we were soon packing up for our return to India. Ted and Mother were to remain in the UK, but we looked forward to Monica joining us at Christmas. On our arrival, we received a warm welcome from the labour who overwhelmed us with gifts of garlands and fruit. They were joined by Kolar Rowther, who, no longer young and unaccustomed to exercise, had made the considerable journey from the plains to present us with a live sheep and an iced cake. He also brought homemade highly coloured marzipan-flavoured sweets of which he was inordinately proud, but which had the consistency of concrete!

After the welcome party had left, the old fellow stayed on. He clearly had something on his mind, but didn't know how to broach the subject until Jim mentioned the new factory. Given his cue, old Kolar launched into his appreciation of the site, the beauty of its design, and the proposal to build it from local materials. He then hesitated, and in a small voice asked if anyone, perhaps the 'Peria Dorai' the Collector, had been chosen to lay the foundation stone?

Hearing the penny drop, Jim asked if he would do the honours. Beaming with unexpected delight, the old man immediately wanted to know when the stone would be laid and would we give him plenty of notice so that he could arrive the night before and be in good trim for the ceremony? On he babbled, clearly relishing his elevated status and a sense of being finally appreciated. Having achieved his goal, off he went, promising to be ready whenever we sent for him. He was a delightful old rascal; short, with a scrubby white beard, scanty white locks, and a single long tooth in the centre of his smile. We knew little about his background apart from the fact that due to his Tamil grandfather's conversion from Hinduism many years before, he was a Muslim. Like other followers of his faith, he had a self-assurance, often absent in those whose inbred self-depreciation and humility was compounded by their conversion to Christianity by missionaries.

Six weeks later, on the evening before the ceremony, old Kolar Rowther duly appeared on the estate accompanied by a large number of hangers-on brought along as publicity agents. He emerged bright and early the next morning, dressed for the occasion in snowy-white garments and a vast turban, which made him look smaller than ever. We then made our way to the factory site where we were joined by Mendiz, the maistry in charge of the building, a motley crew of carpenters, masons and their assistants, and a crowd of children from the lines eager to see what was going on. A small depression had been made in the layer of cement laid for the positioning of the stone, into which and after a short prayer, Kolar placed a silver coin. Each of the artisans, then Jim and I, followed suit. Having completed this part of the ceremony, the old man was assisted with lifting the beautifully dressed stone, which once positioned, was carefully cemented in place. Then came the garlands, ranging from the usual strings of chrysanthemums and jasmine, to magnificent sweet pink roses which, sprinkled with cold water to bring out their scent, cascaded down to my feet. In Tamil, any joyful event in the South is described as 'cool' but they are anything but! Formalities over, we were immediately mobbed by the children who tore at our garlands until every small girl had a flower in her hair and an extra for her mother, whilst not to be left out, each of the boys stuck a flower somewhere about his person.

We went back with the officials for tea and cakes and ended by toasting the factory. Being a Muslim, Kolar toasted with a fizzy soft drink, but any outsider would not have believed him sober! His voice, never the most melodic, rose higher and higher and his laughter louder and more raucous, as he endeavoured to monopolise the conversation and drown any competition. He won hands down, and shouted into submission, we simply sat at peace, letting the tide of the old man's joy flow over our heads. Having had a wonderful time, he and his retinue finally rose to go, leaving Jim and I sunk in a coma, stunned by the whole experience.

Work on the factory, coupled with vital estate and office work, took up much of Jim's time during the months that followed. I made visits to Kardana two or three days a week and called into the Cloudland dispensary whenever Jacob sought my advice. I saw that the horses were fed and arranged for the milk from our cows to be distributed amongst the sick at the little estate hospital and to children who needed it. There were generally a few blood smears to stain and examine, but relieved of dispensary duties in the mornings and evenings, I was able to spend more time in the garden, and with the help of Mundayan, whom I had brought from Cloudland, planted vegetables and flowers.

As planned, Monica arrived early December, and because her time with us was short we decided to take a holiday and show her something of South India.

Having made sundry preparations, we left on 23rd December, setting off for the long, tiring drive to Ootacamund at 4.30 am. and arriving in Ooty at 9 pm. Situated 7000 feet above sea level, Ooty is a lovely place and, at that time of year, sunny with cold, cloudless evenings. It was very much a residence for the privileged, with many beautiful houses and exquisite gardens lined with sweet smelling acacia and gum trees. The gardens at Government House, the summer residence of the Governor of Madras, were glorious, with every kind of English flower blooming in near-perfect conditions.

Although not on their itinerary, we persuaded a couple with whom we'd made friends in our hotel to come with us to Mysore; a place considered unmissable. We took our time driving through the Mysore State teak forest hoping to see some game, but instead passed many large Langur monkeys beside the road. Nearing the city we were treated to a most wonderful sunset, followed at dusk by every street and building suddenly springing to light at the touch of one switch. Illuminated by literally millions of lights, the many palaces on Charmundi Hill looked spectacular silhouetted against the skyline. By a stroke of luck, there was a festival on the night we arrived, so after dinner we went up to the hotel's roof to admire the view of the floodlit city: government buildings surrounded by lovely flowering trees, white fairy-tale palaces, fountains in the many squares, and the temple on the summit of Charmundi which appeared to be floating in the sky. It was a sight that we and our new friends would never forget.

The following day, during a trip through one of the streets in the poorer part of the city, Monica was knocked down by a runaway jutka while taking a snapshot of a wedding procession. She received some nasty cuts and bruises, so we took her to the hospital, where her wounds were dressed and she was given an injection against tetanus. We said goodbye to our friends, and on our return to Ooty en route for Madura, paid a visit to Dr Y, a Swedish doctor. Whilst there, Monica took a violent reaction to the injection she had received in Mysore which could have proved fatal had Dr Y not been at hand. The attack was sharp, but mercifully short, and she was soon well enough to join us at a special party to celebrate the Indian doctors at Dr Y's hospital passing their final exams. It was the first time I had ever witnessed a curious and rather attractive ritual, apparently common among Tamils, to welcome special guests. Once each guest had been presented with a pile of snowy white rice on a banana leaf plate, one of the hosts came round and laid atop a tiny wafer of pure gold; so thin that it could be mixed with the food and eaten without anyone being aware of its presence.

We finally returned to High Wavys via Madura and a night with Bobs, then made the most of Monica's stay by organising picnics at the Surili Falls and a night in camp on a beautiful ridge beyond and above them. Having discovered we could avoid the leeches by wading through water, Monica and I spent the remaining weeks exploring the many streams and waterfalls on High Wavys, Cloudland, and even Kardana, quickly becoming expert in scrambling barefoot over the rocks. Then all too soon, it was time for her to return to her studies in England.

Before continuing my tale, I'll try to provide a picture of the Surili Falls; my holy of holies place. Imagine a bowl with one side broken away surrounded by jungle-clad hills, with a river running down its back and across the base, before spilling over the broken edge. There were times when this river flowed peacefully, and others when it was turbulent with rushing water. The first waterfall descended a sheer rocky face some ninety feet to a ledge, then plunged again, some two or three hundred feet. Thereafter, the river headed in a series of cascades to the plains some four thousand feet below, beyond which rose the Cardamom Hills. A few feet below the lip of the falls was a tiny ledge where I loved to sit listening to the gentle rush of water, the occasional "hoo-hoo-hoo" of the Wanderoo monkey, the chirping of birds and insects, and the distant call of the Giant Hornbill. It was a place where I found true peace and somewhere that brought meaning to the saying: "Be still and know that I am God." During the southwest monsoon however, this was no place of peace, but a raging inferno of wind-tormented water which, as it tumbled over the edge, would be swept high into the air above and far into the jungle in clouds of spray. I have been drenched by this spray more than half a mile away in the tea field and shall always remain fascinated by the glorious battle between wind and water.

Later on, when our son Ted came to visit prior to serving in the North African Campaign, we decided to attempt a climb from the top of the Surili Falls to the bottom, which as far as we knew had never been done before. We could not climb down the sheer rock of the Fall itself, so instead descended one of the sides of the bowl, then down through the jungle. It was precipitous in places and very slippery, but there was a fair supply of convenient roots or branches to use as handholds. Dropping ever lower, we had delightful peeps at the increasingly loud and near full falls and when almost at the foot, found a clearing from which we photographed the magnificent sight of a curtain of tumbling water and rejoiced in its unique, pulsating rhythm. As a guide to the steepness of the climb, it took less time to cover the distance up to the ridge, where we arrived exhausted but triumphant, than it had taken to get ourselves down! I repeated that climb once more after the war and again, as far as I know, it has not been done by anyone else.

Once during the war, two army chaplains came for a holiday during a particularly bad spell of monsoon weather. I took them for a walk to the Falls, suitably protected of course, against leeches and spray. One of them, a Cornishman, was absolutely entranced and told me it reminded him of a clifftop at home from which in rough weather he used to watch the Atlantic crashing against the rocks. We could hardly tear him away, despite him being drenched and frozen cold!

The ridge offered spectacular views of sunsets over the Cardamom Hills. I remember gazing out over the valley one afternoon when suddenly, as if some air pocket had burst, the entire mass of mist lying over the hills turned into a vast waterfall, which streamed over the ridge and down into the plains where it immediately evaporated in the hot dry air and disappeared. During the monsoon, the mist streamed through the jungle making the trees ghostly in the gloom, and in the dry weather, lay in the valleys, shimmering like a lake in which the hills floated like islands. At other times, the mist piled on the top of the Metla Ridge and in the glow of the sunset, appeared to rise like steam from a bubbling cauldron.

It was small wonder that the Falls were regarded by the coolies as something sacred. They could see them from their villages down below and depended upon them for much of the water for their crops. Any Hindu child born on the estate was named after the River Surili and we received a prodigious number of Surilis and Suriliammals at the little dispensary. A festival was held each year at the foot of the Falls, with free meat provided by rich landlords to all worshippers. Any offer of a free meal was hard to resist, even at the risk of contracting malaria, and we often suspected that a considerable number of cases amongst coolies were a direct result of their attendance at that festival.

Land Surveyance, Ratnam and Doctors

Shortly after Monica's departure, we had a request from Pat to spend a week with him surveying land he had bought with the intention of growing cardamom. The land in question could only be reached from High Wavys by walking along wild game tracks across country, but Isaac, the estate watchman, was familiar with the trail and would act as our guide.

Our journey began in leech infested jungle which then gave way to rough grassland. Following almost non-existent tracks over several ridges, we enjoyed breathtakingly beautiful views of the Varusanadu valley as we climbed to 5650 feet then descended to 2400 feet above sea level. It turned out that our guide had only the vaguest idea of the route, but vague was better than nothing, even if we did lose the trail more than once before reaching our destination. We reckoned to have walked well over twenty miles and our knees were literally knocking together with weariness by the time we scrambled up the final ridge to our little grass hut. Pat's supervisor was standing at the door to welcome us and given the state we were in, the hot, very sweet tea which he had at the ready, tasted like nectar! The dogs were also dead tired and like us, had to continually shift position to relieve their aching muscles.

The next morning, the supervisor appeared with food for the road and off we set down a steep hill into a jungle of immense trees and scant undergrowth, then uphill through scrubby jungle interspersed with strips of grassland. Jim was taking samples of soil at various levels, while I was recording the type of jungle growth as an indication of rainfall. That was one of the hardest days of my life. We had scrambled nearly fourteen miles before lunch, which we ate on the bank of a stream, cooling our feet in the water and enjoying the wonderful view over the valley. After allowing our aching muscles an hour's exquisite relief, we were off again, but before long our guide began to flag, and sitting down on the bed of a dried-up stream, declared he could walk no more. A coolie was found to lead us, and we proceeded with our survey. We had been walking on the sides of our feet all day and were beginning to feel the strain, but Jim wanted to get that part of the survey finished, and so we pressed on. Just as dusk was falling, we came out into a clearing in the jungle and a nursery of cardamom plants. Our grass hut was only a mile up the hill, but after being on the move all day that mile was the longest and hardest of my life!

How many miles we had covered I have no idea, but except for our hour's rest at mid-day, we had been on the move all day on steep uneven ground. As we toiled up that hill, I remember encouraging myself with the thought that I could take at least one more step before I collapsed and then perhaps, another and so on until we reached that blessed hut. We drank gallons of tea, provided by the supervisor who had taken a shortcut, then collapsing on deckchairs, watched the sun set over the valley and the advance of a storm from across the plains accompanied by spectacular flashes of lightning. Hot showers followed, Indian fashion, and after eating supper in our pyjamas, we fell into bed. The following days, though strenuous, were less exhausting; we saw some wonderful jungle, and enjoyed some lovely evenings lying in our deckchairs in front of our hut, sometimes looking for game, but more often just relaxing. Our journey back, again over several ridges and this time involving a steep ascent, felt far less arduous now that we had honed our muscles and were familiar with the path. On the way we sighted a few bison in the distance as well as families of elephants and pigs, and after stopping for just an hour for a picnic lunch, we were home and drinking tea, thankfully not flavoured with woodsmoke. By five that evening. Jim eventually accepted the job of visiting the land twice a year after Pat began planting cardamom, so we were to repeat that trek many times, all strenuous, but none as tough as the first. I enjoyed those trips immensely, and would not be without my memories of walking miles through the long grass of the valley, the encounters with wild animals, the glimpses of monkeys and birds, and the joy of relaxing in the peace and silence of the jungle after a hard day' slog.

On our return, the schoolmaster, Aroliah, an odd and sulky man who had gone to his village to get married, brought his new wife to meet us. Jeevaratnam was a slim girl, aged around fifteen, with a heavy plait of hair hanging well below her knees of which she was obviously very proud. Her face wore an expression of serene gaiety and gentle strength, and being of the same Dravidian stock as Amirtnam, I liked her immediately. Not long afterwards, the tea- maker left, taking my crèche helper Dainty with him, so I decided to offer Jeevaratnam her place. Never did I make a happier decision. Almost overnight, the crèche went from being a useful place where mothers could bring their children to be fed and cared for, to a place where it was impossible to keep a child away who was not at work, or ill. All the children, many of them little rascals whom I had often felt beyond my control, became unbelievably virtuous and co-operative. Jeevaratnam, or Ratnam for short, was a miracle-worker! We had all sorts of English nursery games and toys - spinning tops, skipping ropes, balls etc. - but Ratnam invented new games, and gales of delighted laughter would be heard from our queer old shed and the flat piece of ground outside. She then set up a shop selling real commodities to teach the children the value of money. But Ratnam's chief skill, from the children's point of view, was her wonderful storytelling, and after the mid-day meal they would gather round and sit in rapt attention as she narrated stories from the Bible, Indian folklore and a few born of her vivid imagination. Untiring, she could keep the large group of children of mixed ages entranced for hours on end.

One thing we insisted upon in the crèche was the dropping of any distinction between castes. Some of the children were Dravidian or low-caste; others belonged to the Thevar or thief- caste, also Dravidian, but in their eyes, at a higher level, and then came the Pillais, at a higher level still. We had one Pillai girl aged about ten, cheerful and co-operative but very conscious of her superiority. When the supply of banana leaves became limited, I purchased a number of enamel plates on which to serve lunch, and each day asked one of the bigger girls to help either Ratnam or me to wash up. All went well until it came to the Pillia girl's turn. She refused point blank and fled from the crèche. We carried on without her, but some days later, her father spoke to Jim, complaining that his daughter was having her caste endangered by having to wash the food containers of low-caste children. Jim never interfered in my domain, so he told the man to speak directly to me. They had to pass the crèche on the way to the office and by chance, I happened to be washing the dishes. "Well," exclaimed the father, "If the ammal can wash plates without offending God, then, so can my daughter." And from thereon in, his daughter took her turn like everyone else!

Over the three years that Ratnam worked in the crèche her popularity increased amongst all the castes, both high and low, and even her husband, formerly so surly and taciturn, was tamed beyond recognition. One day, they asked if they could discuss something with me. Ratnam apparently wanted to train as a midwife and they wanted my help in getting her accepted at one of the mission hospitals. I didn't know what I would do without her, but the qualification would be a great asset and however much I would miss her, I couldn't stand in her way. It took some time to make the necessary arrangements, then off she went, leaving me desolate. I tried out several replacements, but though willing, no one could match her and the crèche was no longer the Mecca for the children that it had been. The naughty ones began to be naughty again, and the miserable returned to their misery, unless I was there to help with the games and competitions. To the delight of the children, Ratnam blew into the crèche like a spring breeze three times during the three years of her training, bringing laughter and fun. It seemed to come easily to her, though how I never knew!

Jim promised that if she passed her examination she would be appointed official midwife to the estate, replacing the old women who at the time did the job to the best of their limited ability. We both felt sure that Ratnam would be the very person for the job and it was a joyful day when she qualified. By then, largely due to the war, we were suffering an ever-changing succession of bad or very mediocre doctors, and in the gaps often running into months, I was in charge of the hospital. The incompetence of these doctors was frankly unbelievable and my heart often ached for the labour who had to suffer their ministrations. One of these doctors turned up when I had a case of pneumonia on my hands. I hated handing a patient over to an unknown doctor, but since they were paid by the Company, my authority ceased as soon as they arrived. In short, I was merely a stop-gap and had to make way for the 'expert', but the coolies never understood why I could not continue looking after them and why I had to avoid interfering with the doctor.

No longer young, Dr Diaz had qualified many years previously and was supremely confident. After handing over my patient, I went over the list of out-patients, then returned to the bungalow. The next morning he met me on my way to the crèche, and asked whether he could have some limes from our trees. I was delighted since he appeared to share my belief in the benefits of giving the patient plenty to drink and told him to take as many as he wanted. "Drink?!" he almost screamed. "Giving him anything to drink would be highly dangerous! It is a well-known fact that the specific treatment for pneumonia is to rub lime juice over a patient's head!" He went off muttering and shaking his head. Evidently Dr Diaz, if he had ever passed the L.M.P. examination, had never opened a book from that day forth, and returning to the old mumbo jumbo, had forgotten all he had ever learned. We continued undertaking the pathological work and asked Dr Diaz to send all blood smears and specimens to the bungalow. Given that neither Jim nor I had any medical qualifications, we were unable to interfere in his clinical work, and decided that it would be safer to avoid antagonising him if we were to keep an eye on the sick. The coolies however, had no faith in his lack of knowledge and before long he left.

He was followed by another doctor who seemed more capable, and because he claimed to have used a microscope and we would be away on a week's holiday at the start of the malaria season, we foolishly lent him ours. On our return, the week's medical report was waiting for Jim in his office, but as soon as we saw the list of different types of malarial cases, showing an unprecedented high percentage of the very rare plasmodium strain, it was clear that something was awry. I slipped down to the hospital in the morning and happened to see the doctor standing between the microscope and the light and peering down into it with a hand clapped over one of his eyes. Looking up, he then announced: "This instrument is not very good, it is with difficulty I see things in it." I asked if I might try, and re-setting the mirror and standing on the other side of the table, I looked at what he was examining. Not surprisingly, I too saw nothing, since the 6 inch lens was resting on a blob of oil which was covering the blood smear specimen. The microscope came back to the bungalow that evening! Mercifully he did not object, and in truth was probably relieved to have it taken off his hands. He did not last long either, and was dismissed after admitting that he could not recall how much strychnine he had given a patient suffering from food poisoning!

Shortly after the appointment of his replacement, we had a visit from Bobs, and when she went down to the dispensary to meet him, found a number of children with very sore eyes resulting from the high level of malnutrition in the plains. Greeting the doctor, Bobs commented: "We usually find that cod-liver oil works wonders for this sort of complaint. Would you agree?" "Yes! Yes! Of course," replied the doctor, "I always use it." He had done nothing of the sort, but he bustled around and began to drop cod-liver oil into the children's eyes, watched with admiration by Bobs. "Oh", she declared, "What a good idea; I never thought of putting cod-liver oil in the children's eyes in addition to giving it orally." "Of course, I too, always give them a dose as well as treating their eyes," blustered the doctor importantly, and clearly for the first time in his life, gave a child a spoonful! Thus Bobs, with wonderful tact, had got the doctor to treat the children correctly without hurting his feelings.

Before the end of the war, we had one last doctor, who despite knowing more than his predecessors, was the worst of the lot! He was without morals and a hypochondriac, and although Jacob had warned us that something was wrong, he was only found out when Jim was stocktaking at the end of the year. For Jacob to inform us of the situation, and moreover, tell the doctor, was an act which must have taken a lot of courage beyond the comprehension of most Europeans since he was an 'outcaste' and the doctor was a Brahmin. It transpired that the doctor had been treating the masons and carpenters with all of the hospital's most expensive drugs and charging them for 'special' treatment, whilst also treating himself with a selection of injections which unbeknown to us, he kept in his house. Inevitably, as a result of taking incompatible drugs, he made himself seriously ill and after being carried down the ghaut to the government hospital, we saw him no more.

Medical Matters

It is certainly not my intention to condemn Indian doctors. War had taken most doctors and so we had to accept anyone who was willing to live and work in such an isolated location. Most good doctors, of which there were pitifully few, opted for more lucrative posts in town which offered them more varied experience and a far better life for their families. We were particularly unlucky in the doctors we were sent, but alongside the serious shortage of medical personnel throughout rural India, and the presumption that some knowledge was better than none, our provision of those who were not fully qualified, was almost inevitable.

At Cloudland, I ran a dispensary from which I managed to tackle cases of malaria, anaemia cases, colds, coughs, wounds and burns, and since the nearest doctor was four miles away, through leech-ridden jungle, only sent for him in emergencies. It was after we moved to High Wavys in 1936, that my time at the dispensary was curtailed and reduced to spells of varying length whenever the doctor was on leave or we were temporarily without anyone to look after the sick. I derived great satisfaction in my work but my lack of adequate knowledge sometimes landed me in laughable situations.

One afternoon, the assistant tea-maker came rushing into the bungalow in an awful state and when he caught his breath, told us that the tea-maker's wife had been stabbed by her servant. I sped down to the dispensary to gather bandages, disinfectant, needles and sutures, then sent for Ratnam, reliable and unlikely to panic, if the wounds proved serious. Hurrying to the woman's house where Jim was waiting, I discovered the victim lying in a pool of blood on her kitchen floor, moaning and holding her left side, whilst surrounded by women, groaning in unison and clearly getting a great deal of ghoulish satisfaction from the tragedy. Aided by a couple of men standing nearby, we had her lifted onto the bed. I then shooed everybody out, keeping one elderly woman to help me till Ratnam arrived. I removed the blood-soaked clothes, while two pots of water were put to boil on the fire. One wound, on her upper left arm, had evidently severed an artery. I stopped the flow, then proceeded to wash her in order to locate any other wounds; a painfully long business since she shrieked in agony whenever I touched her left side but refused to say anything that would guide me in my search. Fortunately, there were no further wounds and though deep, that on her arm required only three stitches. By the time Ratnam arrived, she was bandaged and propped up in bed in a clean sari. Ignorant as to how much blood a woman could safely afford to lose, I asked Ratnam to sit with her and give her constant drinks of glucose and water, or small quantities of weak, very sweet coffee, whilst I returned to the dispensary to deal with other patients.

I had no sooner arrived, when two messages came from the woman's husband telling me that her pain was "too great" and she "wanted madam." Her pulse had seemed stable, but it was possible that she had lost a dangerous amount of blood, so I checked on her several times during the evening, gave her a sedative, and told Ratnam to fetch me if she was worried. That particular young woman kept me on the run for the next two days. Her pulse and temperature seemed normal and she had not lost her appetite so, reasonably sure she was alright, I left her to it. Then, on the sixth day after the incident, I had a frantic message that the tea-maker's wife was so bad that her family had arrived from her village, and could I come and change her bandage, as the pain was unbearable. The penny suddenly dropped; I had been duped all along! I went over to find a tearful group of relatives standing round the bed and the patient groaning in a most impressive manner. Laying out my medical equipment in a suitably solemn manner, I proceeded to remove the bandage, knowing that the wound, nothing more than a thin line with three little stitches across it, would be unlikely to impress her sympathetic relatives. The stitches came out easily and as I moved back to let the relatives inspect the wound, both they and the moaning patient fell into a stunned silence! I wrapped up my things, and leaving them to their disappointment, returned home feeling vindicated for the many unnecessary walks over to her house.

As I have mentioned, burns resulting from open fires in the labours' confined quarters were often severe. The women and girls' saris or skirts often caught fire, whilst small boys were more often scalded by pulling over a pot of boiling water or rice. In their villages in the plains, people only used fires for cooking, requiring no extra heat in their unventilated little houses and those fires were only of sticks, or more likely, dried cakes of cow-dung. However, when they moved up to the hills to work on the tea estates, they needed fires to keep warm and since firewood was generally plentiful, the fires were bigger and sometimes left burning whilst they slept through the night. I have had terribly burnt babies brought to me, none of whom recovered, alas. Their mothers had left them hanging in primitive hammocks near, or even over, a slow fire, which scorched and then burnt the cloth. Boy babies being the most valued and more likely to be left near the fire to keep warm, were sadly, the most susceptible.

Many tons of charcoal were made for use in the factory and despite being strictly forbidden, on account of danger from the fumes in a closed room, posed a hazard when occasionally commandeered by coolies. I had several cases of poisoning: luckily not fatal but serious enough. There was an instance when one cold night, a family had made a small charcoal fire under a bed fashioned from logs and rough planks. Fortunately, the smell of the fumes was detected by somebody in the next room and the family was dragged out into the fresh air, alive but in need of urgent attention

The dressing of all burns was always distressing, until I evolved a method that reduced the agony, though it was a somewhat lengthy process. I had a large quantity of an ointment made of equal parts petroleum jelly and cod-liver oil, kept in a tin sitting in boiling water. The warm liquid oil was poured into a sterile container, also standing in hot water, and when dripped on the dressings, allowed their easy and painless removal. This same warmed mixture could also be smeared onto gauze, placed directly over a burn, and I recall one particularly terrifying incident where it proved a lifesaver. A man had been cleaning out a blasting hole and when his steel rod accidentally sparked a rock, the blasting mixture exploded, burning him all down one side. His friends wrapped him, practically naked, in a hairy blanket and lay him in the sun whilst they finished their job. They then carried him part of the way to High Wavys and after leaving him there for the night, up to my dispensary. The state of that man was beyond description. Hairs from the blanket had stuck to his burns which in the hot weather were then penetrated by flies. I had a coolie helping me in the dispensary and he and I spent an hour and a half cleaning his wounds with my patent mixture. Why he had not died on the journey and indeed during the cleaning up operation, which was anything but skillful, I shall never know. For a long time he hovered between life and death, but eventually recovered, albeit badly scarred, and able to work again.

Another potential hazard, peculiar to rural life, was rats! I was once visited by a woman whose face was enormously swollen as a result of a deep rat bite on her cheek. Treatment was not very effective and after taking a long time to heal, her wounds left her face misshapen and puckered. That was many years ago, but later, in 1941, we had a plague of rats on the estate. I woke up one night, with the sensation that my nose was being violently tweaked and to my horror, saw a huge rat on my pillow! My movement scared him off, but since the mosquito net was tucked tightly around our beds, it could not escape. Armed with a book and a tightly rolled newspaper, we scrambled about frantically swatting the now thoroughly frightened rat. From being really scared I began to get the giggles, as did Jim, and after eventually catching the rat, went back to sleep. About a fortnight later, Jim was bitten on the back of his neck, but this time the rat remembered the hole where he had entered and made good his escape.

At our little hospital we had many emergencies, some of them serious, some not so, but at least the women on our estate were unafraid to come in and many had their babies there. Midwifery in the East has its own issues and in common with other areas, superstition came into play. I recall helping an increasingly weary Ratnam deliver Neethi's wife, who had been three days in labour. She seemed agitated and when at 11.30pm, her son finally arrived, was broken-hearted that she had failed to hold off until midnight and thus avoid him being born on an inauspicious date! The situation in rural villages was very different. Women seldom had their babies in hospital unless they had been in before, and when difficult labours were charged to village midwives, these generally tough and courageous new mothers were often so badly mauled that they no longer cared whether they lived or died.

During her last two years in India, when acting as a locum to relieve exhausted nurses, Bobs toured remote villages in her hard-working little car which she had transformed into a mobile dispensary, and though initially wary of the white woman from the queer hospital, the villagers came to look forward to her visits. On one occasion, she was asked by a woman to see her daughter whose ear had been torn by a younger brother, and much to the gratitude of the family, Bobs was able to repair both the lobe and the girl's prospect of marriage. Anyone who has seen photographs of women in South India taken twenty to thirty years ago, will have noticed that many had long pendulous ears. It was the tradition for young girls to undergo a painful process of having weights hung from their earlobes until they had stretched to their shoulders. Deemed essential in obtaining a husband, they were kept stretched by the parents in preparation for huge, heavy gold earrings to be used as a girl's dowry. Daughters were expected to look after and carry their baby sisters and brothers and these frail stretched ears were a wonderful handle for babies to pull and liable to tear. A bride with a broken earlobe was unthinkable, and if a tear could not be mended in a village and unless her family could get her to a hospital, the girl would remain unmarriageable.

Such small things can spell tragedy for these people, who know no doctors and fear hospitals. A thorn in a foot may fester, and without proper attention, result in serious blood poisoning: a mother with an abscess in her breast may be unable to feed her baby, who through lack of nourishment, is likely to die. Any wound can become fly-blown, resulting in a really terrible infection, and cleaning a head wound of a child screaming with pain from a mass of maggots under their scalp, is something I'd rather forget!

Thanks to help received from the laboratory at the Madura hospital, we were becoming competent at spotting illnesses other than malaria in samples examined under the microscope, including a case of TB from sputum, and leprosy from an ear clipping. Bobs had cured two cases of leprosy in her staff, but back then, the disease was still greatly feared and when told that she would require treatment in hospital, the woman whom I had diagnosed, was so terrified that she bolted without trace from the estate. My experience with the microscope also proved useful when the man in charge of the building of our factory was constantly taken ill with a curious and continuous low fever. His symptoms were atypical of malaria and there was none in his blood. After searching through my book of tropical diseases, I eventually concluded that he might have Micro-Filaria or elephantiasis, and for confirmation, had to take a blood sample at midnight. In the small hours, we duly inspected the sample under the microscope and lo and behold, there was a little worm-like filaria moving about! Our prognosis did him no good, poor fellow, as a cure had yet to be found, but we regularly gave him leave to rest up at home and luckily his limbs were spared the enormous swelling commonly associated with the disease.

My patients' terrifying faith that the 'Ammal' would make them better, and their willingness to place themselves unreservedly and without any qualms in my hands, is something I still cherish. It required trust on both sides, to override both their ignorance and fear, and my lack of experience. Not untypical, was the case of a man called Alappen who came to me to have an abscess in his umbilicus lanced. Clearly expecting me to dig deep, he told me that he had eaten a meal that morning, and I had to reassure him that I was only going to cut the surface of the abscess. I also remember an instance when a man was brought to me with his face covered in blood. Whilst cutting firewood for the factory, his axe had struck a knot, the axe head had flown into the air and on its descent, almost cut off his cheek which was now hanging in a flap. I washed, disinfected and with great difficulty stitched it up, all the while wishing there was someone more knowledgeable to offer me advice. The next day, the doctor returned from his leave and admonished me for being unaware of the sinuses in the man's cheek. Interestingly, the man's wound healed well but he refused to have his face touched by the doctor!

Children were always my favourite patients. We recognised all the children on the estate, but sometimes a stranger would appear, especially in seasons when famine was reported elsewhere and starving families climbed our hill to offer themselves as labourers. This was naturally forbidden by the Company which was after all a business, not a charitable concern, but it was impossible to refuse help to these pathetic, thin and weary people, who in all probability, had travelled some distance. Hence, easy jobs were found for the adults, and I cared for the children by building them up with cod-liver oil, milk, marmite, raw eggs, tomatoes, bananas, yeast powder and bread. Their recovery was usually very rapid and it was one of my greatest joys to see those wizened children with their pale puffy faces grow stronger, healthier, happier and even naughtier by the day. I remember one under-sized boy, brought to me by a near-skeletal mother. Aged about four, he weighed only twelve and a half pounds! His buttocks and stomach were hollow, and his legs mere sticks barely able to support even his emaciated body. It took just a matter of days for him to begin to fill out, but weeks before he could walk and though with us for over a year, he seemed to have lost the ability to grow. He did, however, regain his joy in living, and as my unofficial assistant regularly brought me other children and offered his opinion on what treatment they should receive!

However, given my lack of formal training, treating very young babies was always a worry. I was once presented with an infant brought in by her mother who did not belong to our estate, and since she had carried the child up the seven miles of rough track to the dispensary, I hadn't the heart to turn her away. Her baby's head was wrapped loosely in a filthy cloth and when removed, revealed an enormous, soft blister covering the whole of the fontanelle. The woman asked me to lance it but not knowing what it was, I told her it would be better to try ointment instead. I then made a soft crown to surround the blister, if a blister it was, and tied on a little bonnet to keep it in place. Arrangements were made for them to stay with one of our coolies and every morning, I gently rubbed the area with ichthyol ointment. The baby appeared to enjoy her treatment and even more so, the sugar that followed, and the blister subsided and disappeared. The woman returned to her family and I never discovered what had caused the blistering or whether it ever returned.

There was a belief amongst the labour in the virtue of a touch of a healer's hands, and I attained a great deal of unmerited fame from my habit of holding a patient's pulse while they told me their troubles. The root of this misguided belief stemmed from a visit to a malarious region to attend to a man with a fever. Samples confirmed he had the disease and he was given a course of quinine, but in the process of examining him, I had taken his pulse and it was my 'holding his hand' as opposed to the medicine, that was considered the reason for his recovery. From then on, every patient, men and women alike, insisted I took their pulse before telling me what ailed them! It soon became a habit which, often unnecessary, was greatly appreciated by patients, many of whom distrusted doctors.

India is a land steeped in ancient tradition and for centuries, people have faithfully revered Ayruvedic medicine. Practiced by healers and handed down from father to son, it has no written formulas or pharmacopoeia, and though often debased and commercialised, can be highly effective.

I myself have witnessed three near-miraculous cures. The first, shortly after WWI, involved a woman on a malarious estate who was suffering from what looked like pernicious anaemia. The drugs we gave her had no effect, and when her condition became progressively worse, she asked our permission to see an Ayruvedic doctor who had offered to cure her. We readily agreed, and a fortnight later, heard that she had been given some huge pills to swallow, one every other day, while reciting passages from the Vedas, the Hindu holy book. She told us she felt better, and indeed made such an improvement that within a few weeks she was able to return to her village. Several years later, I was stopped on the road by a fine healthy woman. "Don't you recognise me?" she asked. "It's me, Veeranmmal, who was cured by the Ayruvedic doctor!" I was amazed, and had I not seen her with my own eyes, would never have believed that this was the same woman who had almost died!

Around the same time, we had a man on the estate who had epilepsy. He too wished to see an Ayruvedic practitioner and this time I was allowed to sit in during the consultation. The 'doctor' told me that with her permission, he was going to transfer the man's fits to his wife. Seeing my look of horror, he assured me that the man's wife, not being a 'natural epileptic', would suffer only a few fits and then no more. In order to proceed, he had to wait till the man had a fit, and a few days later, when the man obliged, a vein in both his and his wife's wrists were opened, placed over each other and bound together overnight. As predicted, the man's wife subsequently had one severe, then three progressively lighter fits, but thereafter and for as long as we knew him, the man ceased fitting altogether!

My third and last experience of Ayruvedic medicine was at High Wavys and the patient was one of Miriam Bibi's sons. His illness began with a swelling in his groin which spread down one leg and then the other, and running a high temperature, he faded in and out of consciousness and was close to death. With no idea what it was, the doctor pronounced the boy's condition incurable, so the father decided to take him to an Ayurvedic practitioner in one of the villages in the plains. Fearing that the child would not survive the journey, I offered to bring the 'doctor' up to the estate, but was told that this was impossible since he was in hiding from the police! It was madness, but with no other option, he left with the child. Three weeks later they presented themselves beaming at the bungalow. The once dying boy though thin, seemed well, and interested to hear what had happened, I questioned Miriam Bibi closely. She had apparently been told that nothing but breastmilk should pass the boy's lips, whilst she herself had to take huge brown pills, presumably as medicine to be passed through her to the child. As in the first case, she too was instructed to recite sections from the Vedas. Remarkably, that was all that it took for the boy to make a complete recovery!

Despite the effectiveness of such traditional medicine, what India desperately needed, and probably still needs, are teams of dedicated doctors and nurses committed to going out to the villages to treat people in their homes. Statistics will tell you that there is just one doctor per 60,000 people; a staggering figure but one which does not give a true picture of the situation. Despite being low, the number of doctors in towns and cities is adequate but there still remain vast stretches of the country, with village populations of several many thousands, who have never seen a doctor in their lives.

The Opening of the New Factory
1937

In 1937, ten months after the laying of the foundation stone, our factory was officially opened, and once again superstition marred the day. Kolar Rowther had been asked to come up to officiate and all the children were invited to a feast in the building. Most of the coolies were delighted, but I was told by one or two that since there was bound to be an accident, they didn't want to put their children's lives at risk. Their fear was based on the belief that any kind of machinery was something of a miracle, and any involvement with it, might anger the gods.

Whilst they considered the machinery a miracle, to us the real miracle lay in the men's ability to carry it seven miles up our long rough road. The engine bed plate, weighing over three tons, and bound to bamboo poles lashed close together along its length, had required no fewer than fifty men to transport it. At the toot of a trumpet, the men had taken the weight on their shoulders, staggered six steps, then let it down before repeating the process. The weight was so great that any fault in timing might have broken a man's back. All in all, it took seventy men ten days to carry the bed plate and fly wheel, weighing 14 hundred weights, from the foot of the hill to the factory. I took a photograph of the teams involved in that feat of endurance and at the end, when I gave them each a copy, was amused to see that because few had mirrors, they recognised their mates but needed help in identifying themselves!

As soon as the formalities were over, the children, bedecked in flowers from the garlands presented at the opening ceremony, were seated on the bare factory floor and given banana leaves as plates, whilst old Kolar Rowther in all his glory, walked among them, beaming like a benign genie. We had prepared literally mountains of rice alongside huge cauldrons of Indian vegetables and the meat of two goats gifted by Kolar. The children's continuous chatter was loud enough to drown out all adult voices, even Kolar's, but having happily adopted the role of host, he was too busy examining the curries and the rice to talk. Suddenly, the room fell silent and every little sleek oiled head turned in the direction of the cooks who had begun to serve the food. Two men carried each pot whilst another ladled out generous portions with a coconut shell.

The speed with which that mountain of rice and curry disappeared was almost frightening. One small boy sitting close to me, was in such a hurry to finish

Cloudland

Cloudland and Bungalow

Tea factory 1937

Carrying stones for factory

Carrying machinery, pelton wheel and dynamo

Ratman with children from the creche.

Estate staff family

Estate children waiting for Christmas presents

High Wavys bungalow 1938

Looking towards Udamulpet from High Ridge

Estate staff families

Estate staff families

and qualify for a second helping, that he swallowed a mutton bone and began to choke. I immediately jumped to the rescue, put my finger down his throat and got it up before anybody noticed. The sharp edge of the bone had made a small cut and there was a little blood, but none the worse for wear, he finished his second helping with undiminished gusto!

I then watched fascinated, as a small girl aged about four and wearing nothing but a flower in her hair and a silver fig leaf on a string tied round her waist, attacked an extra-large portion. I remember remarking to the tea-maker's wife that it would be a miracle if the child managed to eat it all, but sticking grimly to her task, she ate every last crumb and accepted a second helping. I watched in astonishment, for it seemed physically impossible for that small anatomy to hold any more. Determined not to be defeated, she carried on, then pushing a last, large handful into her mouth, suddenly keeled over. Flopped on the floor, flat on her back, tummy distended and fig leaf awry, she had fallen fast asleep and was still slumbering when her father carried her home! By the time the children had finished and filed out of the factory, we were starving. The smell of curry is one of the most hunger-titillating aromas in the world and one by which we had been tormented for far too long! Devoid of any anticipated tragedy, the opening had been a great success and everyone was happy.

Among the many heavy pieces of machinery carried up from the plains were a Pelton wheel and dynamo to provide power and electric light for the factory. It also meant that for the first time ever, we had electric light in the bungalow; a momentous and much welcomed development since up until then, we had depended on oil and paraffin lamps and lanterns. A dam had been built to supply the Pelton wheel with water and everything worked well until early the next year, it burst during a freak storm. The huge pipes, one foot in diameter, along with their steel props were torn up and washed downstream. Jim, several fitters and dozens of coolies worked all day, waist-deep in rushing water, making temporary repairs to the dam by erecting supports from hurriedly felled jungle trees, and reinstalling the salvaged pipes. It was an immense job, but they eventually got it done without holding back factory work for more than a day. In due course, a new, and higher dam was built which as far as I know, is still there today.

Sewing Classes and Corruption

In addition to the factory, Jim was kept busy with the construction of other new buildings, including redesigned dwellings for the labour and a purpose-built school, which sited mid- way between the two divisions on the estate, was a vast improvement much welcomed by Aroliah. I, meanwhile, had begun to run a sewing class where some of the brighter girls were taught to make and mend. The latter was not at all popular so, to make it more appealing, I collected together a bag of dressmaking relics and provided the girls with patches of various fabrics and colours which they could appliqué over the holes in their garments.

At the end of each class, the girls were given a sweet, but I was surprised to see that as soon as they accepted it, they bolted outside. Intrigued, I ran through the bungalow and from a window facing the road, discovered that once out of sight, the girls popped their sweets from their mouths and wrapped them carefully in a corner of their saris. When asked for an explanation at the next sewing class, the girls looked guilty and told me that they saved their sweets for the babies at home. Thereafter, I let them have their sweets earlier in class and ensured they enjoyed them! They had clearly been taught to consider their siblings, especially brothers, before themselves; a situation further illustrated when one day, I found one of the girls sitting by the road crying. A beautifully embroidered jacket over which she had taken great care had been snatched by her elder brother. I tried to intervene by tackling her mother, and as I might have expected, was told: "But he's a boy and he wanted it, so what could I do?!"

One day, when returning from the tea field, we were stopped by a coolie with a complaint about a 'kangany' or overseer. The previous year and in need of money, the man had borrowed the sum of two rupees, and since then had been paying the kangany two annas per rupee per week in interest. As there are but sixteen annas in a rupee, he had paid the kangany back many times over, but had never been able to save up a whole two rupees to get out of debt. Kanganies were not allowed to lend money on usury, as it led to all sorts of what Jim called 'monkey tricks', and this was flagrant robbery! Furious, Jim sent for the kangany and whilst severely reprimanding him, unintentionally used the word 'nasamapochi', meaning 'you are done for.' The man gave a sudden yelp and flung himself on the floor crying, "Dorai, Dorai I will pay back the money and promise never to lend any again, but please, take back that word!" Jim agreed, whereupon the kangany galloped home and returned shortly afterwards with the man's receipt and the money he owed.

After this incident, Jim announced that if ever coolies needed money, they could borrow it from the office. It would be free of interest and repayable in small, manageable amounts, but they would be required to deposit jewellery which would be returned after the loan had been cleared. The idea was welcomed and from time to time, Jim's safe was awash with treasure! Unfortunately, about a month after this episode, the kangany in question had his room burned down, and of course, that 'word' was believed to be the cause. It says a lot for Jim's popularity, that the labour bore him no grudge.

The following incident occurred some years later but rounds off this story. The young man we had taken on at Kardana was offered a better job by another cardamom owner and to replace him, we employed Vurkey, an apothecary with knowledge of malaria. He was someone we knew and trusted, since many years previously, he had bravely stood by us during that awful night spent fighting off cholera on Munji. He was not afraid of hard work and seemed ideally suited to the job. However, he was also a married man with a big family and had been without a job for some time. Cardamoms are a peculiar crop, accepted as currency in shops run by Indians, and that proved a terrible temptation for Vurkey. We began to notice that a considerable amount of our best fruit was not coming into our store, and after making enquiries, found that Vurkey was deflecting a proportion of it to his home. This could not be allowed to continue; we could not afford it and besides, we had a partner, albeit a sleeping one, but still a partner who had invested in the business. Jim sent for Vurkey, who must have known the reason, for the moment he entered the office, he declared: "I will go quietly and give no trouble, if the Dorai doesn't used that word! Please don't use that word!" As he spoke, he held up his hand as if to silence Jim and it appeared that even amongst the more educated, 'narsamapochi' was a word to be feared. Jim had never intended to use it of course, but the culprit was not to know. Vurkey was dismissed, but as he had a family, had been under considerable temptation and had proved his courage in the past, that was the end of the matter.

Yurghese

There had been no cholera scares on the estate for years, though it was endemic in the villages in the plains below, but one day coming back from the field, we were met by a carpenter, who said that one of the masons was very ill with the disease. The very word 'cholera' was enough to fill us with dread, and knowing the dangers, we were horrified. The doctor, when asked, said he suspected cholera, but unsure, was keeping a close eye on two other men with similar symptoms. We had very little faith in that doctor, but he was the only one we had so we let him get on with his job. It was an anxious time. The original patient died but, thankfully, the others despite nearly dying of fright recovered and with no further cases, we presumed it was not cholera after all.

As our long serving 'boy' Francis was no longer young nor very strong, we decided to hire an under-servant to help him, preferably one who could drive a car. One of the estate staff was going on leave, so we told him what we wanted and asked him to make enquiries. He returned from his holiday accompanied by a cheerful young man who presented himself as we were having breakfast on the verandah, by announcing that he was our new 'chokra'. Just like that; as if there was no doubt in his mind that he was the very man for us! I took a fancy to him, a quite unreasonable fancy, but I solemnly asked whether he had any 'characters' to show me from his previous employers. In response, he beamed - in fact he was always beaming - and produced two rather battered bits of paper. The first mentioned that he had carried tea trays in the YMCA meeting house every week for two years, whilst the second, longer reference, had been written by a missionary who after raving about his reliability and honesty, ended with the astonishing remark that it had been a privilege to live under the same roof as such a sweet Christian soul! Even this did not damn him, for by then I was well taken by his cheery smile and self-confidence. I then asked whether he could drive. "Oh yes." he replied somewhat over-cheerfully. "Have you ever driven a car?" I continued. "No," he replied, "but I know how." It was a sound reason for not employing him and waiting until we found what we wanted, but Yurghese won the day! He knew nothing and had to be taught everything. He must have been a perfect nuisance to poor Francis, but he worked his charm, until tolerating his failings, the old man told me: "He will learn soon Madam, he is a good boy." So Yurghese stayed.

In our part of the estate there was very little game. Sometimes, coming home in the evening, a sambhur would flit across the path or some Wanderoo monkeys would abuse me from the trees, and while Giant Hornbills were rare, I might catch a glimpse of a Malabar squirrel slipping silently along a branch. Elephants, however, were becoming a real nuisance elsewhere on the estate. We had been planting grass along the top of the banks above the paths to both help retain the soil and as fodder for the cattle and horses. Unfortunately, this highly succulent grass was nectar to elephants and having discovered it, they proceeded to devastate the banks. I remember one particular section which looked as if Hannibal had ridden through, for at least a dozen elephants had systematically torn out all the grass, filling the drains with earth. Curiously, their droppings had been left neatly along the edge of the road as though they had been tethered.

We were now due to make another visit to the distant cardamom estates that we had surveyed in September. This time, we would take a different route, so that we could spend the night at Mr G's place and have a look at his crops. He had no furniture to speak of and after zig-zagging our way down the path laden with camp beds, we arrived at our friend's primitive hut and ate sitting on wooden boxes! Meanwhile, Yurghese had been charged with leading our porters along our original route involving six miles through leech-infested jungle, followed by a further twelve over of hot grassland. He had set off beaming but we wondered what he would make of it all and what condition he would be in at the end of it!

The next morning, Mr G walked with us for the first few miles, as much for company as to put us on the right track. Shortly after he left us we heard three shots, and later learned that he had run into a small herd of elephants which for some reason had taken a dislike to him, and to drive them off he had climbed a tree and fired his rifle into the air. However, at the time we had no reason to think he was in any trouble, and with a long trail ahead, continued on our way.

Tramping on, we passed a holy bell hanging in a sacred tree in a cattle laager. Very old, it had been there for many years and though quite unprotected, had never been touched by elephants. Large numbers had clearly been rubbing themselves against the tree trunks and had pulled off branches from the surrounding trees, but as in other jungles of Southern India, had respected this primitive little primitive Hindu shrine.

Rounding a little hill into a small strip of jungle flanking a stream, we spotted elephant droppings, still hot and steaming. Elephants were clearly very close and before long we saw a little family of Ma, Pa, and their big son. Having seen us, they turned onto our path and proceeded to amble along, stopping every now and then until we had almost caught up, and becoming increasingly irritated by us following them, delayed moving off for longer and longer periods. There was only one path and it would have been impossible to navigate the saw-sharp elephant grass growing six feet high on either bank without lacerating our hands and faces. There were also deep, narrow gullies in the airless undergrowth, and because the grass held the heat of the sun, taking such a detour would have been extremely tiring. The elephants' patience, however, was running out, and when the bull began to stamp his feet and blow through his trunk, we had no other option than to take to the hillside and try to rejoin

the path via a gap about two miles ahead. Anyone who has tramped through that sort of landscape in the heat of the day can imagine the next hour of our journey as we blindly groped and tumbled our way uphill, through razor-sharp grass, feeling increasingly hotter and desperate. We finally reached the gap to the path, sweating and exhausted. Hating the sun, elephants usually prefer to travel in the cool of the evening, but having made their point, that particular family could still be seen ambling along the path behind us.

Thanks to the detour we were late but comforted by the thought that Yurghese and the porters, who should have arrived the day before, would be ready to welcome us with water for baths, tea and a meal. However, much to our dismay, no one was there! We had camp beds but no food and just as we were wondering what on earth could have happened, up came Yurghese and the porters, looking footsore and weary. It transpired that they had been stopped at the top of the valley by a herd of elephants which had refused to move, despite the men's shouting and banging of tins. The party had thus been forced to stay put for the night, guarded by the best fires they could make from grass and small woody shrubs. By morning, the siege of elephants had lifted but after setting off, they then lost their way and had to walk several miles before retracing the path. The porters were bemoaning their trials, and small blame to them. Yurghese, however, though obviously very tired, was looking remarkably cheerful and when asked whether he had had a terrible time, replied: "Yes; but I had never seen wild elephants before and I can't wait to tell my wife Mary!" That settled Yurghese's fate: He loved adventure and was unafraid of wild animals; in short, a man after my own heart, a treasure not to be lost! We would put up with his many faults to keep him, for that alone. As for Yurghese, he was considered quite a hero when he got home, and Mary bathed in his reflected glory.

Our land survey was less strenuous than the first, but strenuous enough. We were taken to Gandamanayakanur Zemindari and a section of land cleared and planted with cardamom, and also shown the great elephant track that ran through the jungle all the way to the great grass plateau in Travancore where, many years ago, we had run the camp for the Simon Commission. Elephants are great road-makers, and as a rule their roads are well traced and often used by motorised vehicles, especially in rough country. This track however, was particularly spectacular, since covering a distance of some thirty miles and fifty feet in width, it ran straight through the heavy jungle without deviation, up steep hills and through valleys; every mile of it, clear of undergrowth and trees and carpeted over the centuries with the dried dung of wild game.

I wish we could have travelled its length before we left India. It would have been a truly wonderful experience to have built a machan in one of the big trees by the track and watch the elephants migrate either west towards Travancore and the south-west monsoon in June, or on their return to Gandamanayakanur Zemindari in October for the northeast monsoon. But alas, the opportunity never came.

Remembering Elephants

I have mentioned elephants often in these pages and as I write have come to realise what queer, individual and unpredictable creatures they are. Why, as in the case of the bell we had passed on the way from G's, do they ignore little Hindu shrines, but refuse to tolerate secular buildings erected by Europeans? I know of several of these shrines, two in grassland and the others in the jungle, and all are equally safe from harm. It is an extraordinary phenomenon, especially with regard to a shrine located in the heart of the jungle seventeen miles from any dwelling, bar a tiny hut inhabited by an unarmed priest. Clearly respected by herds of passing elephants, it remains intact year on year, ready to welcome the pilgrims' annual visit.

Another shrine, near the estate, was likewise left alone. The elephants, however, took great exception to a bungalow built beside it and knocked it down. Stranger still, when a pumping house was built to replicate that shrine, it too was destroyed whilst the shrine itself though completely unprotected remained inviolate. The shrine and the pump house were within a few hundred yards of each other beside a river which had been the meeting place of elephants for centuries. One was continually attacked but the other remained safe and no one will ever know the reason why.

With the exception of a few rogues, wild elephants belong to a tightly knit herd and are generally peaceable and non-aggressive towards other animals, including humans, so long as they aren't challenged or feel under threat. However, if enraged they are mighty in battle, and are especially dangerous during the mating season when the bulls in musth will fight each

other ferociously for leadership of the herd. Once, when out walking, my Father and I heard a curious noise which I can only compare to the sound of a drummer humming whilst gently striking his drum. It seemed to be coming from the hillside and, creeping towards it, we found two bull elephants with ears outspread, facing each other, about fifty yards apart. Rippling with rage they continued their drumming whilst rubbing their trunks on the ground, presumably softly trumpeting at the same time which would have explained the humming sound. Now and again, they turned away then changing position, faced each other once more and resumed their drumming. Whether it was an invitation to fight we couldn't tell, but the one with broken tusks and sporting the scars of many battles was obviously old, so perhaps the younger bull was challenging him in an effort to take over the herd. If he succeeded, the old bull would be exiled and forced to live a solitary life, develop deep-rooted grudges against the world and become highly dangerous. Once cast out, the once all-powerful old bulls will usually follow the herd at a distance but dare not join it, and given the overt lack of concern displayed by their families I couldn't help but pity the plight of these sad and lonely beasts.

I never witnessed an actual fight, but Jim and I did see the scene of a battle in a dry riverbed, which the hillmen told us had lasted for several days. The whole place was in shambles. The bank had collapsed, small trees had been felled, and on the sandy bed splattered with blood, pitted with holes and littered with branches torn from larger trees, lay the bodies of the two badly wounded combatants. On another occasion we came across a bull elephant standing belly-deep at the edge of the Periyar Lake and rocking to and fro. Flies had penetrated a deep tusk wound high on one of his forelegs, resulting in his entire leg becoming enormously swollen, with rivers of pus oozing from the wound. He was obviously in great pain and close to death. We wanted to put him out of his misery, but at the time elephants were sacred in Travancore, and having applied for and refused permission by the authorities we were told that the forest officers would deal with it. Nobody came, and tragically that grand old elephant was left to suffer until he died some days later.

At the end of the dry season and in anticipation of the monsoon, hillmen burn off the grass to encourage new growth on which to graze their cattle, and, though usually very cautious, elephants will sometimes burn the soles of their feet on the hot ash. The pads of an elephant's feet are extremely sensitive, and an elephant in pain is a dangerous beast that will look for something on which to wreak vengeance. In such instances, and if you happened to be a V.I.P whom the Travancore Government wished to honour, rules would be bent and a permit issued for the animal to be shot. When the hunters conformed to the rules of 'shikar' all was well. However, sometimes an elephant would be wounded rather than killed, and the V.I.P. would go off leaving behind a dangerous beast for us all to worry about. One such elephant proved particularly troublesome for several years prior to the first World War. The wound on his mouth must have caused him a great deal of pain, and moreover made him angry and a threat to humans. He was the only rogue elephant I knew who did not fear fire, and ignoring the camp fires burning all through the night, would regularly attack carts bivouacked by the roadside as they made their way to the coast with loads of tea. He eventually disappeared, but what happened to him I do not know.

Elephants have the reputation of being wise with good memories, but even elephants sometimes make mistakes. One night, after a long dry spell in the hills, a small herd came down to the plains and raided some of the villagers' fields. Among the crops was a field of millet called Kambu, which is poisonous at a certain stage of its growth. The next morning, the villagers found not only their fields laid waste, but eleven huge bodies. The forestry department was informed and had the unenviable task of removing and burying them.

One of the miracles of the jungle is the ability of elephants to move through heavy undergrowth in complete silence. When feeding, they crash and squeal with a lot of breaking of branches and trampling of feet, but afterwards or if frightened will move away at speed without making a sound. In his book 'The Jungle Tide' John Still claims to have used tracks through the undergrowth known only to jungle dwellers and travelled by elephants. I have found what looked like tracks, but they are so narrow that even with my small bulk I had difficulty in making my way through the undergrowth of long barbed thorns of cane and branches that press in from either side. Despite being proven it is impossible to imagine elephants following such tracks.

Whilst these 'secret' routes remained largely unknown, the locals were very familiar with the many others which, creatures of habit, elephants have used for generations, and it was along those, traps were set to capture elephants for domestic use. Elephants are extremely suspicious, easily scared, and very careful where they put their feet, so the pits must be heavily camouflaged. Using traditional and well-honed skills, a hole is dug, fifteen feet deep and the mouth covered first with slotted bamboo, then a light layer of soil on top of which are scattered leaves from the forest floor. Though beautifully constructed it is a cruel form of trap, for the great beasts are often injured by their fall, and if a cow and calf fall together, she may crush it or, highly distressed, kill it. The elephants remain in their traps whilst fed on succulent material, which because they are hungry, they enjoy even though it provides them with very little strength. As they become accustomed to both their captors and being fed by hand, the pit is slowly filled, gradually raising the floor, and once at a sufficient level to enable the elephant to get out chains are put round its legs. The ends of these chains are then placed in the mouths of a couple of tame, fully trained elephants, who heave up the captive. By that stage, the wild elephant is in no condition to express its resentment and through continued feeding and kind attention becomes resigned to his new conditions. In due course, his two guardian elephants are no longer required. The man who has fed and cared for him from the time of his capture becomes his mahout, and bonded with the animal, often for life, is responsible for washing, feeding, riding and training him and eventually, supervising his work.

Wives, Mothers and Daughters

Returning to life on the estate I was increasingly enjoying the company of wives of the Indian staff with whom I had formed close friendships. Mrs. Matthews was very much 'down-to-earth' with few inhibitions, whilst Mrs. Devamani, though rather unstable, was a highly intelligent and delightful woman who spoke several languages. She was also a voracious reader and she and Dainty Matthews would come up to the house in search of reading matter: Mrs Devamani for romance, and Dainty, highly scornful of her friend's preferences, demanding adventure or crime. Mrs Anthonymuttu, meanwhile, was too busy having babies and caring for the ones she had to take much part in the group. She was also a Pillai who considered herself our superior, and I never got to know as well as the others.

I still kept up my friendship with both Amirtham by then the mother of two daughters, Daisy and Lily, and Assirvatham, the Cloudland tea-maker's wife, and visited them frequently on my trips to and from Kardana. Amritham, very much a traditionalist, believed that a woman should fulfil the life for which she was created - marriage and children - and never enthusiastic about Monica training to be a nurse, was delighted to hear that she had become engaged. Tragically, before Monica married, dear Amirtham lost her young daughter Daisy. The child had fallen ill whilst the family was on holiday in their village, but before arrangements had been made to take her to Madura, Jacob's old mother had secretly given Daisy a native drug. She reacted badly, and although still alive on arrival at hospital died soon afterwards. Sadly, it was yet another example of both the widespread fear and suspicion of hospitals, and a refusal to confront and accept change that continued to exist amongst illiterate families in rural communities. Educated Indians from illiterate families often have much to contend with, which in this case proved fatal.

They still had their baby, Lily, which helped them both, and Jacob was soon involved in an emergency in which he distinguished himself. Early one morning we received a message that he had discovered a case of suspected measles amongst some newcomers in the lines. He reported that he had arranged for a small grass hut to be built on the other side of the stream in which he had isolated the family and hired a watchman to ensure they didn't return to the lines. Thanks to Jacob's quick response we had no new cases, but over in High Wavys the disease had been imported from a nearby village, and because Dr. Menon was not informed until several people had been infected, an epidemic developed in which several children died. In typical fashion and thanks to his diligence Jacob had saved Cloudland from a similar epidemic. He always appeared hesitant and apologetic, but if left to deal with a situation took sensible action and never panicked. He had a keen desire for knowledge, and whenever either of us used a word he didn't understand he would fish out his little notebook and write down its meaning. He seldom had to ask twice.

During this period a team of surveyors came up for a few weeks to survey and demarcate the boundaries on Cloudland and High Wavys. One day, Jim returned from a round of field work unusually concerned about Jacob. He had appeared to be doped, and because he had been unable to take in what was said to him Jim wondered if he was taking drugs. I came across Jacob the following morning, staggering along the road as if drunk, and clearly having difficulty in understanding what I was saying. It certainly appeared that there was something very far wrong, but as soon as the surveyors had left he was back to his old self. I asked Amirtham if she knew the cause of the trouble and after further enquiries discovered that

Jacob, ever eager for knowledge, had spent every evening studying with one of the surveyors, then continued on his own by the light of a hurricane lamp till the early hours of the morning. Of course, being Jacob and despite severe sleep deprivation, he was out as usual at six a.m. mustering the coolies then working all day in the field! Years later, when we were stuck for a surveyor to make a rough plan of new land to be opened, Jacob offered to do the job and produced a very fair plan.

The Indian staff increased and with more wives on the estate we decided to form a Ladies' Club. Though initially an opportunity for chats and get-togethers its remit quickly expanded to include sewing, knitting, dressmaking and later on, cookery classes. As usual, I began by being the instructor, but soon found myself learning from the others. The women were of all classes and races: the wives of the two clerks and Mary, Yurghese's wife, were Travancoreans and all three 'Jacobites' or Syrian Christians. Mrs. D., the head conductor's wife, was a Hindu who, unusually in the south, spoke Rajput, whilst Mrs. A. was a Roman Catholic Pillai. We also had many Dravidians amongst who were Ratnam and Amirtham, who now living four miles away across a leech-infested jungle only attended now and again. As the only British member I insisted upon one rule: in order for us to meet as equals all castes and races were to be dropped at the Club door. That rule was kept and worked very well.

Dravidians are descendants of the race that invaded and populated the peninsula around 3,200 - 2,000 B.C. driving out the aboriginals from whom the Ooralis and Munnans are descended. India's so-called higher castes have roots in the various waves of northern invaders - Nordics, Mongols, Syrians and Muslim Arabs - who in turn, became overlords of both the earlier immigrants and the indigenous people. As time went on they all became Indian, but were ranked as different castes according to the point in history when their ancestors invaded. With each successive invasion the Dravidians found themselves pushed further down the scale, and also down the peninsula. However, despite centuries of domination they remain positive and exceptional people, and thanks to the missionaries can rise to become valued citizens: the new generation is literate and finally able to escape the stultifying poverty of village life,

One morning, I received a deputation from some of the men who had hauled our heavy machinery up to the factory, asking if their wives, who had helped carry the cement for the factory floor, could have their photographs taken. I happily agreed but, seeing the men hanging around in bashful silence, I knew that another request was coming. Finally, after a few embarrassed coughs, one man stepped forward and asked if I would also let the women see over our bungalow. Again, I agreed and one day in December conducted my first tour of the bungalow, which though not large, seemed immense to them and full of surprises. I had other parties of women in the years to come but none as enlightening and entertaining as the first!

Fifteen women arrived dressed in their best with fresh flowers in their hair (no mean feat after a seven mile climb up our hill) all eagerly smiling and obviously out to enjoy themselves. We entered the verandah with its open windows and rattan chairs which had to be stroked, sat upon and minutely examined. Next came the sitting room, named by the servants as the 'flower room' on account of its many bowls of flowers, furnished with easy chairs by the fireplace, a wireless and my writing table. They were suitably impressed with it all, but even the wireless, which I turned to a Tamil programme for their benefit, paled in comparison to the photographs arranged on my writing table. Amongst portraits of my parents, Ted and Monica, in place of honour, sat a frame containing four snapshots of Monica's first baby, born a few months previously. As they crowded around, I explained that it was Missie's baby daughter. There were gasps of amazement then, amidst the excited chatter, I heard a woman cry: "Fancy! Missie had four babies at once!" Nothing I said would convince them that these photographs were not of four babies, but rather four photographs of one baby, and from that point on Monica was famous in the villages for being the mother of quads! Having eventually managed to peel them away from the wonder photo, we continued into the dining room which they found most amusing. Why, with all this space, couldn't we eat in the sitting room or on the verandah? Everything in and on top of the sideboard had to be handled, and in some cases tasted, with mixed reactions. The bookcase was opened with exclamations of approval. It was quite obvious that these women were going to milk every drop of enjoyment from this tour and intended to miss nothing out. We came at last to our bedroom where, of course, the bed had to be tested. Suddenly, there was a cry of delight as one of them caught sight of herself in the full-length mirror on the wardrobe door. All else was forgotten and the whole party pressed around to look upon this fresh wonder. They waved their arms and giggled to see their reflection imitating their actions. One of them had a small baby who was held up and made to laugh and move its hands, much to his mother's delight. The bathroom and kitchen were gone over with meticulous care and intense interest, but the two highlights were undoubtedly the picture of the 'quads' and the long mirror. After their photographs had been taken and a few sweets distributed to take down to the village for their children, they left happy and satisfied.

We had meanwhile acquired a new doctor, a cocky little Travancorean and a high-caste Nair, and when he asked for leave to get married, we agreed, thinking a wife would help him settle. As was the custom the bride had been chosen by his parents, but before his departure Jim reminded him that it would be him and not his parents who would have to live with her. He was given a fortnight's leave, but within a few days Dr. M. was back, looking rather gloomy and minus a wife. Apparently, when presented with the girl, he had refused to marry her; an awful solecism. His mother had immediately taken to her bed, refused all food and threatened to die, until in despair Dr. M. told her: "Choose me another wife Mother, and whoever she is I will marry her even if she looks like a buffalo." Springing from her bed she ate then immediately renewed her mission. The wife, chosen some six months later, was a nice enough girl who cooked beautifully and sang well to the accompaniment of some sort of zither. However, she had an air of cool superiority and neither I nor the other staff wives ever knew her well.

Another new recruit was a Muslim junior clerk employed by the estate's office. Some months after his arrival, Ratnam discovered that he had a wife hidden away in their gloomy little house and, together, we decided to pay her a visit. The door was opened by a timid and highly nervous woman, little more than a child, with two healthy little boys, one aged about three, clinging to her sari, and the other a baby in her arms. Employing her usual charm Ratnam managed to reassure her that we meant her no harm, and it became clear that in addition to being kept in complete purdah within those four walls for fear of being seen by men, she was terrified of the jungle. She was also illiterate and without any handwork skills. Apart from her children she was all alone, and her entire existence seemed to centre round her young family, their needs, and those of her husband.

It took more than one visit to extract these facts. She was particularly wary of me with my white face and terrified of appearing disloyal to her husband. Ratnam was more successful than I in gaining people's confidence, so I left most of the talking to her while

I played with the boys. Before long, Miriam Bibi began to look forward to our visits. Being shut away in that dark little house was no way of life for any woman let alone two little boys, so I decided to take unfair advantage of my position as manager's wife to force her husband to do something about it. I therefore waylaid him one evening as he was returning from work and told him that unless he permitted his wife to attend the Ladies Club with precautions taken to respect her purdah, and allowed her to take walks outside, veiled if necessary, the manager would insist that he take his wife to her family in the plains. "I cannot do without my wife" he replied sulkily. "Who would cook my meals?" I explained that his wife was unlikely to keep well if forced to continue living as she was, and nor was it healthy for his sons. The mention of his precious sons hit him where it hurt, and I was finally given leave to make whatever arrangements I liked for his wife and the children, so long as I respected her purdah.

Ratnam invited her to the next club meeting, but I have seldom seen a more miserable creature than Miriam Bibi, who from the moment she arrived looked like a mouse surrounded by a large gathering of cats. She found the other women's kindly advances pure torture, and had she not been afraid to venture out into the open without Ratnam and been able to carry both children, she would surely have fled back home. Following my advice Ratnam ignored her imploring looks; laughing and chatting with the club members as though Miriam were not there. It happened to be a day when one of the women was giving a cooking demonstration and with the others distracted, Miriam became less agitated and appeared calm by the time we had tea and even tasted the samples. Her two boys meanwhile were having a merry time with the other children, and laughing and chuckling, relishing their freedom after being confined for so long at home.

However, when the next meeting came round Miriam refused to come and her husband told me smugly that she didn't like it. Unwilling to give up on her I insisted on her attendance, and albeit with a bad grace, he said he would see that she came. Miriam went through several days of misery before she got over her intense shyness but eventually, helped by the friendliness of the women and her boys' happiness, became an enthusiastic member. Between us we taught her to knit, and, keen to learn after admiring what we had made, she worked on a little jersey. Once finished, tears ran down her cheeks as she sat stroking it on her lap murmuring "for my son, I made it for my son". Her conversion complete, she lost her timidity, and one red-letter day she gave a demonstration to a full meeting on how to make Muslim sweetmeats. Now a 'graduate' she learned to sew and, having honed her skills making clothes for her husband and children, became an enthusiastic participant in making things for the Red Cross during the war.

A New House Guest and Entertaining at High Wavys

In the late summer of 1938 we received word that Mother was suffering very high blood pressure and wanted to come out to India to make her home between those of her two daughters. Arrangements were made and in October she sailed from England to Cochin, the newly opened port on the south-west coast of India. Just before I went to meet her, I lost the filling from one of my teeth. It was extremely painful but knowing I would soon be somewhere comparatively civilized with access to a dentist, I took the temporary measure of stuffing the hole with oil of cloves.

Like all journeys, my trip to Cochin began with the seven-mile scramble downhill to the plains. My tooth jarred unbearably with every step of that rough road, and, since the next seven miles cross-country in the bullock cart were not much better, I arrived at old Kolar's house in the village more dead than alive and in no mood, I'm afraid, to listen to him roaring about the latest news. I managed to eat my sandwiches in the cool twilight of the room, and after a long wait caught my bus. The route retraced the one taken with Mother when visiting Jim before we were engaged, then on through the district where we had lived for many years, and down to the rubber growing district beyond. There were the usual leisurely formalities at the Travancore frontier, during which I sat nursing my tooth dreading the thought of the many miles ahead. Then after staying the night with a friend, set off on the final lap to Cochin.

It was a journey I always loved. Crossing the rolling grass hills, the road winds its way down to the plain where the dull lines of rubber trees are relieved by small villages and clusters of houses sheltered by palm and mango trees. Amidst a scattering of coffee bushes, pepper vines climb over indigenous trees and when in flower give off a wonderful spicy scent. Leaving the rubber plantations behind, we entered the cultivated western plains and along the road passed a Travancorean family: a father carrying his youngest child on his shoulder followed by the mother with sleek black hair coiled in a neat bun at the back of her head, andtheir elder daughters walking as straight as rods in long full skirts and plaits reaching down their backs. In contrast to the adults in their snowy-white clothes the children, like little golden cherubs, were all but naked. I never failed to be struck by the Travancorean peoples' natural beauty and elegance, despite their poverty and the very hard lives they led.

As soon as the bus arrived at Ernakulam, on the opposite side of the water from Cochin, I rushed to see a Japanese dentist who was reputed to be careful and confident. However, when asked to extract it he insisted that since the tooth was sound it would be a pity to lose it. Like a fool I gave in and agreed to have it refilled. I met the ship next morning, accompanied Mother ashore, then found a chair for her in the customs shed while we waited to have her luggage checked. It was still a very new port and we were highly entertained by the sight of customs officers bustling about trying to appear highly efficient. After a while, a smart official strode up and asked why we had not prepared a box ready for him to inspect. I asked which box he had in mind and sounding slightly flummoxed he replied: "Any box you please". I dutifully opened one of mother's cases but he hardly glanced at its contents and we left with an amusing story to tell back home! To make the journey easier for Mother we returned to the estate in stages, hiring a car and staying with several friends along the way. Our last stop was Munji, and after getting Mother to bed I spent an hour wandering around the lovely garden that we had made and left with much sadness, six years before. The following morning, we were met by old Kolar who had kindly provided his own cart for Mother's comfort, and as was his wont, generous quantities of his revolting sweets, sticky cakes, and sweet fizzy drinks. He then insisted on accompanying us to the hills and waving aside our protests, and much to the discomfiture of the bulls and driver, perched himself on the foot of the cart and settled down to entertain us with polite conversation. At least it began that way, but when he discovered that Mother did not understand Tamil, he employed his usual tactic of acting as though she were deaf and raised his voice to a bellow. By the time we got out my ears were ringing, but luckily Mother was indeed a little deaf so was spared the worst! Sustained by a picnic lunch sent down by Jim, we then faced the long, hot climb to the bungalow; Mother in a dhooly and me on horseback.

My tooth meanwhile was throbbing, so determined to get rid of the brute once and for all, I sterilised a few ancient forceps inherited from Bobs and sent for Dr. M. Having no knowledge of dentistry, he was very reluctant to extract it, but I insisted and he eventually agreed. Mother was lying down in her room and even though I assured him that I would not make a sound, he asked me to turn on the wireless so that she would not hear my cries! I expected him to be clumsy, but when he finally screwed up his courage to do it, the extraction was quick and painless and relieved to be rid of the tooth I felt better at once. Doubtlessly intended as a compliment, he commented "You are one bold woman", then left, still visibly shaken by the ordeal!

It was lovely having Mother with us though she must have been very lonely at times since I was often over at Kardana, and both Jim and I were out and about for much of the day. She had never enjoyed remote, isolated places, and even though she had lived alone it took a lot of courage to leave her beloved London for India, albeit to stay with her daughters. She often felt nervous at night but her health improved, and better still, Yurghese adopted her and soon became her willing servant. Mother found Yurghese a difficult name to remember so decided to call him George, which later became Porges. They got on famously though how they managed to communicate I do not know for Porges, despite understanding more than he admitted, spoke no English and Mother had forgotten all her Tamil.

Old Francis had fallen ill and when Mother arrived was in hospital and died soon after. We felt we had lost a friend as well as an excellent cook who, left to his own devices and aided by an ancient and enormous copy of Mrs Beeton's cookery book, had concocted a constant stream of delicious and succulent dishes. In this regard, he had been one in a million and though Porges managed the tasks of a head servant wonderfully well he was certainly no cook, and nor for that matter, was I! However, not to be defeated and having inherited that book, Porges and I spent hours poring over recipes and planning our meals. It was a lengthy process that involved me translating the English into Tamil and then Porges writing it down in Malayalam, his native language. Cooked on a wood-burning stove of considerable age and uncertain temperament the results were sometimes surprising, but usually fit to eat!

It was only after coming to High Wavys that we began to entertain Indians at home on a regular basis and through trial and error, learnt a lot about strict rules concerning food and drink which differed from caste to caste. Some would only accept fruit with unbroken skins and would only take milk from our cows if collected in their own pots by either themselves or their servants. Some would accept food from us, but had to cook it themselves on a fire in the bedroom fireplace. Others would eat food cooked by Porges, but only on the assurance that it was strictly vegetarian, whilst Muslims, who generally ate anything, insisted that meat was slaughtered in accordance with their religion. Porges became quite clever at dealing with our various guests' requirements, with very few exceptions. On the rare occasions when we couldn't meet their needs our guests were quite prepared to go without, but there were always bananas, oranges and milk which even the highest caste could consume.

After-dinner conversations usually began tentatively, then once the ice was broken and our guests relaxed, we would talk well into the night, often about politics and religion. Recognising our genuine interest, our guests eagerly provided us with fascinating insights about their lives and it was always intriguing to hear views and opinions from the 'other side' as it were. They in turn, often seemed bewildered by some of the British customs and laws and I remember one veterinary officer, a keen politician, who admitted being puzzled by the way the British kept the very top jobs in Government for themselves. "Are we not able?" he asked, "Are we not honest? Have we no sense of responsibility?" We agreed that Indians had all these qualities. "Then why is this the case?" he demanded bitterly "Please tell me!" He went on to assure me that he would not take offence and so I told him: "If you were the Viceroy wouldn't you give the highest positions to your nearest relations, regardless of their suitability?" "Of course;" he replied somewhat indignantly "Why wouldn't a man help his own family? It is his duty!" I tried to convince him that it would do the country no good if successive viceroys were to sack all the men holding high positions in Government to make room for members of their family. He saw my point and was rather worried. "But a man's family would put great pressure on him for shouldn't they have a share in his good luck?" It was an interesting and very much traditional perspective which hard to change, illustrated the deeply ingrained loyalty and sense of duty inherent in Indians families. Though quite unrelated, his response reminded me of a story about a very wealthy breeder of Kangayani cattle, so famous that they were sold all over the country. He was illiterate but sent his two sons to schools and then universities in Britain where one graduated with a degree in agriculture, and the other in veterinary science. Both, however, retained a profound admiration for their father and admitted to readily seeking his advice since his knowledge was far greater than theirs.

Christmas Plays, Other Dramas and the Arts and Crafts School

It was now nearing the end of 1938, the situation in Europe was worsening and amidst ever-growing fear and rumours war seemed increasingly likely. One evening, when Jim was staying the night at Cloudland and I was alone listening to the news, I heard a speech by Hitler to a rally somewhere in Germany. I understood not a word, but the mad rhetoric of the man and the disciplined howls of the audience made my blood run cold. I had a sleepless night and was thankful to see Jim back in the morning.

He then went down with what seemed to be a typical attack of dengue fever, known as 'three- day' fever. Along with a continuous blinding headache his temperature remained high and his aches severe. Nothing seemed to improve his condition and as he grew increasingly weak I began to fear that he might have contracted typhoid, though I couldn't imagine from where. In despair I wrote to Bobs, sent her his chart, and asked her advice. She didn't reply, but being Bobs did something far better. My letter had arrived just as she was going into the operating theatre, but leaving her patient in the hands of her assistant, she jumped into her hardy and adventurous little car, drove to our foothills and tramped up the seven miles of steep uphill road to our bungalow with only a villager as guide. She finally arrived at ten at night, still cheerful despite being soaked to the skin and freezing cold.

She was well over fifty and after a hard day at the hospital her trip was a feat of endurance, but above all a wonderful gesture of friendship. The very sight of her seemed to do Jim good, and when she had given him something for his headache and taken a Vidal test in case it was typhoid, he was at last able to have a good night's sleep. The next morning, after talking with Jim and offering me advice, she set off down the hill to her car and the hospital leaving two much relieved and grateful people behind. Jim improved, his test was negative and he was soon up and about, somewhat gaunt and pale, but none the worse.

We then had an unexpected trip to Madura. I had a very sick woman who I wanted Bobs to see and Jim had some business to discuss with the Collector. Once finished, we decided to go to the cinema. The 'pictures' being shown were a series of Laurel and Hardy films; not exactly our first choice, but better than nothing. As usual, gramophone music was played before the film began but we were most surprised when a full harvest festival preceded the slap-stick comedy! It was a very odd combination, but even if they had understood it, one which the Indian audience who made no distinction between religion and entertainment would not have found at all extraordinary! The next morning, I accompanied Jim to the Collector's bungalow, and while the men were working his wife offered to show me the famous 'Lotus Room' which I had always wanted to see. It was a beautiful room filled with ornate pillars and arches designed to resemble the petals of a lotus flower, and she had added her own artistic touches to make it very welcoming. I loved it as much as she did but was told that it had been known to touch the nerves of the bachelor Collectors who found it eerie and ghostly. Some had been driven to drink by it which, lovely as it was, I could well understand!

Back at the hospital, Bobs took me to see a blood transfusion being given to a small Muslim girl brought in a few days before with severe anaemia. Having gradually overcome their fears and superstitions, many Indians had begun to come to the hospital for blood transfusions. Times were changing for the better, and one of the most extraordinary examples was the willingness of Brahmins to accept blood donated by a Harijan, when in any other situation they would not dream of allowing a member of this despised caste anywhere near their food, nor even take water from the same tap. In this instance, the girl's father had offered his blood, which was unusual as a man would rarely give blood for a mere female. Lying immobile, the child looked like a pale ivory doll, very beautiful but fragile, whilst in contrast her father was so seized by panic that he was in danger of fainting. The child made a full recovery, but when he saw her the man had apparently been furious that no longer anaemic, her cheeks had darkened, and she had lost her greatly admired pallor.

The festive season was now upon us and on the estate, preparations were being made for Christmas; usually marked by dances performed by groups of labourers and a drama, written and produced by Aroliah. The plays, usually religious or highly moral in flavour, were enormously popular and the goal of being allowed to act in the Christmas play spurred many a reluctant pupil to attend to his lessons in order to qualify. Much to the schoolmaster's credit even the wildest boys seldom forgot their lines and showed no signs of nervousness. It was all in the vernacular, of course, except for a welcoming speech in English; a gesture greatly appreciated and loudly applauded, since for us much of the Tamil language was unintelligible.

Snags were inevitable but always dealt with calmly without ever disturbing the flow. One year, for example, in the first scene of the Christmas story, the Archangel Gabriel found it impossible to control his wings. Made of plywood and lavishly painted in gold, they were clearly far too heavy and awkward, and instead of flapping kept slipping down and sliding forwards becoming entangled with his robes. The scene was momentarily interrupted and from the audience two small boys, naked and none too clean, were pressed into service and positioned on either side of the angel as wing supporters. It was all done with the utmost reverence without a hint of laughter from anybody. The play itself was very well acted but the performance was constantly interrupted by members of the audience climbing onto the stage to place garlands around the necks of actors or characters they most admired. Before the end, Mary and Joseph were laden with garlands, and though considered right and proper by the majority it was a tradition that we Europeans found both incongruous and tiresome.

In a previous year Aroliah had staged a highly moral temperance play with an early Victorian flavour. The father had spent all the family's wealth on drink, forcing the mother and children to beg. The children then befriended a mission doctor, and weeping at his feet, persuaded him to cure the father of his drunkenness. We still had Dr. M. with us, and the Indian staff had yet to lose faith in his medical ability. The small boy chosen to play the doctor was short and tubby like Dr. M. and a natural actor. Suppressed laughter greeted his entrance on stage and even Dr. M. himself appreciated the joke. The climax came when the stage doctor, having got the drunkard into hospital, produced his homemade stethoscope - beautifully made I may add - and placing the earpieces in his ear requested in the manner of Dr. M. that the father stick out his tongue. He then proceeded to place the other end of his stethoscope on the tongue and listen intently! There was a strangled noise from among the staff sitting in the front seats then Dr. M. fled with his handkerchief held to his face, followed by the head conductor, almost in hysterics! The play ended with a genial scene in which the family was happily reunited, and the 'doctor' strung with so many garlands that he was in danger of suffocation!

I had begun to give the girls lessons in knitting, sewing, and carpet and net - making. We also made Christmas cards from rough handmade paper into which we inserted greetings written by the children in their own language on finer paper supplied by me. With her ever-insatiable appetite for learning new things, Ratnam proved her weight in gold in these classes and before long we had developed an arts and crafts school. Such skills, however, would be of little use to boys so Aroliah, who had already been instrumental in teaching the boys carpentry and building skills, approached Jim with a request that one afternoon a week a mason or a carpenter be spared to teach the best of his pupils. Jim was enthusiastic, ordered some tools for the class, and another popular initiative came into being.

Java

1939

When Mother had been with us for about a year we decided to take a trip to Java to visit Monica and her husband Stephen and meet the 'quad'. Excited to be seeing a new country, and of course spending a whole month with the family, plans were made for Mother and I to leave on 2nd August, with Jim following on later. Our long journey began at five on a wet and blustery morning with our descent down the hill, Mother in a dhooly and me on foot. We were then driven to Madura where after a night with Bobs, boarded a train for Danushkudi, then the ferry to Columbo. A day later, we set sail for Java on the Dutch Ship Indrapura.

The first port of call was Sabang, an island off the coast of Sumatra, with heavily forested hills coming right down to the water's edge, and beautiful tropical bays. There, for but an hour or two, we only had time for a short stroll and were soon on our way to Belawan Deli, the port for Medan, the capital of Sumatra. The weather was not unduly hot, and we were surprised to see scattered about the landscape bushy trees covered in white berries, which from a distance looked rather like hawthorn. The land around the port was flat and intersected by drainage dykes edged with vetch in full bloom and could easily have been mistaken for somewhere in the low countries of Europe. Our next stop was Singapore where Mother and I toured the city in a taxi. At dusk, in the cool drizzly weather, the European sector looked for all the world like London, with buses and traffic and wet streets reflecting the traffic lights and shop fronts, whilst, in contrast, the Chinese district offered a far more exotic and quite definitely Eastern flavour with streets filled with gaily dressed crowds and brightly coloured shop fronts.

Stephen met us in Batavia, now Djakarta, where after being treated to a snack at the famous Hotel des Indes we continued to the airport for our first ever flight to Bandoeng, followed by a car ride to the estate where Stephen was a tea planter, and Monica and her daughter Gillian were waiting to greet us. It was wonderful to see them and to be able to enjoy time together in Kertasarie, which at 5000 feet above sea level had fine cool weather and a short spell of daily rainfall.

Used to those on our own tea estate, we found the differences in customs and management of particular interest. Men pruning in the fields while smoking pipes would have been unthinkable in India; the women pluckers wore large straw hats in which they kept a change of clothing to wear after being soaked by showers. The land was flat with drains six-feet deep intersecting the fields to carry the water that gushed down from the surrounding hills. These drains were also used by the labour as latrines, so there was none of the soil pollution typical of the estates in India and hence, no hookworm or the sores that covered the bodies of the children on our estate, picked up from the filth that collected around the lines. Likewise, the labour's dwellings were clean, airy and much better than anything we had at home. We were, however, struck by the lack of friendly interest shown by locals towards the Europeans in their midst, except in the case of Monica who had opened a medical clinic for mothers and children, and gained popularity through her treatment of burns and wounds.

Mother's birthday, August 17th, was celebrated by taking photographs of the four generations, Mother, me, Monica, and Gillian, in the garden of their little bungalow. Jim then joined us having flown in from Belawan Deli, and arrangements were made for us to see something of the country. Leaving the estate early one cold morning we set off for a nearby sulphurous volcano, Papandayan, where, following paths marked 'safe', we climbed down to the shimmering yellow crater. The glare of the sun intensified the stench of sulphur which bubbled and sizzled on the surface of the crater like brew in a witch's cauldron. Stephen then made matters worse by driving his walking stick into the ground at the edge of the path, releasing a foul-smelling jet of steam. We almost choked on the fumes which felt as deadly as fire and brimstone, and indeed, the whole scenario conjured up images of Hell!

A second later trip to Papandayan was far more pleasant. This time we climbed the great ridge behind the crater which offered magnificent views. On one side, 8000 feet below, was the sea, studded with boats and with waves crashing onto a palm-fringed beach. On the other, stretched the hilly country of Java with several other volcanoes, Tjikorai, Tjermai, and in the distance, Slamat: An impressive panorama indeed.

We were also taken to a low-country tea estate where we were royally entertained by a friend of Stephen's, a host with but one fault; he had no sense of time. We had meals at such unusual hours that we were sometimes hard put as to know what time of day or night it was! On another excursion we visited Batavia with its canals and Dutch architecture. Our hotel was very smart but with no fans and unbearably hot and airless, whilst the meal in a Chinese restaurant of ants' eggs and asparagus soup, though revolting to look at was, surprisingly, quite delicious. The day ended in a nightclub where we drank beer and watched people of all races, in all manner of dress, dancing to an excellent band. We returned to the hotel at 4 a.m. It had all been quite fun, but I'm afraid I found the gay life too much like hard work!

I far preferred the many delightful glimpses, encountered on our travels through the villages, of the country folk going about their daily lives. Rice was ripening in the fields and I was struck by how picturesque the locals looked, walking along roads lined by tall trees, carrying sheaves of golden grain hung on bamboo poles slung across their shoulders. On our arrival back at Kertasarie, where Mother and Gillian had been keeping each other company, we visited the estate's market held each week for the convenience of the labour. Walking amongst them we again experienced an apparent lack of interest from the locals, but realising that they expected us to talk to them first, and after learning the right word to use, were instantly rewarded by friendly smiles and warm greetings! There were some magnificent rams for sale in the market and we were told by Stephen that almost every Sundanese, the most predominant race in the area, had one. Ram fighting was a popular sport; betting was keen and the combatants so powerful that the sound of their heads crashing against each other could be heard at a considerable distance.

We tried not to let it spoil our holiday, but all the while a dark cloud of war was hovering. None of us could ever have foreseen its devastating impact on the world, but listening to Mr. Chamberlain's declaration on the radio, it was clear that serious trouble was brewing in Europe. We then received word from the Dutch Shipping Line that they had been ordered to return all their ships to Holland *via* Cape Town, so would only be able to take us as far as Singapore from where we would have to find our way back to Colombo. That was a bit of a blow, but there was nothing we could do about it. After driving to Bandoeng we flew into Batavia. Everything seemed the same as before, but behind the facade of cheerfulness was an awareness of coming change. Little did the Dutch know what they would face in the future.

Our ship was the same vessel on which Jim had travelled to Java a fortnight before, and he was welcomed with open arms by the quartermaster and carpenter with whom he had made friends. Like most Dutchmen both spoke English. September 15th, 1939, is a day none of us will ever forget. We arrived in Singapore around 6am and as soon as we had passed through immigration

Jim left us on board and dashed off to see what could be done about our return to India. Mother and I waited anxiously for news, entertained at intervals by his two pals, the carpenter and quartermaster, who tried to relieve our anxiety by cheerful talk. Finally, Jim returned having had no success at all, but as we could not stay on board indefinitely, he collected us and our belongings and took us up to Cook's office where we were prepared and fated to wait for hours. Apparently, we had no claim on the Dutch Shipping Line and since Jim and I had pretty well spent all our money, with just enough to take us home from Colombo, we might have been badly stuck. Fortunately, Mother, to be on the 'safe side' and unbeknown to us, had quite a sum in travellers cheques. Growing increasingly hot and weary, Jim continued to pester other shipping lines until at last, late in the afternoon, he managed to get two cabins on a Japanese boat sailing that evening. We thought our troubles were over but not a bit of it! Having got our tickets we then had to go through another lot of immigration, but when we got to the Immigration Office the place was closing and it was with great and obvious reluctance that the official was persuaded to do what was needed. Racing back to the docks in a taxi we discovered that the gates to the quayside had been locked and were told that no further passengers could board. Jim dashed off again with us in tow, and after making himself a nuisance thankfully found an official, less particular about the letter of the law, who allowed us in through a side gate and onto the ship.

Though better than nothing our cabins were dark and dreary, there was barely any deck space, and a curious attitude amongst the stewards. They were perfectly, in fact oppressively, polite, but there was an underlying something that, hard to pinpoint, suggested that we didn't know what we were in for! The mix of passengers was equally curious and included people of unrecognisable races, prosperous men from the Middle East, and several Roman Catholic priests. There were three characters who particularly caught our attention. The first two were an R.C. priest and his companion, a huge, dark, greasy looking man who might have been a Levantine, who spent their time eavesdropping on conversations on deck, snooping about the cabins at night, and becoming very excited whenever we neared land or arrived in port. We reached Penang too late to be allowed ashore whereupon the pair became highly agitated, and after complaining in what sounded like several languages went into a huddle as if devising some plot. However, despite having the appearance of archetypal smugglers or spies from some melodrama, they were probably quite ordinary citizens with unfortunate looks and manners.

The third man was a different character altogether. Small and mouse-like he tried to avoid notice, seemed to have no friends, and looked pale and ill. Jim spoke to him and by spending a good deal of time in his company discovered him to be a Jew who had fled Germany after losing all his family in one of Hitler's pogroms. After a series of terrible adventures he had arrived in China and set up a business, but just as it was beginning to prosper the Japanese invaded and he was forced to escape once more. It seemed odd that he had chosen to sail on a Japanese ship, but he was now on his way to Tel Aviv hoping to find peace and security. Having held his silence for so long the relief of having a sympathetic ear was so great that his words fairly tumbled over each other in an effort to get told. It was the same old story of persecution, murder and pursuit of people whose only 'crime' was their race. He told Jim that his first glimmer of hope was when, entering a British port, people had seemed not to notice the 'J' branded on his back, and indeed many did not even know what it meant. Whilst talking to Jim the man would often burst into tears too overcome by emotion to continue and revealed that he was unable to sleep. Despite being teetotal and refusing Jim's offer of brandy he was eventually persuaded to have some beer, and next morning confessed he had slept a little. On the day we arrived in Colombo he was desolate to be losing his one and only friend and inviting Jim down to his shared cabin - a horrible hole in the bowels of the ship - presented him with a bottle of clear liquid which he had received from a Jewish friend. We later discovered that the name of the drink was Arak-du-Vin and what potent stuff it was, but sadly, we never heard what became of that man.

Colombo was already a changed place. Sailors and troops filled the hotels and guns were out on the Galle Face. At nightfall hotel lights were blacked out, cars and buses drove with dimmed lights, and on the train all the way from Colombo to Veyangoda we travelled in complete darkness. Our arrival in Madura, however, was as usual a joyful occasion. It was lovely to be back and after settling my weary mother in bed Jim and I talked with our dear friends and folk at the hospital until 2 am. Then, after two hours' sleep, set off on the final leg home. Early in the morning on our first day back I was awakened by the heavenly yet tuneless song of a Malabar Whistling Thrush and, looking outside, saw a male with deep iridescent blue plumage and a long tail, which he would spread out now and again. For whatever reason this shy bird, seldom seen so near a dwelling, had come right into the verandah outside our bedroom window. It was a wonderful welcome home and one I shall always remember.

We felt as though we had been travelling for ten weeks instead of ten days, and though it was a relief to stop moving there was a lot to get on with. Once again, Jim took up the reins of the estate, whilst I took charge of Kardana amidst looking after Mother, visiting the creche and resuming my sewing classes at the arts and crafts school. Then, just before Christmas, the doctor departed and I was saddled with running the dispensary which, despite being enjoyable, meant additional work.

The Splendours of Kashmir and the Taj Mahal

The war years were years of intense work, worry and crises. Jim was now looking after both estates in our hills as both his friend E.C.S and Christopher, his assistant at Cloudland, had joined up. We still had guests in the bungalow, mainly Indian Government officials, and Jim was having to provide supplies of food, clothing and blankets for the estates' population of around 2000. There was also the worry over news from Europe, which seemed all the worse in the absence of neighbours with whom to confer. We heard of the fall of France and of Singapore, and the sinking of the two battleships in the China Sea and it all lay heavily on our hearts. I remember, when fighting really started in Europe, Jim getting out his old maps which he had used in Flanders, but they were already out of date and useless, and in a matter of days we had lost all the land that had been fought for and won during WWI.

It soon became evident that Jim needed real leave, not just a day or two here and there. His Home leave was due in 1940 but of course that was impossible, so his firm decided to provide a locum and send Jim to Kashmir for three months. We had planned to leave in late September, but since the locum didn't arrive until mid-December, we eventually arrived in Srinagar just before Christmas and sadly missed the autumn colours.

The journey took us through country neither of us had seen before, revealing miles and miles of excellent, jungle-free land along the peninsula which, hilly or flat, required only water to make it highly productive. After three days on a train to Rawalpindi we drove to Srinagar in a hired car shared with two officers who were spending their leave in Kashmir. The steep road wound its way through the mountains, surrounded by sheer cliffs with fir trees clinging precariously to every possible ledge, whilst down below in the valley the river Jhelum roared in its rocky chasm, and when the gorge opened out for a short distance we were able to see logs being floated downstream from Kashmir to the plains of India. As we descended it seemed impossible to imagine that a valley, with houseboats on the river and lakes, could be found at the end of such a road. Then, as if a curtain had been swept aside, we found ourselves in a flat, beautiful plain in which fruit orchards and farms nestled along the now becalmed river. Our fellow travellers were heading for Gulmarg, many miles away and 8000 feet higher than Srinagar, but since one was looking particularly the worse for wear after the journey we persuaded them to stay with us the night. We had booked a houseboat complete with staff, but it was all a bit of pot luck since we had no idea about the state of the amenities. They were happy to accept our offer and so we drove to the club in Srinagar where we were directed to our boat which lay in the river close by. Our two servants, though surprised to see four instead of two guests, managed to rustle up a hearty meal, and after piling on heaps of blankets to ward off the bitter cold we climbed into bed to sleep the sleep of the exhausted.

We awoke to frost and after breakfast unpacked and explored our domain. It was quite a roomy boat, with a sitting room heated by a wood burning stove, a bedroom and bathroom. The kitchen was accommodated in another boat attached to the first, and beyond that, a smaller boat contained the servants' sleeping quarters. We also had use of a small rowing boat or 'shikara'. The houseboat next to ours belonged to the owner, Mrs B. Hailing from Ceylon knew many of our friends and relations, and we in turn became great friends, though admittedly she slightly disapproved of our queer habit of mixing with the Kashmiri shopkeepers! It was out of season and with no tourists the shopkeepers were less desperate to make sales than they would have been in summer. We were obviously not big spenders but, ever-courteous, they made us very welcome by offering us tea in priceless little porcelain cups. Highly scented, it had been carried by mules in the form of bricks all the way from China; a journey of several weeks through Tibet. Only slightly darker than light ale the brew looked very weak, but actually tasted delicious, even when flavoured with cardamom or cinnamon, and very refreshing. One of our new friends also treated us to a Persian meal served by our host's two stalwart sons as we sat on cushions on the floor of his wonderfully warm room. That too was delicious. Mountains of rice appeared, garnished with succulent mutton, cooked in various ways, and a dish of little discs of mutton, delicately spiced and grilled over the coals until they were crisp and literally melted in the mouth, was one of the nicest I have ever tasted!

When the meal was over, we were shown around the mosque where we took photographs and visited the tomb of Jesus of Nazareth. The locals believed that, rather than ascending to Heaven, Jesus simply disappeared into the sky then returned to Earth in Kashmir. Here he remained, preaching and gathering disciples until he died and was buried on the site now marked by the huge and highly impressive mosque in the centre of town. We were also taken, this time by Mrs B, to an ancient Hindu temple built of soft green granite around 750

A.D. Whilst taking photos I noticed a charming, wide-eyed little girl watching us; her curiosity clearly stronger than her fear of strangers. I had a square camera with knobs on two sides and a viewfinder on top, so pretending to photograph the temple I was able to take a perfect shot of her without her even noticing.

Life on the river was fascinating. Alongside the usual fishing boats families had set up home on primitive houseboats and planted vegetable gardens on floating rafts. Most curious of all was the way in which people kept themselves warm by making small charcoal fires in earthenware pots, carried in basketwork containers under their voluminous robes. A highly unusual method and apparently the cause of a great deal of abdominal cancer. There is little or no wind in the vale of Kashmir so the river and the lake are always as clear and smooth as a mirror, reflecting the snowy mountains, the boats, the floating gardens, and the trees and houses on the banks. Autumn and winter are dry and apart from patches of snow the landscape is colourless, bar the blazing scarlet of new growth in the willow groves. However, Kashmir in spring, with her hills covered in wildflowers, fields of croci cultivated for saffron, and masses of irises and roses marking villages' burial grounds, must be a wonderful sight. In the poorer quarters, sods cut from the hillside to insulate the corrugated roofs of the mud-walled huts are also in flower and look so beautiful that we heard of a wealthy American who, regardless of cost, ordered a fully intact roof to be shipped to the States!

We visited many of the famous gardens around Srinagar: the Shalimar, the Ghash-Ma-Shai, and those made by Akhbar so that he and his harem could escape the summer heat of the plains. The journey must have taken weeks, and how he managed to transport his huge retinue by horse, camel and elephant on roads which back then would have been far worse and steeper than those we travelled, I cannot imagine. There is a poplar-lined road to the Banihal Pass through which we had intended to leave Kashmir, but having gone up it and found the pass blocked by snow we realised we would have to return the way we had come. In fact, all the passes had been blocked by snow making it impossible for me to fulfil a long-held dream of travelling the mountain road, known as the Golden Road, to Samarkand, Gilgit, and the Gangabal Lake, reputed to be the source of the Ganges. We did, however, manage a trip up to Gulmerg, although it was terribly snowy there too, and spent a lovely day enjoying glorious views of the Pamirs, some of which rise above 17,000 feet.

I was also delighted to catch a glimpse of a yellow-bellied blue magpie, looking especially lovely against the snowy landscape. The last few miles had to be done on horseback on tough little mountain ponies that looked too small to take Jim with his long legs!

After a wonderful break in Kashmir we continued to Behar to pick up my mother from my sister's house, and naturally couldn't resist visiting some of the many famous sights *en route*: the old fort in Delhi, the Taj Mahal in Agra, and Fatehpur Sikri, a city abandoned without ever having been inhabited. One hears much about the beauty of the Taj Mahal, but it was a revelation; no painting or photograph does it any sort of justice. Although I had never admired pictures of the building, which seemed too perfect and almost impersonal the reality was, I repeat, a revelation. Even though its dome was sheathed in scaffolding, we were, like most people who see it, bewitched by its wonderful workmanship; as perfect in the hidden corners as much as the more visible areas. We were sadly unable to visit it at either dawn or sunset, and I can well imagine how its ethereal qualities would be intensified on a still moonlit night. Some of the walls in the old fort in Agra are decorated with semi-precious stones, and we were fascinated by the almost prehistoric method involving a vice and a bow strung with fine wire, used to cut them to shape. It must have been a seemingly endless and highly laborious task but, apparently, time was of no consequence.

The fortnight spent at my sister and brother-in-law's house allowed us time to meet some of their friends and join in many of their activities. They ran several tiger shoots for wartime V.I.P.s but knowing our dislike of that sort of thing very kindly arranged an alternative expedition into the Bettiah jungle. We stayed in a jungle rest-house and spent two days wandering through the area on the backs of elephants, not seeing much in the way of game, but enjoying the lovely countryside in what must be the best way possible. Our elephants travelled quietly, cleverly removing branches and other obstacles as they went along and made me long to travel likewise through our Yarushnaad Valley where, unlike the Bettiah, game had no cause to fear elephants, having never been shot at from one's back. I resolved to manage at least one such trip before we left India, but Jim was too tired by the time the war ended and alas, we retired without fulfilling that vow.

Years had passed since my sister had been south and since her husband had never been to that part of India, they decided to come back with us. They loved our beautiful hills but could have done without the leeches, despite their number being low at the beginning of the year. Interested in wildlife, they spent many hours walking in our jungle, which different to theirs, offered opportunities to spot new species of birds and once, by sheer luck, a black leopard appeared on a rock beside the stream where they were sitting.

Wartime Rationing
1942

Not long after my sister and brother-in-law had left, our troubles over food for the labour and our Indian staff began. Rice, their staple diet, was becoming increasingly difficult to obtain and rising steeply in price. The Company continued to sell rice to the coolies at a set price taking a loss themselves, but as stocks ran low, we were forced to make unwelcome changes. At the time, various types of pulse were comparatively easy if not cheap to source, but when we told the coolies that they would have to eat their curry with pulses they were horror- struck! Whoever heard of pulse and curry? Pulses were acceptable as an accompaniment to rice, but as a substitute? Impossible! Jim had started a canteen at which the labour could get a mid-day meal, but even the cooks refused to entertain this new diet and our attempts to convert the coolies failed once more. In an attempt to remedy the situation, I asked Porges to cook a huge vat of pulses then bring it down to the canteen for the cooks to serve with one of their special curries. The coolies viewed their helpings with deep suspicion then watched furtively as Jim and I, to set an example, ate ours with relish. Though rather too peppery for our taste it was exceedingly good. First one and then another of the coolies tried a mouthful, and eventually most of them ate their portions. Jim and I ate with them for a day or two while this new regime was launched. There were no ill effects and much to our amazement the coolies were convinced by this curious new way of mixing traditional food

However, within a few months the supply of pulses, besides being terribly expensive, began to dry up and we had to think again. We managed to source wheat, which being closer to rice was less suspect, but again we ran into trouble. The coolies helped themselves as liberally to the wheat grains as they would to rice but given that it is less easily digested suffered stomach-aches, which in turn fuelled a rumour that Indian people could not eat wheat. Again, Jim and I went to the canteen, this time to explain to the labour that wheat, being stronger than rice, had to be eaten in smaller quantities. They were very polite, if seemingly unconvinced, but we heard no more complaints except that their stomachs were never really full. When finely ground, wheat is more digestible and easier to cook, so Jim installed a power-driven mill in the factory for everyone to use whenever they liked. It proved very popular, and we too took advantage of the mill, using the rougher ground wheat as porridge, and the finer as flour to make the most delicious brown bread. We were particularly glad of the latter since the quality of white flour, delivered each month from Madura, was becoming worse and worse. Later still, as the war progressed, wheat also became scarce and it was necessary to ask the coolies to put up with yet another kind of food; this time maize. It was a most unfortunate business. The first consignment, unfortunately very large, was weevil- ridden and had to be ground very fine to make it edible and the labour hated it. What would have been pleasant to a Bantu labour force was purgatory to Tamils; they moaned, of course they moaned, but to our amazement persevered then submitted.

Thankfully, unbeknown to the labour, I began exploring the use of jungle plants as a form of nourishment. As children we had often eaten nettles and since there were many local varieties, I wrote to the agricultural college in Coimbatore to seek their advice. How we laughed when snubbed by their appalled response that Indians never ever eat nettles! Adapting to new food is far more difficult for anyone used to just one or two staples than those who enjoy a more varied diet, and we prayed that no further changes would be necessary. Sadly, this was not to be and before the war ended we had to ask those poor people, once again, to live on a strange and alien food; rye. This upset them more than anything else and we were most sympathetic, given that they had already put up with so much of their diet being mucked about with good grace and patience. Women and children then began to fall ill with severe stomach ache, and indeed the health of the whole labour force was affected. We rightly guessed that this was being caused by black-market rice, which at the time was entering Travancore via its jungles. In an attempt to arrest the problem the Government had ordered Jim to post printed notices warning: "It is illegal to bring rice into the estate. Anyone seen doing so will be severely punished." He duly displayed the posters around the factory and in various places where everybody could see them regardless of the fact that few could read, but I am afraid he had no intention of 'seeing' anything! Often, when walking round the estate, Jim would stop to examine a bush or gaze at the view and catch a glimpse of a furtive figure laden with what can only have been rice, slipping out of sight. However, having watched these people endure years of disruption to their diet, he always turned a blind eye!

One Monday morning towards the end of the war, Jim announced that he had no food at all for the weekend and didn't know where any was coming from. With 2000 people depending on us for their food supply we had an anxious week ahead. Our labour was flexible, but in many villages in South India what can be eaten is centred around people's religious observations, and despite having access to maize and wheat they were on the brink of starvation. It was a curious illustration of how people will adhere to the rules of their caste to the point of death and reminded me of an incident witnessed at an Anglo-Indian wedding during the worst of the food shortage. I have no idea how they sourced it, but there was enough for a handsome feast. At the end, servants began to throw away enormous quantities of leftover rice and horrified, I told them that it should be given instead to the dozens of the beggars who were currently starving in the city. "But madam," came the reply "these beggars are high-caste and would rather die than touch any food cooked or touched by us!"

Another of Jim's worries concerned the supply of clothes. The rationing in force in the hot plains of India was all very well but caused difficulties in our hills where the weather was often cold and wet. As far as I can recall women were allowed seven yards of cloth per year: six for a sari, and one for a short jacket, whilst the men's ration was five yards. Very young children in the plains do not wear clothes, so their ration of two and half yards only applied to those over three years old. We were a tiny minority, of course, and special laws could not be made just to suit us, but the men and women working in our fields were regularly soaked by either the dew or rain and their clothes wore out very quickly.

On one of our trips to Madura we went round various places hoping to find a solution to our problem, and after a long search found a funny little mill making woven vests for men and boys. During the assembly process the selvedges were trimmed off and seeing a huge pile lying in the yard we bargained with the owner and took it back to the estate. The carpenters were asked to make large numbers of knitting needles from bamboo and we set every girl to knitting. They made vests for baby brothers and sisters, followed by clothes for themselves. They also taught their mothers to knit, and before long practically every female and even a few of the boys were knitting! This certainly helped, but men's shorts and shirts could hardly be knitted and nor could the women's saris, all of which were fast wearing out. To see what could be done, Jim made a quick trip to the cotton mills on the outskirts of Madras. He was cheerfully met by one of the managers who, eager to help, asked how many yards were required then almost fainted when told 2000 yards! He initially offered just 100 yards, but after numerous phone calls and many delays Jim finally got his cloth. Meanwhile, in search of fabric for the women's saris I had gone round the Madura bazaars and managed to amass a queer assortment of cotton material, some of high quality from abroad, some hand-woven khaddar cloth, and some highly coloured thin cotton which although unlikely to be durable, had the advantage of being very cheap. Though not enough to cover their needs it would tide the women over. Having returned to the estate with our booty I decided to issue the women with their fabric myself by setting up shop in the creche. The bright colours of the cheap material deceived nobody and the good stuff went first, but the whole experience was fun and gave rise to a couple of illuminating incidents.

A sweeper-woman came to the shop asking for one yard of a rather nice material to make her baby a jacket. I measured the yard and cut it off, but when I gave it to the lady she held it up saying: "This is not a yard Ammal!" and burst into tears. I could not imagine what was troubling her so made her watch as I measured it again. Yet still she murmured: "It is not a yard; I've never seen such a yard!" And then it all came out. Because of her caste, she was prohibited from entering many of the cloth shops and made to take what she was given, usually less than she had paid for. Hence, her tears were tears of joy! It was sadly very common for poor Dravidians, especially the uneducated and illiterate, to be cheated by shop owners who, taking full advantage of the fact that these villagers could ill afford to travel further afield, charged whatever they pleased.

Whilst running the shop, I quickly noticed that the labour disliked being given change in old notes; something that continued to cause resentment despite my reasoning that they were just as good as the new ones and had the same value. Eventually, one man explained: "That might be fine for the Dorai and you but for us it is different. Whenever we give the shopkeeper an old note he refuses to give us change and we are made to take goods to the value of the whole note. We are forced to have to buy things we do not want." I reported back to Jim, and from then on wages were paid in new notes ordered from the bank in Madura. It was yet another example of the many unjust situations with which the illiterate and uneducated had to contend. The Indian Government was doing a great deal to stop it, and to my mind the money-lenders and shopkeepers should have been held accountable, but it was so ingrained in society that finding a solution was terribly difficult and education was really the only answer.

Angus, Snakes and a Troublesome Tiger

]Towards the end of the war, Jim was sent an assistant who had been too young to serve as a soldier. A lover of snakes, Angus regularly sent skins to both the South Kensington Natural History Museum and the Bombay Natural History Society. Prior to him leaving us, and to his credit, he discovered two new varieties of known species as well as one completely new species which was named after him. Indians hate snakes, whether poisonous or not, and so Angus's habits were a great source of anxiety to his servant. I would often see his 'boy' taking him tea in the early morning, whereupon he would open his door a crack, peer in fearfully in case some of Angus's pets might have escaped during the night, and then advance towards the bed slowly, ready to put down the cup and fly at a moment's notice!

There were many snakes in our jungle, few of which were poisonous. Angus taught me which ones were safe to handle, and I came to enjoy the feel of their slim bodies and admire their graceful movements. Before his arrival I had handled the little green grass snakes, but now became bolder and thanks to Angus learnt more about them. Curiously, the normally poisonous snakes seemed to be less venomous up in our hills; something which Angus attributed to the high altitude. Be that as it may, we still had several cases of snakebite including one man who was bitten twice on the neck by a particularly poisonous pit viper, although he thankfully recovered. Down in the lower valleys, snakes were as poisonous as anywhere else. They were rarely seen, but I remember hearing an alarming story about a snake found by a man in the valley through which we walked when visiting distant cardamom estates. Hillmen had captured it by pinning its head to the ground with a pronged stick, and assuming it was a constrictor, the man shot it and bought the skin. He then sent it to be cured by a firm in Madura with a note saying that he wanted to have the enclosed python skin made into shoes for his wife. Much to his surprise, he received a letter by return notifying him that the skin was, in fact, that of a black cobra, a Hamadryad, one of the deadliest snakes and in this case, at over 18 feet, the longest they had ever seen. When one realises that a cobra, when striking at its prey, lifts a third of its length off the ground, one can imagine what a terrifying creature that must have been when alive.

Not long before we left India, we had a difficult time on the estate with a tigress. She began by killing our tiny transport donkeys; one every other day.

Often there was nothing but a few scraps left, for those little donkeys were not much more than a fully grown tigress could manage in one meal. On occasion, she was disturbed and left her meal and Angus would then keep watch nearby in an attempt to shoot her. That tigress, however, seemed to lead a charmed life. Shooting at night without the proper equipment is very difficult and the 'Heath Robinson' style gadgets we rigged up were all in vain. We tried strapping a torch onto the barrel of his rifle or placing it within easy reach, but something always went wrong and he became more and more frustrated. Then one night, when he was lying in wait on a flat grassy patch behind a tree, she came up behind him and in Angus's words, "sat so close beside me that I could hear her licking her lips as if her mouth were watering at the thought of a change of diet." Angus admitted he was terrified, but the tigress passed him by and walked to her kill in the ravine below. Angus switched on his torch and fired, but at the last minute his torch slipped and he missed. He returned to the bungalow crestfallen but after dinner, determined not to be defeated, announced he'd give it another go. This time we helped him make a rest for his rifle so that he could train it on the kill, whilst leaving a hand free for his torch. Within half an hour the tigress was back, but once again Angus missed.

By this time we were beginning to think that the animal might have been wounded, and if so, would pose a possible danger to human life. She then killed a young bull, unfortunately in a location unsuited for the erection of a machan or somewhere safe where Angus could sit in wait. Angus therefore decided to take Christopher along and after drawing lots it was decided that Angus would wield the torch, and his companion, the rifle. The kill was in a gully with a rock face above and a strip of jungle with a stream running through it below. We spied out the land and reckoned that the tigress would almost certainly be lying up by the stream, waiting till dusk before returning to her meal. About thirty feet above the kill lay a small mossy platform about the size of a large sofa which afforded good views of both the kill and the surrounding rocky hillside. It was unlikely that the tigress would be able to approach from any other direction without being seen so around five o'clock in the afternoon the two young men took up position, eyes glued to the little piece of jungle below. However, just as it was getting dark they heard an animal cough somewhere above them, and along strolled the tigress directly towards them! Between the tigress and the men were a few strobilanthus shrubs, not large enough to prevent a fully grown tigress from passing through, but enough to effectively hide her, making a shot difficult. Just as she drew level she swung towards them whereupon Angus directed the beam of the torch towards her and Christopher, as he put it afterwards, fired into a "wall of stripes". The tigress leapt in the air and disappeared over a rise on the hillside. They then faced a dilemma: should they sit there all night in fear of being attacked by a wounded tigress, or make for the bungalow with the same fear of attack, but with a restful night ahead if they made it? They decided on the latter and the pair turned up around nine o'clock excited to tell us their story. The next morning, we all went to the ledge where they had been sitting and seeing the tracks of the tigress only six feet away, followed her trail for some 80 yards to a spot where the animal lay stone dead.

She was in good condition thanks to an adequate diet of donkey, but one of her front paws had been pierced by a porcupine quill and the pain would have prevented her from being able to hunt her natural prey. It also explained the 'licking of her lips' that Angus had described, since the poor beast must have continually stopped to lick her festered paw. Her persistence in returning to her kill, even after being shot at, showed how desperately hungry she had been and had her diet of donkeys run dry she might easily have turned into a man-eater. It was therefore just as well that she had been destroyed. And as for her corpse, every last bit of that tigress's meat was naturally devoured by the men of the estate.

Rajan, Rabid Dogs and Donkeys

In the aftermath of the war there were fewer Europeans available to run the tea estates and many British companies were forced to break their closed - shop policy and take on Indians as assistants, one of whom was contracted to Cloudland. Rajan, from the Malabar coastal area, was an intelligent, very pleasant boy with beautiful manners. His parents and siblings were well educated and literate in English, and also accustomed to speaking it. Rajan, though able to speak his own language, could neither read nor write Malayalam. After initially living with us, and once versed in what was expected of him, Rajan moved to Cloudland where Jacob could teach him all he needed to know about estate work. It must have been very lonely for a young Indian boy living away from home for probably the first time in his life, but between weekends with us and occasional visits from his sisters, brother and uncle, he managed very well. His brother, Rabindra, was an officer in the Indian merchant navy, and though less highly educated than Rajan he was an exceptional and intelligent young man. He also harboured an unusual appreciation of western classical music and whenever they stayed with us it was delightful to hear Rabindra whistling some well-known aria or a bit of some symphony as he went about the bungalow. The firm then decided to transfer Rajan to another estate; a move that filled him with trepidation. Because of his background Rajan had no self- esteem, and though sometimes tearing strips off him in private, Jim did all he could to boost his sense of authority by publicly backing all that he did. We parted in sorrow, and sadly, without Jim's level of support, his progress was curtailed. Poor Rajan was such a nice lad, but for all his Western ways he was a product of the East and in his case ill-equipped to face life's harsh realities.

We were therefore surprised when one day he paid us a visit looking particularly happy and lively, and when asked what had happened to make him so cheerful, he replied: "It is my lucky day. A beggar came to my bungalow this morning." To Indians a visit from a beggar is considered lucky since it provides an opportunity to practice charity. Westerners are apt to judge Indians as ungrateful without realising the subtle difference between their perception of gratitude and ours. For them good deeds are done to please God, or to acquire merit, and thus the donor is more likely to be grateful to the recipient as opposed to the other way round, for giving them the opportunity to do good.

I have lived long enough in the East to become accustomed to that point of view, and in many ways prefer it. Since moving to Britain I have been told by many folk that they can't feel any compassion for refugees, since no matter how much help they receive they show no gratitude. But perhaps they would feel differently if instead they recognised that the gratitude lies in their being given the chance to help those in need!

During the war years we had visits from our son, serving in India prior to being dispatched to the African campaign, Christopher, stationed on the Burmese frontier, and several naval men and soldiers on short leave. These visits provided the perfect excuse for treks into the jungle and expeditions to see game, all of which was great fun. One or two of our guests, having experienced what we had to offer, came back again and again, whilst others, finding the jungle and leeches unbearable, felt that once was enough!

One day, when Mother and I were sitting on the verandah one of the load coolies, who came up from the plains with supplies, arrived in a great hurry to tell us that four weary Dorais were walking up the hill and could we send down some drinks? I rustled up some coffee and sandwiches along with a note inviting them up to the bungalow for lunch. We were curious to meet them and after waiting a while four officers appeared; three British, and one Indian. Sent by their unit to see if any land in these hills was suitable for jungle training camps, they had not intended to bother us, but since the weather was cold and wet readily accepted our invitation to stay and use the bungalow as a base. All four were keen to know more about our remote estate and the Indian, a doctor, was particularly interested in the general health of the labour and the presence of malaria. Much to his surprise, Jim returned from lunch on Cloudland to find the floor of the verandah strewn with men examining maps, and after hearing their story arranged for me to escort them in the direction of areas in our main jungle most suited to their needs. As usual, I was delighted for an excuse for a trek and we set off early the next morning, stopping on our usual rock to de-leech and survey the jungle below, then walking for several more miles. However, despite being otherwise ideal, they decided that our jungle's leeches, which had to be seen to be believed, and difficult access, made the area unsuitable for training. We had, nevertheless, enjoyed a very pleasant day together and the Major, a butterfly enthusiast, later kept his promise to return and collect some interesting specimens.

That evening, when the creche was about to close, their doctor asked if he might take a spleen count; a request that was met with great excitement by all of the children. He was, however, only interested in those under ten and when told, the older children were deeply offended that the doctor Dorai did not want to poke their tummies and demanded to know what was so special about the 'babies'. Highly amused, the doctor proceeded to poke everyone's tummies and even practiced a few phrases in Tamil, not his native tongue, which equally delighted the children.

It was around this time that we experienced what might have turned into a very nasty incident, though it was bad enough as it was. Jim and I were walking to the factory one afternoon, leaving Mother reading on the verandah, when suddenly, a thin, strange looking dog ran out from behind the arts and crafts school, causing our own dogs to give chase. We then heard a howl from the stray, and entering the factory, found everyone in a terrible state. The dog had run into the building, up the stairs to the withering lofts, and from there off towards the lines and our bungalow. I dashed off in a panic; there were children in the lines and Mother sitting in the open verandah. As soon as I got to the bungalow I told Mother to shut the door nearest to her while I shut the others, but just as she pushed hers shut the dog flung itself against the other side! It then jumped through the open dining room window, bit a servant in the leg, and sped off towards the lines.

Jim, meanwhile, had given the estate watchman a rifle and sent him to hunt down what we now realised was a mad dog. It was eventually shot, but not before biting the watchman in the stomach. The dog's head was sent away to be examined, and just as we feared reports confirmed that it had had rabies. Neither of our dogs had been bitten, but as a precaution both they and the two men who had been attacked were sent to the nearest Pasteur Institute for treatment. They all returned after three weeks having had all the necessary injections, and thankfully, little the worse for their horrid experience.

Late in 1944, we were sent to Britain for six months' leave and during our absence, Jim's relief manager had a bright idea on how our transport difficulties could be eased. Our food supplies were still being carried up from the plains either on men's heads or on the backs of tiny Indian donkeys, so he decided to invest in a number of South African donkeys; strong beasts, sure-footed and hence, supposedly ideal for the work involved. The donkeys were duly bought and delivered to the estate, but from the very outset proved an utter headache. It soon became apparent that there was not nearly enough grass for both them and the cattle which were essential for milk, and over and above the special food provided to compensate the lack of grazing, they ate everything they could get hold of, including the palm leaf walls and roofs of the latrines! The leeches were also a problem; every bite became septic as did every other wound they sustained. Forced to live in such an alien environment, they became increasingly thin and out of condition and eventually died. It was an unfortunate episode, and lessons learned we decided to make do until the end of the war when an outlet road could be built for cars and lorries.

By now, practically all the women on the estate were knitting, but while most of the very young children had some sort of garment to keep out the cold I was still very concerned about the newborns. For some reason, perhaps to avoid tempting providence, the women did not stock up in advance of a birth, and susceptible to the cold and damp, babies could fall ill and die. Since most of my leisure time was spent knitting, I decided to focus on making tiny garments to be laid aside ready to protect any new babies that arrived.

Riots and the Dawn of Independence
1945

In the period running up to Independence, India was torn by riots during which many people died or were brutally murdered. Amongst those who had narrow escapes were my sister and brother-in-law, as well as Monica, Stephen and their three children, who were staying with them at the time. Behar was very much a trouble spot, and the whole family had to flee at the dead of night to get to the nearest town.

Our journey back to the estate after Home leave in 1945 was a series of unfortunate occurrences. We arrived in Bombay to mutiny by the Indian navy; a nasty situation which soon turned very threatening. The harbour outside our hotel was afloat with naval vessels from which men began shouting through megaphones: "You shoot, we shoot. We have guns trained on the Taj Hotel and the Yacht Club". The hotel was barricaded and outside many were killed in the riots that filled the streets. Despite the fires, lit to prevent cars driving through, we watched two buses, one full of Hindus and the other of Muslims, careering along and swaying dangerously close together while their passengers hurled insults and abuse at one another.

It was critical that we catch the Madras train that night by whatever means available and we managed to hire, at a fabulous cost, a taxi whose driver, a Persian, was willing to run the gauntlet of the rioting crowds. Our offer of the spare seats to anybody prepared to come with us was accepted by a young couple and together we made a dash for the station on the most alarming drive I have ever experienced. Our driver, who seemed to have a particular aversion to anybody wearing a Congress or 'Gandhi' cap, insisted on charging towards them, and then proceeded to crash through fires in the road, mercifully avoiding setting the car alight and the stones being hurled from one side to another! It was a blessed relief to arrive at the station in one piece, and moreover on time for our train, which enabled our escape from Bombay. Our troubles, however, were far from over. The staff at our hotel in Madras had gone on strike leaving the guests to fend for themselves. We then heard that the train from Madura had been heavily stoned and when forced to stop some passengers had been murdered; particularly alarming news since we were booked on the night mail train from Madras to Madura.

It was therefore with some trepidation that we boarded our train, whereupon we were further warned of riots *en route* and, as a precaution, advised to close the steel mesh shutters and not to show ourselves at any of the stations. Nevertheless, Jim, being a friendly soul, struck up a conversation with two Indians in the next carriage, and after joining them for a long and pleasant chat found them warm and friendly. Every station along the way was teeming with people shouting and wearing Congress caps, and noticing that they paid special attention to our carriage, it began to dawn on us that our next-door neighbours were in some way connected with the rioters. Our suspicions were raised when we were met by a particularly loud throng at Trichinopoly in the early hours of the morning. There was always a long wait at this station and we had been dreading it, but we need not have worried. Hearing the din, one of our neighbours put his head out the window and shouted: "No noise please. There is a lady trying to sleep next door!" His authority had clearly been recognised, for things quietened down considerably, and much later we learned that one of those men had, in fact, been the South Indian Communist leader!

We had been wondering what Madura would be like but were not surprised to find a mob as large and unruly as those at the other stations. With no chance of a porter, we began to hump our luggage from the carriage, and using Tamil vernacular I joked to Jim: "We're all coolies now!" A roar of laughter immediately arose from the crowd. One of the men standing nearby took our tickets and cleared the way to the exit, whilst others picked up our bags. It was all quite fantastic and feeling somewhat bewildered, we were soon winding our way through the streets following a procession of rioters carrying our belongings! I can only attribute their hospitable reception to our speaking vernacular Tamil. They were as friendly as you please, but as soon as we had paid and thanked them, they quickly reunited with the rioters who continued to shout and boo at the passengers and brandish the carriages with such slogans as "Go back, white dogs!"

Tamils laugh easily and are not ideally suited to rioting. Mr S., the D.S.P. and a friend of ours had a curious experience during these same riots. He was a most remarkable shot with a revolver and had become quite famous in and around Madura. A furious mob had gathered on the dry bed of the River Vaigai and he and some of his police had gone down to deal with the situation. Identifying the ringleader, he drew his revolver and shot the man in the arm. The D.S.P. was fluent in Tamil and as the man was being put in his car to be taken to hospital he cracked a somewhat questionable earthy joke which made the crowd laugh. They dispersed quietly and the patient was left in the doctor's hands. Later that evening when he went to the hospital to enquire after the wounded man, he heard gales of laughter coming from the ward. Peeping around the door he saw his victim, arm bandaged, sitting up in bed, keeping the whole ward entertained with a vivid description of what had happened. "Imagine", he exclaimed, "The D.S.P. himself shot me and furthermore, took me in his own car to this hospital!" He continued by repeating the earthy remark made by the D.S.P. which was greeted with even louder roars of laughter. Mr S. then walked through the door and apart from being greeted like an old friend was proudly introduced by the patient as the man who had shot him!

A New India and a New Road

The rest of our journey home passed without incident and all was well on the estate. It was now 1945 and we were nearing the end of our life in India. Men began to trickle back from the forces, swelling the European population. E.C.S. and Christopher returned and overnight Jim changed from being a 'jack of all trades' to a group manager.

Some years previously, Jim had traced an outlet road running eastward from the estate to the plains, and now that our community was increasing it was revised to create a road fit for motorised traffic. It was a difficult trace, requiring whole sections to be blasted out of solid rock, but before we left in 1948 the entire length of twenty-three miles had been completed and was regularly used by jeeps and lorries albeit with some difficulty.

On Independence Day, Jim gave the coolies a feast whilst I hosted a party for the Women's Club. A table was laid in the factory, with a centerpiece of the Indian flag which I created from flowers. Though not a thing of beauty it was much appreciated by our members. Then came the shocking news that Mahatma Gandhi had been killed. It was a tragic day for all of India. If, as initially feared, his assassin had been Muslim there would have been unprecedented bloodshed the length and breadth of the land, so it was therefore something of a relief to learn that he had been killed by a fellow Hindu. All the Indians on the estate took the loss of their beloved Mahatma very badly indeed, and in sympathy Jim gave everyone the day off and hosted a dinner for one and all. There then followed a procession to the muster ground where, under the Indian flag flying at half-mast, speeches were presented by Jim, the doctor and Aroliah.

Little by little, we began to accustom the labour to the fact that we would be leaving, but despite our best efforts, they held firm to the belief that we would one day return. We now had a fully qualified doctor, who with much help from his wife ably covered the two estates.

They were Brahmins and liked by everybody, but Ratnam was still the goddess as far as the women were concerned. I remember a Pillai woman saying to me "When Ammal goes we will have the new doctor and his wife which is good, but better still our Swami nurse Ammal" This was a great compliment to Ratnam, since it was very rare for a member of a 'superior' caste to praise a despised Harijan.

Just before we were due to leave, we invited a preacher to hold a service in the factory. He was head of a small party who were going round the estates in the surrounding districts hoping to gather enough funds from their congregations' collections to buy a portable harmonium. The preacher was a good singer and a master raconteur who made the story of the flood as vivid and dramatic as an exciting whodunnit. A skilled orator, he gave each character a distinctive voice, and that of God, deep and resonant with an undertone, which filled the audience with a curious thrill. Delivered in the vernacular, it was more akin to a play than any bible reading ever heard before or since, and I would not have missed it for the world.

As you have gathered, the labour had a pretty grim time during the war, so, to give them a little fun now and again we bought ourselves an 8mm cine-projector. Films were hired from a cine film library, and our fortnightly shows became tremendously popular stimulating much interest and discussion. Held in either the factory or in the creche, they were scheduled to begin at 7.30pm, but by 4pm, every nook and cranny was packed to suffocation point, and when I eventually came down to start proceedings, often found it quite difficult to find room for myself and my projector! The only thing they ever complained about was the length of the films, since unlike Tamil versions which usually last for several hours, mine seldom ran more than an hour and a half. Charlie Chaplin was easily the favourite, followed by the adventures of a gang of little American boys and their dogs. 'Rin-Tin-Tin' featuring a German Shepherd dog and Bob Hope were also popular. They were all silent films of course, but none of the audience could read the captions, so the better the miming, the better their understanding of the plot. Having exhausted the selection available, we tried repeats and found them just as popular as the first-time round. There was, however, one film they would happily watch again and again. I had taken a roll of people working on the estate and whenever anyone they knew appeared on screen, the audience would greet them with cheers and hand clapping.

With the exception of missionaries, I felt that we gained a better understanding of Tamils as people than most Europeans, and for that reason alone my story is worth telling. Many expats live insular lives, consciously distancing themselves from the local community, and I doubt whether anything they gain as a result can ever be as rewarding or worthwhile as what they stand to lose. A little friendliness brings such a wonderful return. I remember when travelling to Madura one wet and windy day our bus broke down, requiring all passengers to get out and push. I immediately joined them, and whilst there were exclamations of horror, everyone thought it a wonderful thing for a white woman to do. Those who had been friendly on the bus became even more so, and when the bus came to life, I was first to be lifted by many willing hands onto the moving vehicle. When we eventually arrived very late in Madura, one of the passengers raced off and collected a jutka to take me to the hospital. My suitcases and I were meanwhile bundled into a phone box, and though they were just as wet as me, some of the women passengers formed a screen to protect my privacy whilst I changed out of my wet clothes.

There always was a huge fund of goodwill to be tapped, if only we white women relinquished any notion of false superiority. This unfortunate trait, though common amongst mem-sahibs, was strangely more prevalent amongst Anglo-Indians. Inordinately proud of their white blood, the Anglo-Indians would rather starve than do anything that might insult their dignity and to honour their European origins would rather wear worn and ragged Western clothes than dress in saris.

I remember an occasion when the Anglo-Indian nurse who had helped deliver Monica's third child, fell ill and was discovered by the local parson lying on a mattress on the floor whilst her husband, an absolute rotter, commandeered the only bed in the house. Appalled, he told the man in no uncertain terms that he was good for nothing, bar going to the liquor shop and squandering all his earnings on drink and had no chance of getting a job or keeping it unless he changed his ways. He also ordered him to immediately relinquish the bed to his genuinely sick wife. With great indignation, the nurse leapt up and exclaimed that her husband always paid a boy to carry home his liquor; clearly more insulted by the accusation that he had demeaned himself by going to the liquor store than by wasting all their money on drink or making her sleep on the floor!

The notion that carrying anything was beneath them was widespread. I recall seeing Anglo- Indians coming to a mission in Madras for their weekly ration of rice, and despite living in extreme poverty, paying 9 rupees to a small Indian child to carry their rice back to their horrible shanty huts. It was small wonder that the Anglo-Indians with their ridiculous insistence on their British origin had a bad time of it soon after Independence, and indeed, it took some time before they bowed to the inevitable and called themselves Indian.

Final Adventures and Ongoing Injustices

I suspect that to the reader the camps described sound very similar but allow me the indulgence of describing our last: a two-day expedition to a high hill with a cousin and her son who had never camped before. Accompanied by Angus and Christopher, we arrived at the campsite in the early afternoon then went off exploring while load coolies erected our tents, built a small grass hut and prepared our meal. The three young men would sleep in the hut, Jim in the inner part of our little tent, and my cousin and I under the shelter of the outer part, spread over some bushes to keep off the dew, but open at the sides so that we could see out. After dinner we sat by a campfire singing songs and telling stories till it was time to go to bed. As always, I was too excited to sleep on the first night, but there must have been a big cat on the prowl and the calls of alarm from the sambhur and the muntjac kept everyone awake. It quietened down eventually, although the monkeys still had a lot to say in the small hours of the morning!

The next day was spent trekking to the nearest boundary of the land belonging to the estate, from where we could see right into the grasslands of Travancore and in the mist, beyond the great stretch of jungle, Periyar. Unaccustomed to walking long distances over rough ground, our guests had had enough by the time we got back to camp, and after stand-up baths and a good supper, gratefully retired to bed. However, as soon as I lay down I became aware of a queer buzzing sound coming from somewhere inside the tent. I switched on my torch and unable to see anything that might be causing it, lifted the edge of my mat to be greeted by a roar of wings, as a dozen bluebottles flew into my face. Then, lifting the mat a little more, shuddered when hit by a second, mightier wave of these enormous, egg-laden brutes. I roused my cousin and to our horror, discovered that they were everywhere and had covered our blankets with their revolting eggs. We called the men to our rescue, but since they were either sound asleep or pretending to be, we were forced to deal with the problem ourselves. Having dragged our mats to the fire, we raked up the embers, and scorched off the bluebottles as much as we could. We then used torches of flaming wood to sweep the shelter and burn the flies on the ground. After being exposed to the cold mountain air we were frozen, and though highly unappealing, rolled ourselves up in our now scorched blankets and finally fell asleep. Not surprisingly, the men heard exactly what we thought of them when they awoke refreshed the next morning! Whilst our gear was being packed we went for a ramble and not far from camp discovered the rotting carcass of a sambhur and the cause of our plague of flies.

By that point, my cousin must have felt that there were far more amusing things than camping. She was, however, slightly appeased by Angus' proposal to erect a grass hut among the branches of a big tree beside a small lake on a hilly slope, about three miles from the bungalow. At an earlier date, he had shot a strange new dove from that same tree, which he sent to the Bombay Natural History Society for identification. In response, he received a long and detailed letter containing a passage which at the time had amused us and now seemed particularly ironic given my cousin's frame of mind: "We have received only one specimen before, and that was sent to us in 1917 when a certain Reverend Father went up into some mountains called the High Wavys to collect orchids and explore the forest. If you intend to go to these mountains, we must warn you that the track is very rough and arduous, the forest is thick, and the leeches terrible!"

Once completed, my cousin and I decided to spend a night in Angus' tree house. Accessed by a very steep ladder constructed from rough poles of bamboo, it sat some twenty-five feet above the ground and offered a magnificent view of the lake. However, despite being comfortable it was really too small for more than one person and would also have been better if the weather had been warmer and the moon had been full. I, nevertheless, managed to spend quite a few memorable nights up there, simply enjoying the sounds of the jungle. There wasn't much game to be seen, but one night, gazing across the lake, I noticed a ripple on the water and illuminated by the bright moonlight, the ghost-like form of a sambhur doe drinking at the edge of the bank. She stayed for a while then silently faded into the forest. On another of my vigils, this time at dawn, I was rewarded by the sight of a family of wild dogs, and trotting along with their red coats shining in the light of the rising sun, they looked for all the world like domesticated collies rather than the fearless hunters they were. Though not particularly exciting such simple pleasures filled me with joy, and with our departure now imminent both Jim and I treasured every poignant moment of our last two years in India.

One of the greatest advantages of the tree house was that it was beyond the reach of leeches! There is, however, one last tale to be told of these pests before I cease to mention them. Just a few months before we left India for good, Jim was looking for a new site on which to build a bungalow, as more accommodation would be needed for new assistants and managers when the estate expanded. He had only intended to set the team of surveyors off then return directly home, but the jungle looked so inviting, and though inadequately protected against leeches, I persuaded him to go just a little way in. However, whilst searching for a water supply, we somehow got lost and it took at least half an hour before we found our way out. The leeches were legion, every dead leaf on the jungle floor had its leech, waiting and praying for blood. By the time we reached the tea field we were in a sorry state: our shoes were full of blood, and great clusters of leeches covered our legs as if jockeying for position on the vein of their choice.

We hurried home and after Jim had washed off his masses with bowls of salt water the bathroom floor was red with his blood. Curious to see how many I had collected I made a quick count, and believe it or not, found ninety on one leg and seventy-four on the other! It was only after first applying a tincture of iron, and then stronger benzoin, and encasing our legs in yards of bandages, that we were fit to enter the bungalow. I felt no ill effects from my bleeding, but not so Jim who had bled for much longer. He still needed bandages the next morning, and later that day suffered a sort of black-out, possibly from loss of blood. I'm sure his tally was greater than mine, but he refused to demean himself by counting them!

The time then came for our last trek to the cardamom estates, and now that we knew we would not be along that way again, every mile previously taken more or less for granted seemed to hold some special fascination: a Malabar squirrel slipping silently along the branch of a tall forest tree, an elephant family moving across a hill, a distant view of a herd of bison, huge and black against the green grass, all seemed more beautiful than ever. Rather than taking our usual route we had to return home by way of Madura, where Jim had business.

Descending a steeper and rougher track, we were met by our agent in the plains and after a meal and change of clothes in a rest house, caught our train.

In the period of unrest following the declaration of Independence the rioting continued and we fully anticipated trouble in Madura, and, as Europeans, a degree of hostility from Indians. We were therefore pleasantly surprised when the group of Indians with whom Jim had chatted on the platform went out of their way to be friendly, and at every station on the journey called into our carriage to ask whether we wanted anything to eat and drink from the platform. We had been dreading trying to shop in Madura, but as it turned out nothing could have been easier, and once again locals were more than friendly and very helpful in their advice as to which streets and shops to avoid. We finished our shopping, and with nothing else to do whilst Jim spent time with the Collector, I sat in the car knitting. I then became aware of two women watching me from the courtyard and as they came closer, heard one ask the other: "What is she doing?" Seeing the second shake her head I invited them over, and delighted that I spoke their language, they chatted away as I showed them my knitting.

It transpired that they were calling on the Peria Dorai or Collector in an attempt to resolve a dispute over a piece of land that had belonged to the elder woman's late husband but had been taken from her following a claim by a relative. "It is awful," she said, "We have no other language than Tamil and when the interpreter translates what we say into English, the Peria Dorai gets angry. Nothing we say could possibly make him angry, but then again we have no idea what the interpreter is saying about us!" The two women begged me to come in and explain their situation to the Peria Dorai, and when I in turn told Jim what was happening, he spoke to the Collector on their behalf. Thanking Jim, he promised to look into the matter and see that the women were protected from their greedy relatives. We left hoping that we had made things easier for the widow and her daughter, though unconvinced, they continued to weep and beg for help. It had been the same old story of such high interest being charged on a loan that the original sum had been repaid many times over yet never been cleared, resulting in foreclosure on the debtor's death, and a life of beggary for his surviving family.

The next day we awoke to rain at 4.30am, and throughout our journey home it continued to pour heavily, flooding the roads. Along the way, we reached a village where a torrent of water rushed down the road laden with crops and bushes, and with no hope of crossing it we would need to turn back to Madura and try another, longer route to the foot of the hills. Wondering what to do, we watched as water swirled around the little mud huts, corroding their walls until the thatch roofs collapsed and, along with the occupants' belongings, float out of sight. Heaven knows that villagers in India have little enough to lose, and when that disappears so too does their livelihood.

Sadly, there was nothing we could do to help, so we returned to the city and managed to reach our agent's village via the alternative route. We were then advised that since our usual road to the foot of High Wavys' ghaut was flooded, we should take a bullock cart to the foot of the Cloudland track. Seeing the bullocks battle the truly terrifying sea of mud, rising to their bellies and threatening to wash around our feet, was like reliving the arduous cart journeys travelled many years before. Every jolt seemed likely to shoot us into mud as thick as pea soup and I shuddered to think what filth it contained. We were late in reaching our foothills where our horses were waiting, but because riding was difficult on the flooded trail, had to dismount halfway and wearily lead them on foot up the steep rocky path in the pouring rain. The horse-keepers had been sent ahead to the Cloudland bungalow to dry themselves and be ready to deal with the horses, and on our arrival, provided a very welcome pot of tea to set us up for the last four miles of leech-infested jungle to High Wavys.

It was a very dark night, and the rain continued to pour as if it would never stop. Both of us had forgotten that prior to leaving the estate, Jim had given orders for the re-cutting of the path between the two places. To our sorrow, the last two miles were strewn with debris and mess caused by cutting the road in wet weather. Still dressed for the heat of the plains, in thin cotton shirts, shorts and sandals, and still having to lead our horses, we were far from equipped to deal with either the mud or the leeches. Stumbling over loose stones left by the road-cutters and wading through liquid mud, we grew more disheveled with every step. Though very hungry, utterly exhausted and generally fed up, we began to see the funny side, and when I lost a sandal and almost got bogged down in mud trying to retrieve it, we couldn't help but collapse in a fit of giggles! Then just as we were growing desperate, we spotted the lights of the bungalow across the last little valley. When we finally walked through the door we were not a pretty sight. Our legs looked as though we were wearing red stockings on account of numerous bleeding leech bites, and our clothes, and indeed our whole persons were smothered in reddish mud. Porges and the kitchen coolie rallied around, providing salt water for the leech bites, drinks for us, and running hot baths in which we were soon luxuriating. It had taken us seventeen hours to cover the ninety miles from Madura to High Wavys, and by sheer coincidence, the very next morning, we read in our newspaper that a mosquito aircraft had flown from London to Delhi in exactly the same time!

Farewell to Forty Years in India
1947

Our life in India ended on the day during the monsoon when we left our bungalow for the very last time. After spending the night with one of the new managers, who happened to be an old friend, we were driven by jeep back through High Wavys to Cloudland and down through the new road to the plains.

The road was lined with weeping coolies and at each of the muster grounds Indian staff who also wept as they waited to shake our hands. I don't mind admitting that I too cried bitterly, though being a man and disinclined to display his emotions, Jim sat as looking as though he had swallowed a poker; a ploy that fooled no one. Garlands of every description were hung around our necks until we were almost smothered, and with all these frequent stops it seemed like we would never get away. It was a terrible parting, made even sadder by the fact that because so many of our people were illiterate, we would never communicate again. At last, it was over and we sped towards Madura where we would catch our train to Madras. The hundreds of garlands that filled the car were now redundant, so I amused myself by throwing them out, one by one, in front of any woman I saw walking along the road, the poorer the better, then watched in delight as her face lit up when she picked it up and carried it home. It was a small act that helped ease my sorrow.

One of the worst effects on western civilization is a proliferation of stuff which purports to increase our leisure time, but which seems to do the opposite. Few men or women in Britain, or at least none that I have met, are aware of what they lack in life. Busy from morning to night, they focus on whatever seems important at the time, but how can precious memories be stored if no one ever takes the time to stop, think and wonder? The exceptions are those perhaps closest to nature, gardeners, farmers, birdwatchers etc, and of course, parents.

The love of the jungle which had so long lived in my heart would now need to live in my memories too. What a curious thing memory is. It retains what it likes to remember and is inclined to leave out the rest. I attended many planters' meetings in Bangalore and Ootacamund and enjoyed holidays in Kodaikanal, but though I remember them the details are blurred. On the other hand, many of our adventures and encounters in the jungle are as clear to me now as the day they happened.

If I close my eyes and turn back the clock, I can see the old bull elephant with his magnificent tusks, ears outspread, standing beside his family on that lovely ridge on the plateau in 1920. I can once again feel a squirm of fear when the old sloth bear reared himself up deciding whether to attack us in defense of his timid wife, and earlier still, the moment of terror when my beloved father and I gazed into the eyes of that furious boar. I tingle with pleasure when picturing that beautiful hillside and the little shoulder of jungle where, standing at the entrance of our little white tent, Jim and I watched two bears gamboling in the sunset, and can experience the delight of my first glimpse of the Paradise Flycatcher back in 1908. The sounds of the jungle, amassed over forty years, are likewise packed in my memory, ready to come at the call of this luckiest of women.

Sitting on the plane to Bombay, I found it hard to believe that this was really the end of an era, and we would no longer have any part to play in the villages slipping away beneath us. But all is not lost, for I often revisit India during sleepless nights when with plenty of time, I can relive moments of joy through treasured memories.

To

Mrs. M. E. CANTLAY,
High Wavys Estate,
CUMBUM P. O.
(Madura Dt.)

Respected Madam,

We, the members of the Staff of High Wavys Estate, the Kanganies and labourers, take this opportunity to express our happiness and joy in receiving you back in our midst, quite healthy and well after your recent operation. We thank the Almighty for the successful outcome of the operation.

Madam! it is no exaggeration when we say that you have had been very kind and generous towards us and our families during the past fourteen years - from 1934 onwards - and no words can express our gratitude for your kindness. We deeply felt your recent seperation, though short it was, and we were all very anxious about your health. It was only after hearing from our generous Group Manager that your operation was a success, we felt happy again.

Your profound knowledge in our welfare and the kind and benevolent treatment you extend to the poor labourers, staff and their families is really a boon and beyond human expectation. Your kindness and unfailing sympathy towards the sick are real blessings and relief to the sufferers; and there were occasions when you have actually saved the lives of the poor sufferers by your careful and deligent attention.

Your unfailing interest in the depressed classes is really a virtue in you, and we have to express with full confidence that you have had been doing much more substantial work towards the uplift of the depressed classes, than many of our National leaders.

Madam! you have been very kind to organize a lady's Club in this place, and your efforts to develop the spiritual and temporal sides of the ladies of this Estate is really marvellous. We are all enjoying now the benefits of your kind & social enterprise.

It is really a touching sight to see the children of the Estate cluster around you and cling on to you, whenever you come out of the Bungalow to receive their share of sweets and eatables at your hands and they all consider you as their God-mother.

Your keen interest and enthusiasm in the welfare of all the people around you have no comparison and we feel that we are Divinely blessed to have you as our patron.

Dear Madam! please permit us to place before you this, as a token of our esteemed love and devotion towards you. We sincerely hope and wish that we should be blessed to enjoy many more years under your kind and loving guardianship.

"**L**et Almighty shower upon you and your beloved husband - our Group Manager - His choicest blessings and bestow upon you both, long, prosperous and happy life". This is the ardent prayer of us all.

Yours respectfully,

High Ways Estate,
21st November 1947.

The Staff, Kanganies and Labourers of
High Wavys Estate.

(Written by:- K. BALAKRISHNAN NAIR.)

Rajaji Press, Madura:-47.

Acknowledgements

A very big thank you to Laura Hamilton
for your unwavering support and enthusiasm
expertly guiding me through the two year process
of editing the manuscript.

To my nieces Jess and Fran for your
invaluable feedback and proofreading.

My son Dominic for your digital assistance.

Mary for your time and expertise in
preparing the photos.

Pete, not only for your unfailing encouragement,
but giving me the space to make it all possible.

And of course to my Grandmother for
this gift to her family.